THE BAD APPLE EFFECT

A Compassionate Parent's Guide to Harmful Influence, Family Systems and Raising Resilient Children

Greg Doney

Paperback ISBN: 978-1-7646377-6-3

First edition, 2026.

This book uses Australian English spelling conventions throughout.

MEDICAL DISCLAIMER

This book and its contents are provided for informational and educational purposes only. The author and publisher make no representations or warranties regarding the accuracy, completeness, or applicability of the content. They disclaim all liability for any errors, omissions, or inconsistencies that may be present.

The content in this book is not intended to diagnose, treat, cure, or prevent any condition or disease. It is not a substitute for professional medical, psychological, psychiatric, paediatric, family-therapy, child-protection or legal advice. Always consult a registered healthcare professional, registered psychologist, family therapist, or qualified specialist before making any changes to your child's care, your family's arrangements, or any health regimen or treatment plan. The use of this book implies your understanding and acceptance of this disclaimer.

This book does not constitute advice to start, stop, reduce, or change any medication or prescribed treatment. Never alter or discontinue any medication for yourself or your child without first consulting the prescribing doctor or psychiatrist.

The author and publisher do not guarantee any specific outcomes or results from following the suggestions or strategies in this book. Individual results will vary, and the examples or composite scenarios provided are not intended to guarantee similar experiences.

All clinical examples in this book are composites. Names, ages, family configurations and identifying details have been changed or invented to protect privacy. Any resemblance to a particular family or child is unintentional.

If you, your child, or another person in your household is in immediate danger or in mental health crisis, contact your local emergency services. In Australia, call 000. Lifeline Australia can be reached on 13 11 14, Kids Helpline on 1800 55 1800, and 1800RESPECT on 1800 737 732. If you are reading from outside Australia, please use the equivalent services in your country.

By reading this book, you accept full responsibility for your decisions and actions and agree that the author and publisher are not liable for any decisions or actions you take based on its content.

AUTHOR'S NOTE

This book uses the phrase "The Bad Apple Effect" as a metaphor. It is not a label for children. Children are not bad apples, they are not rotten, and they are not disposable. Even when a child's behaviour becomes aggressive, defiant, cruel, manipulative, withdrawn, disrespectful or destructive, there is almost always something further beneath the surface than the behaviour itself.

That something can take many forms. It might be fear, shame, abandonment or betrayal. It might be unmet attachment needs, unprocessed trauma, anxiety carried across years, or peer pressure that has reshaped the child's sense of who they need to be in order to belong. It might be a neurodevelopmental difference that nobody has yet named, or modelling at home that has taught the child to handle distress in the only ways the adults around them ever did. Sometimes it is plain nervous system dysregulation: a young body that has run out of capacity to stay calm. And sometimes it is a child who has learned, through slow accumulated experience, that harmful behaviour is the most reliable way to gain power, belonging, attention, protection or control.

This book does not exist to shame children. It exists to help parents understand patterns.

The bad apple effect is what happens when harmful behaviour, emotional dysregulation or unhealthy culture begins to spread through a family, a friendship group, a classroom, a team or an online space. One child's aggression can change the emotional climate of a home. One toxic friendship can shift a child's values over a school term. One online community can normalise cruelty until it stops registering as cruelty. And one dysregulated parent can make an entire household feel unsafe, even on the days when nothing visible has gone wrong.

But compassion must not become avoidance. A child's feelings may be valid while their behaviour still needs to be stopped. A child may be hurting and yet cannot be allowed to keep hurting others. A child may need understanding at the same moment that the rest of the family needs safety. Holding both of these at once is the daily work of parenting.

One useful way of capturing this balance, in a phrasing now widely associated with the parenting work of Dr Aliza Pressman, is the line:

All feelings are welcome. All behaviours are not.

In practice, this means that a child is allowed to feel angry but not allowed to hit. They are allowed to feel rejected, but not allowed to humiliate someone online. They are allowed to feel jealous, but not allowed to bully a sibling. A teenager is allowed to feel frustrated by a boundary, but not allowed to lie, threaten, intimidate or manipulate to escape it. The goal is not harshness. The goal is calm authority.

The parent's task, then, is to become Bigger, Stronger, Wiser and Kinder: big enough to hold the child's feelings, strong enough to set limits, wise enough to look beneath the behaviour, and kind enough to correct without shaming. This is difficult work, because parenting does not happen in theory. It happens in the middle of noise, exhaustion, sibling conflict, work pressure, financial stress, relationship strain, trauma triggers, sleep deprivation and the thousand daily demands that stretch a nervous system thin.

Many parents arrive at this work carrying guilt. They look back and see moments when they yelled, withdrew, overreacted, ignored warning signs, minimised sibling distress, excused harmful behaviour, or treated the dysregulated child as the whole problem. This book is not here to shame those parents. As Maya Angelou is often quoted as saying, "Do the best you can until you know better. Then when you know better, do better." That is the spirit of this book. Not blame, not perfection, but awareness, repair and growth.

Parents are not to blame for everything their child does. Children are shaped by many forces: temperament, biology, peers, siblings, school culture, digital environments, nutrition, sleep, trauma, neurodevelopment, family stress and the wider culture around them. But within that long list, parents do matter deeply. A parent's nervous system is itself part of the child's environment. If the parent is chronically overwhelmed, anxious, reactive, shut down, burnt out or carrying unresolved trauma, the child will often feel it before they can explain it, and may then act it out through behaviour.

This is one of the hardest truths in family work:

The child is often the signal, not the problem.

In many families, the child who appears to be the problem is the child carrying the signal. They may be the one melting down, refusing school, bullying a sibling, lying, withdrawing, exploding, clinging, controlling or constantly demanding attention. On the surface, it can look as though the child is the issue, but behaviour is rarely random. A dysregulated child may be communicating something the family has not yet been able to name. They may be responding to parental stress, inconsistency, emotional absence, conflict, unresolved trauma, poor boundaries, sensory overload, unmet attachment needs, or a home environment that does not yet feel safe enough for their nervous system.

This does not mean parents are bad. It means parents matter.

Many parents do not take this easily at first. They come seeking help for the child, and it can feel painful or even insulting to hear that the family system itself may also need to change. But this is not about blame. It is about power. If the family system is contributing to the dysregulation, then the family system can also become part of the healing. The child is not bad. The parent is not bad. But the pattern may need to change.

This book also asks parents to look beyond the loudest child. In families where one child takes up most of the emotional space, another child often learns to take up less. They become the easy one, the helpful one, the mature one, the child who does not make a fuss. Parents may feel grateful for this child's independence, especially when family life is already stretched. But sometimes the child who seems fine has simply learned that their needs are inconvenient. They may not be regulated; they may be resigned. They may not be coping well; they may be coping alone. In many families, one child carries the noise and another carries the silence, and both need attention.

This book is about both children. It is about the child who acts out and the child who disappears. It is about the parent who reacts and the parent who withdraws. It is about the sibling who dominates and the sibling who becomes invisible. And it is about the peer group that rewards cruelty, the classroom that normalises disruption, the online space that teaches contempt, and the family system that may slowly drift away from safety without meaning to.

Most importantly, it is about repair.

Children often do not have the words to explain what is happening inside them. They may not be able to say, "I feel ashamed," "I feel abandoned," "I feel betrayed," "I feel unsafe," or "I need you to notice me." Instead, they communicate through behaviour. They melt down, withdraw, lie, cling, rage, control, refuse, bully, people-please or shut down. The behaviour may be difficult, but it is often the child's best attempt to express something they cannot yet name. The parent's task is not simply to stop the behaviour, but to decode the message underneath it, while still holding clear and loving boundaries.

Throughout this book, we will return to a simple formula:

Validate the feeling. Name the behaviour. Hold the boundary. Repair the relationship.

Another way to say this is:

Decode first. Discipline second. Repair always.

This is the heart of compassionate parenting. It is not permissive, not punitive, not fearful, and not controlling. The child is loved. The behaviour is held accountable. The family is protected. The parent stays regulated. That is the foundation of The Bad Apple Effect.

CONTENTS

Introduction

"Do the best you can until you know better. Then when you know better, do better."

Commonly attributed to Maya Angelou

When One Influence Changes the Whole Child

Most parents recognise the moment. Your child spends time with a particular friend, joins a new group, moves into a different classroom, follows a new online personality, becomes attached to a particular peer, or starts copying an older sibling, and something shifts. Their tone changes, their attitude changes, their language changes. They become more secretive, more defiant, more anxious, more negative, more aggressive, more withdrawn or more disrespectful. Sometimes the change is subtle. Sometimes it feels sudden and alarming. Sometimes it feels as though your child has been pulled into another emotional world entirely.

You may find yourself thinking: where did this come from, who are they copying, why are they suddenly behaving like this, how do I protect them without controlling them, and how do I set boundaries without pushing them further away? This is what I call the bad apple effect. Not because children are bad apples, they are not, and that distinction will be repeated throughout this book.

Children are developing human beings. They are learning who they are, where they belong, how to manage emotion, how to handle rejection, how to gain approval, how to stand up for themselves and how to survive socially. They are influenced by the people and cultures around them because they are meant to be. Human beings are relational. We learn through imitation, attachment, belonging, modelling and emotional contagion.

But while children are not bad, environments can be. A friendship that started warm can sour into mockery and exclusion. A peer group can drift toward cruelty when the loudest voice sets the tone. A sibling pattern can lock two children into the roles of aggressor and target long after either of them remembers how it began. Classroom cultures, coaches, social-media feeds, an emotionally absent or chronically stressed parent, the wider family system itself: any of these can begin to shape a child's behaviour in ways that look, from the outside, like the child has changed. In most cases, the child has not changed. The child is responding, accurately and biologically, to a shift in the field around them.

The bad apple effect, then, is what happens when one dysregulated person, one destructive pattern, or one unhealthy culture begins to shift the emotional and behavioural climate around it. One child's aggression can change the tone of a classroom. One sibling's constant dysregulation can dominate a household. One friend's cruelty can reshape a child's sense of self-worth. One online group can normalise disrespect, pornography, self-harm, misogyny, bullying or contempt. One emotionally immature adult can make a child feel unsafe in their own home.

This book is not about fear-based parenting. It is not about judging other people's children, controlling every friendship, monitoring every conversation, or wrapping children in cotton wool. It is about helping parents understand influence. More importantly, it is about helping parents raise children with enough internal strength that they do not collapse into the strongest personality in the room.

What that internal strength looks like in practice is fairly specific. A resilient child still wants to belong but does not abandon themselves to belong. A grounded child can be kind without being easily manipulated. A confident child can walk away from cruelty without needing to become cruel. A connected child is less likely to outsource their identity to the peer group. A regulated child is less likely to be hijacked by the dysregulation of others. A values-led child can recognise when something feels wrong, even when everyone else is laughing.

That is the deeper purpose of this book. Not to raise suspicious children, not to raise judgemental children, not to raise children who believe they are better than others, but to raise children who can recognise harmful patterns, protect their own character, choose better influences, and, in time, become a positive influence themselves.

Children Absorb the Atmosphere Around Them

Children do not develop in isolation. They are shaped by the emotional atmosphere around them, absorbing tone, tension, rhythm, stress, facial expression, body language, conflict, repair, silence, warmth, criticism, fear and belonging. A child does not simply live in a home; they live inside the nervous system climate of that home.

That climate is registered at a level beneath language. They notice whether adults are calm or reactive, whether conflict gets repaired or buried, whether one sibling receives all the attention, and whether the quiet child is expected to stay quiet. They notice whether anger is safe to express and whether sadness is met with comfort or dismissal. They notice whether love feels steady or conditional, and whether the parent in front of them is present, distracted, overwhelmed, unpredictable or emotionally absent. Even when children cannot yet explain what they are noticing, their bodies keep track.

This is why behaviour is so often communication. A child who is constantly defiant may be trying to regain a sense of control. A child who bullies a sibling may be discharging shame or powerlessness. A child who lies may be terrified of disappointing an adult. A child who becomes clingy may be carrying abandonment fear. A child who becomes hyper-independent may have learned that no one is reliably available. A child who copies a harmful peer may be choosing belonging over self-respect because, to their nervous system, belonging feels like survival.

When children do not have the words, their behaviour speaks for them. This does not mean every behaviour is acceptable. It means every behaviour deserves to be understood before it is corrected.

The Family Is an Emotional Ecosystem

A family is not just a group of individuals living under one roof. It is an emotional ecosystem, and in an ecosystem, everything affects everything else. If one part becomes unstable, the whole system adjusts. If one person is chronically dysregulated, the rest of the family adapts around them: when one child is constantly explosive, another may become compliant; when one parent is anxious, the child may become hypervigilant; when one parent withdraws, the child may escalate to regain connection; when parents are misaligned, children can feel unsafe and confused.

This is why focusing only on the identified child often fails. A child may be the loudest symptom but not the deepest source. When parents bring a dysregulated child for help, they often, understandably, see the child as the problem. The child is the one refusing, yelling, hitting, lying, melting down, withdrawing or causing disruption. The child is the one who appears to need fixing. But very often, the child is showing us something about the wider system.

What that something is varies from family to family. The child may be showing us that the parent is exhausted, or that the home lacks predictable boundaries. They may be showing us that a sibling has been unsafe, that the family is organised around avoiding conflict, or that the parents are carrying unresolved trauma. They may be showing us that the household is overstimulated, under-rested, under-nourished or emotionally disconnected. They may be showing us that no one has had the capacity to notice what they need until their behaviour became impossible to ignore.

This is not about blaming parents. It is about giving parents their power back. If the family system can shape dysregulation, then the family system can also shape healing.

Shame Makes Families Hide

One of the reasons family patterns are hard to change is shame. When parents are invited to look at their own dysregulation, many do not initially feel curious; they feel accused. They may feel exposed, ashamed, judged or blamed. Shame is powerful because it does not simply say, "I made a mistake." It says, "There is something wrong with me."

When a parent hears the suggestion that their child's behaviour may be connected to the family system, shame can quickly turn into defensiveness. The familiar lines arrive almost on cue: "He is just difficult." "She has always been like this." "It is the school." "It is the phone." "It is the other parent." "You do not understand what we live with."

Sometimes these things are partly true. Schools matter, phones matter, peers matter, the other parent matters, temperament matters, diagnosis matters. But shame narrows the lens. It searches for a villain instead of a pattern. Shame rarely helps a family heal. It makes parents hide, makes children hide, and turns behaviour into identity.

A more helpful path is responsibility without self-attack. The question is not, "Who is bad?" The question is, "What pattern is asking to be understood?" Shame shuts the system down. Compassion opens it up. Responsibility changes it.

This is true for parents and for children. A child who feels guilt may be able to repair: "I hurt my brother. I need to make it right." A child who feels shame may instead collapse into: "I am bad.

There is no point trying." A parent who feels guilt may be able to repair: "I yelled. That was not okay. I need to do better." A parent who feels shame may collapse into defensiveness, denial, rage or despair.

The goal is not to remove accountability. The goal is to remove humiliation from accountability. A child can be held accountable without being shamed. A parent can take responsibility without being destroyed by guilt. A family can change without anyone being labelled as the problem.

The Quiet Child Still Needs You

In many families, the loudest child receives the most attention, and this is understandable. A child who is aggressive, explosive, self-destructive, defiant, anxious or constantly in crisis naturally pulls parental focus. Urgency tends to organise the household.

But while the dysregulated child is taking up emotional space, another child may be learning to take up less. This child may become mature, helpful, quiet, independent, high-achieving or emotionally low-maintenance. They may seem fine. They may even be praised for being the easy one. The risk is that, sometimes, the easy child is not secure. Sometimes they have simply learned not to need anything.

What that learning looks like, over time, is a quiet narrowing of what the child believes they are allowed to bring home. They learn that their sibling's needs matter more, that their job is to keep the peace, that their sadness creates more stress for the adults, that being good is the safest way to be loved, and that anger is not allowed. They may begin to parent the parent and to take care of themselves too early. This is parentification. It can look like maturity, but underneath it there may be loneliness, resentment, anxiety, perfectionism or emotional self-abandonment.

The quiet child is not always the okay child. Do not only check on the child who is loud. Check on the child who has stopped asking.

The Biological Floor Matters

Before we describe a child as difficult, we should ask whether their nervous system has the basic conditions required to regulate at all. Children need more than discipline. They need a biological floor that supports emotional stability, and that floor is built out of unglamorous, daily inputs.

Those inputs are not exotic. Children need enough sleep to consolidate emotional learning. They need protein and steady blood sugar so the prefrontal cortex has fuel for self-control. They need movement and sunlight to keep mood-regulating circuits online. They need rhythm and predictability to lower baseline arousal, and reasonable distance from the constant stimulation of screens. Layered onto those biological conditions are the relational ones: safe adults, reliable connection, and the experience of repair after rupture. A home that does not constantly overwhelm a child's nervous system is, in itself, a clinical intervention.

When those conditions are stripped away, behaviour follows. A child running on poor sleep, unstable blood sugar, chronic stress, excessive screen stimulation, low movement and emotional disconnection becomes far more likely to look reactive, impulsive, anxious, defiant or shut down. This does not excuse harmful behaviour. It explains why so many children have so little capacity to regulate when the moment arrives.

If we want better behaviour, we have to build better conditions first. A later chapter draws this biological floor together in more detail, and points to the broader work of integrative mental-health writers, including my own previous books on trauma, depression and blood-sugar health, for parents who want to understand the cellular and metabolic story underneath behaviour.

The Parent as the Safe Harbour

When a child is caught in a harmful pattern, parents often feel pressure to find the perfect consequence, the perfect script, or the perfect disciplinary strategy. In many moments, what matters most is not the script. It is the state of the parent's own nervous system.

A dysregulated child does not need a dysregulated adult trying to win a power struggle. They need an adult who can be bigger than the storm, stronger than the behaviour, wiser than the surface reaction, and kinder than the child expects. This is not permissiveness; it is calm authority. It is the experience of the child feeling loved while the harmful behaviour is clearly stopped. In ordinary language, it sounds like:

“I can see you are furious. It is okay to feel angry. It is not okay to hit your brother. I am going to help you calm down, and then we will work out what happened.”

That is compassionate parenting. The feeling is welcomed, the behaviour is limited, the child is not shamed, and the relationship remains intact.

The Aim of This Book

The aim of this book is not to help parents find the bad apple. It is, instead, to help parents recognise harmful patterns before those patterns take over the family, the friendship group, the classroom, the team or the child’s inner world. Practically, that means helping parents respond without shame, panic or harshness; understanding why children are vulnerable to harmful influence; protecting siblings who are quietly carrying the cost; examining their own dysregulation without collapsing into blame; and giving families practical tools for connection, boundaries, repair, discernment and resilience.

The world is contagious. So are fear, shame, contempt, aggression and hopelessness. But so are courage, kindness, calm, responsibility, honesty and strength. The aim is not only to protect your child from the bad apple effect.

The aim is to raise the good apple.

Not the perfect child. Not the compliant child. Not the child who never struggles. The aim is to raise a child who knows who they are: a child who can belong without abandoning themselves, who can feel anger without becoming cruel, who can feel rejection without collapsing into shame, who can recognise harmful patterns and choose a different path, and who can become a safe, steady, kind and courageous influence in the room.

And that begins with us. Not because parents are the problem, but because parents are the most powerful part of the solution.

CHAPTER 1

What Is the Bad Apple Effect?

The Phrase, the Metaphor, and the Disclaimer

A child does not need to be surrounded by chaos to be changed by it. Sometimes one powerful influence is enough. One friendship can shift a child's language, values and confidence over a single school term. One sibling pattern can change the emotional climate of a home. One peer group can make cruelty seem normal, one classroom can teach a child that disruption earns status, and one coach can confuse humiliation with discipline. One online space can reward contempt, pornography, aggression, shame or hopelessness. One dysregulated parent, even a loving one, can leave a child's nervous system in a state of unsafe alert. This is the bad apple effect.

Before we go any further, this distinction needs to sit clearly on the page, because the metaphor is sharp, and a sharp metaphor in the wrong hands can cut a child. Children are not bad apples. The bad apple is the pattern, the influence, or the culture, not the child.

Take the most common examples. A child who is hitting is not a bad apple; the hitting may be a warning sign of nervous system dysregulation, attachment distress, sensory overload, trauma, peer modelling or unmet need, and while their behaviour may need to be stopped, their dignity does not. A child who is bullying is not a bad apple; the bullying may be a discharge of shame, a survival strategy in a peer group that rewards contempt, or a learned imitation of cruelty the child has been exposed to, and while their behaviour requires accountability, their personhood does not. A teenager who is lying, manipulating, withdrawing or hurting siblings is not a bad apple; they are a developing human being caught in a pattern. The pattern can change. The child remains.

Throughout this book, the phrase is used to describe what harmful behaviour does to a system, never to describe a person. When the metaphor is read in any other way, the rest of the book stops working.

Where the Idea Comes From

The bad apple effect did not begin in family work. It began in workplaces. For decades, organisational researchers had assumed that a healthy team could absorb and reform a single difficult member. The wider group, the thinking went, would simply pull the difficult member up to its standard. That assumption did not hold up.

In 2006, three researchers, Will Felps, Terence Mitchell and Eliza Byington, reviewed the evidence and reached the opposite conclusion. In their landmark paper, How, When, and Why Bad Apples Spoil the Barrel, they argued that a single negative group member could exert powerful, disproportionate and corrosive influence on a team, even when the team was otherwise functional.[1]

Their finding was clear. The destructive person did not have to be the most senior, the loudest, or the most obviously toxic. They simply had to persistently exhibit one or more of three patterns: withholding effort, expressing negative affect, or violating important interpersonal norms. Once those behaviours were established and unchecked, the rest of the team began to organise around them. Trust dropped. Cooperation narrowed. Energy that should have gone into shared work was diverted into managing, monitoring and defending against the harmful member.

Their work was not isolated. A growing body of organisational and management writing has reached the same conclusion from different angles. Stanford organisational psychologist Robert Sutton, in The No Asshole Rule, argued that systems must hold an absolute and unyielding standard against persistent interpersonal cruelty, regardless of the offender's perceived productive value. Sutton's point was confronting and necessary: when an institution tolerates one person's contempt because they appear talented or strong-willed, the institution is silently teaching everyone else that contempt is acceptable.[2]

Adrian Furnham and John Taylor, in Bad Apples: Identify, Prevent and Manage Negative Behavior at Work, offered a complementary clinical framework for recognising destructive behaviour patterns before they took root. Their argument was that toxic behaviour is rarely a single explosive event. It is a slow, repetitive pattern that erodes the operating capacity of the surrounding group.[3] Alan Cavaiola and Neil Lavender approached the same phenomenon through a psychiatric lens. In Toxic Coworkers, they catalogued the personality patterns that drive sustained interpersonal harm in shared environments and offered evidence-informed strategies for containing them.[4] Even in the popular leadership literature, the same pattern has been named: John Maxwell, in The 17 Indisputable Laws of Teamwork, called this the Law of the Bad Apple, and stated it bluntly. Rotten attitudes are infectious, and a team that ignores them will eventually be ruined by them.[5]

Different fields, different methods, different decades, the same finding. A single dysregulated, hostile or chronically destructive person can shift the climate of an entire group. It is not because everyone else is weak. It is because human beings are relational, and groups are systems.

The Three Patterns That Spoil a Group

Felps, Mitchell and Byington named three repeating patterns that account for most of the damage caused by a destructive group member. They were studying workplaces, but the patterns translate intact into families, friendship groups, classrooms, sporting teams and online spaces. Anywhere humans share an emotional environment, these three patterns do the same work.[1]

The first pattern is withholding effort. At work, this looks like coasting, free-riding, or refusing to carry a fair share of the load while still expecting the same recognition and reward. In a family, it looks like a child or teenager chronically refusing to participate in reasonable responsibilities: not helping, not contributing, not cooperating, not studying, not cleaning up, not attending family activities, not making any effort unless forced. Over time, this creates resentment in siblings, exhaustion in parents, and a household culture in which expectations become negotiable.

Withholding effort is rarely about laziness in the way adults sometimes describe it. Underneath, there may be depression, anxiety, shame, executive function difficulty, ADHD, demand avoidance, trauma, sleep deprivation, hopelessness or learned helplessness. The point of recognising the pattern is not to shame the child. It is to notice that when one person consistently opts out of shared responsibility, the rest of the system adjusts, usually by carrying the absent contribution, and often by quietly resenting it.

The second pattern is persistent negativity. At work, this is the colleague whose chronic complaining, contempt, pessimism and hostility drains the bandwidth of every meeting. In a family, it is the child, teenager or adult whose constant negative tone shifts the emotional climate of the home. Joy becomes harder. Playfulness disappears. Siblings become cautious. Parents become reactive or avoidant. The family slowly organises itself around avoiding the next outburst, criticism or collapse.

A parent may think, “That is just how he is,” or “She has always been dramatic,” or “Everyone is just tired.” But over time, persistent negativity changes the atmosphere. The home stops feeling emotionally safe. Both research and clinical experience show this is not personality. It is a pattern, and the system is paying for it.

The third pattern is violating interpersonal norms. In a workplace this is harassment, intimidation, contempt, dishonesty, manipulation, sexualised behaviour or coercion. In a family or peer group, the same patterns appear in age-specific forms: aggression, bullying, sibling intimidation, manipulation, lying, humiliation, coercion, cruelty, online shaming, sexual pressure, stealing, threats or repeated boundary violations. These behaviours cannot be minimised as personality quirks or normal developmental phases when they repeatedly harm others. Compassion can explain the behaviour. Compassion does not excuse the harm.

A child may be dysregulated, traumatised, impulsive, ashamed, anxious or under peer pressure. They may still need a firm boundary. The family still needs safety. Siblings still need protection. The child causing harm still needs to learn that their feelings are valid and their behaviour has limits.

All feelings are welcome. All behaviours are not.

From Workplace to Family

A workplace and a family are not the same thing. Families are bound by love, biology, history and obligation in a way no team ever is. There is no resignation letter from a sibling, no exit interview from a parent. And yet a family is a system in the same way a team is a system. It has roles, rules, hierarchies, norms, emotional currents, patterns of reward and punishment, and a steady ambient temperature. Children learn very quickly what earns attention, what creates belonging, what brings power, what avoids shame, what keeps them safe and what gets them rejected. They are reading the room from the day they arrive in it.

A child is always learning from the system around them, and what they learn is broader than what the adults consciously teach. They learn from what adults say, but they learn more from what adults tolerate. They learn from what gets laughed at, what gets ignored, and what receives attention. They learn from what makes them belong, and from who has power in the room. They learn from what happens after someone causes harm, and from whether repair happens or whether everyone simply moves on. Across thousands of small incidents, those observations accumulate into a working model of how the world responds to behaviour.

This is why harmful behaviour can spread inside a family even when no one is formally teaching it. A child may not be told to mock others, but if mockery earns laughter, it becomes powerful. A child may not be told to lie, but if lying avoids shame or punishment, it becomes useful. A child may not be told to bully, but if bullying brings status, it becomes attractive. A child may not be told to shut down, but if no one is emotionally available, shutting down may become the only available form of survival. A child may not be told to take care of everyone, but if the adults are overwhelmed, parentification may quietly become their role.

The bad apple effect inside a family is not always loud. It can show up in a child becoming cruel, or anxious, or controlling, or invisible. It can show up in a parent slowly lowering the family standard because they are too tired to keep intervening, or in siblings adjusting around the most dysregulated child until the whole household is walking on eggshells. Sometimes it shows up in nothing more dramatic than everyone pretending something is normal because naming it would be too painful.

Why One Person Matters in a System

Parents sometimes hear a description of the bad apple effect and quietly think, "That seems like a lot of weight to put on one person." It is. And the research says it is also accurate.

Felps and his colleagues found that the influence of a destructive group member is asymmetric. Negative behaviours, hostility, withdrawal, contempt, dishonesty, spread more efficiently through a group than positive behaviours do. They are stickier. They are louder. They demand more cognitive and emotional bandwidth from the people exposed to them.[1]

In a family, this asymmetry is even more concentrated, because children are still building the very nervous system they are using to process what is happening. A workplace colleague exposed to a hostile coworker can usually go home, decompress, and arrive the next morning with most of their internal world intact. A child cannot. The household is the world. There is no decompression zone. The hostile or dysregulated person at home is also the person who tucks them in, drives them to school, and shapes their first models of relationship.

This is why parents matter so much in this work, and why this book is written for them. A parent cannot remove every harmful influence from their child's life. The world will keep arriving with its own bad apples. But a parent can do four things, all of which sit at the centre of this book. They can recognise the patterns early, while the patterns are still small. They can refuse to normalise harmful behaviour, in themselves and in others. They can build the conditions, emotional, biological, relational, in which a child develops enough internal strength to recognise a harmful influence and walk away from it. And they can repair, again and again, every time the family system slips.

Repair is not a bonus. Repair is the mechanism.

Looking Ahead

The next several chapters stay with the mechanism. We will look at why one child's dysregulation is so easily caught by a sibling, what is happening neurologically when emotional contagion takes hold, why family systems are particularly vulnerable to a single destabilising member, and how to tell the difference between a true bad apple pattern and a child who is unconsciously carrying the family's pain.

The chapters that follow look at where the bad apple effect actually shows up: between siblings, in the marriage that holds the household, in the parent who has become dysregulated themselves, and in the peer groups, classrooms, online communities and adults around the child. From there we look at how it takes hold, the slow drift of normalisation, and the subtle ways parents can talk themselves out of acting on what they are seeing. A short bridge chapter then puts the body underneath the behaviour, because the biology matters and a regulated nervous system is not optional in this work.

The practical heart of the book is ten chapters of what parents can do: becoming the safe harbour, exercising calm authority, holding the line that all feelings are welcome and all behaviours are not, monitoring and protecting without controlling, solving problems collaboratively, engineering a positive peer culture, holding visiting adults to the same standards, and repairing after rupture with accountability but without shame. The closing chapters are not just about protecting your child from the bad apple effect, but about raising the good apple: the child who knows who they are, who can belong without abandoning themselves, who can recognise harmful patterns, and who, in time, becomes the safe, steady, kind and courageous influence in the room.

That is where the book is going. We start in Chapter 2 with the line the rest of the book stands on: children are not bad apples.

Key Takeaways

- The bad apple effect is a metaphor for how harmful behaviour, dysregulation or unhealthy culture can spread through a group or family system. It is never a label for a child.
- The phenomenon was first formalised in organisational psychology by Felps, Mitchell and Byington in 2006, and has been described from different angles by Sutton, Furnham and Taylor, Cavaiola and Lavender, and Maxwell.

- Three patterns reliably damage groups: withholding effort, persistent negativity, and violating interpersonal norms. They translate directly from workplaces into families.
- Negative behaviours spread through a system more efficiently than positive ones. The asymmetry is concentrated in families, where children cannot leave the environment to recover.
- Compassion explains behaviour. Compassion does not excuse harm.
- Parents cannot remove every harmful influence from their child's life. They can recognise patterns early, refuse to normalise harm, build the conditions for resilience, and repair when the system slips.

References

1. Felps, W., Mitchell, T. R., & Byington, E. (2006). How, when, and why bad apples spoil the barrel: Negative group members and dysfunctional groups. Research in Organizational Behavior, 27, 175–222. Https://doi.org/10.1016/S0191-3085(06)27005-9
2. Sutton, R. I. (2007). The No Asshole Rule: Building a Civilized Workplace and Surviving One That Isn't. New York: Business Plus / Warner Books.
3. Furnham, A., & Taylor, J. (2011). Bad Apples: Identify, Prevent and Manage Negative Behavior at Work. Basingstoke: Palgrave Macmillan.
4. Cavaiola, A. A., & Lavender, N. J. (2000). Toxic Coworkers: How to Deal with Dysfunctional People on the Job. Oakland, CA: New Harbinger Publications.
5. Maxwell, J. C. (2001). The 17 Indisputable Laws of Teamwork: Embrace Them and Empower Your Team. Nashville, TN: Thomas Nelson.

CHAPTER 2

Children Are Not Bad Apples

No Child Is Rotten

No child is rotten. No child is disposable. No child should be reduced to the worst thing they have done, the hardest season they have lived through, or the most difficult behaviour they have shown. This is where we have to begin.

If the title of this book is misunderstood, it could easily become harsh. It could sound as though some children are good and some children are bad, that some are healthy fruit and some are rotten, that some should be protected and some should be rejected. That is not the message of this book.

Children are not bad apples. But the harmful patterns that surround them are real. Cruelty is real. So are bullying, aggression, manipulation, lying, coercion, online humiliation, sibling intimidation, emotional contagion, family dysregulation and peer pressure. So is the truth that a child can be deeply worthy of love and at the same time caught in a pattern that is hurting others. A child can be traumatised and still need boundaries. A child can be dysregulated and still need to learn responsibility. A child can be anxious, ashamed or abandoned and still need to repair harm. A child can be influenced by peers and still need help finding their own values again.

Compassion does not mean pretending behaviour does not matter. Compassion means refusing to confuse behaviour with identity. The child is not the behaviour. The behaviour is a signal, a strategy, a symptom, a habit, a survival response, a learned pattern or a cry for help, and sometimes it is several of these at once. But it is not the whole child.

Behaviour Is Not Identity

One of the most damaging mistakes adults make is turning behaviour into identity. A child lies, so they become "a liar." A child hits, so they become "violent." A child refuses, so they become "defiant." A child melts down, so they become "dramatic." A child withdraws, so they become "lazy." A child seeks attention, so they become "manipulative." A child copies a harmful peer, so they become "badly behaved." Labels may feel efficient, but they are rarely healing.

A label can trap a child inside the very pattern we want them to outgrow. If a child begins to believe, "I am bad," they may stop trying to be good. If a child believes, "I am the problem," they may either collapse into shame or fight harder to protect themselves from that shame. Children need adults who can name behaviour clearly without making the behaviour their identity.

There is a world of difference between "You are cruel" and "That behaviour was cruel, and we need to repair it." There is a world of difference between "You are a liar" and "You lied, and now we need to understand why telling the truth felt unsafe." There is a world of difference between "You are out of control" and "Your nervous system is overwhelmed, and I will not let you hurt anyone while we help you calm down." The first set of statements attacks identity. The second set addresses behaviour, responsibility and safety.

This distinction is not soft. It is precise. When we separate the child from the behaviour, we make change possible.

Why Children Do Harmful Things

Children do not always understand why they do what they do. Adults often expect children to have adult-level insight. We ask, "Why did you do that?" and then become frustrated when the child says, "I don't know." But often, they really do not. They do not yet have the language, the emotional literacy, the self-awareness, or the nervous system capacity to pause, reflect and explain.

A child may not yet be able to say, "I felt ashamed when you corrected me in front of my brother," or "I felt abandoned when you were always busy with work," or "I felt replaced when the new baby arrived," or "I felt unsafe when you and Mum were fighting." They may not be able to name jealousy when their sibling gets all the attention, or anxiety when they tried to control everything, or rejection when their friends pushed them out and they wanted someone else to feel small. They may not be able to admit they copied a harmful peer because they were scared the peer would turn on them, or that they lied because telling the truth felt dangerous, or that they hit because their body was already in fight mode before any thought arrived.

Instead, the child acts. They yell, hit, refuse, lie, withdraw, mock, cling, control or shut down. They become the class clown, the bully, the victim, the rescuer, the perfect child or the invisible child. When children do not have the words, their behaviour speaks for them.

This does not mean the behaviour is acceptable. It means the behaviour is meaningful. Parents do not need to choose between understanding and boundaries. Children need both. They need adults who can say, "I want to understand what happened inside you," and, "I will not allow this behaviour to continue." That is the balance.

The Hidden Wounds Beneath Behaviour

Many harmful behaviours are built around hidden wounds. The three wounds we will return to often in this book, and which receive a fuller chapter of their own later, are shame, betrayal and abandonment.

Shame is the wound of: "There is something wrong with me." Betrayal is the wound of: "The people I trusted were not safe." Abandonment is the wound of: "I am on my own." Each of these wounds shapes behaviour in a recognisable way. A child carrying shame may become defensive, dishonest, aggressive, perfectionistic or avoidant, because admitting fault feels like being exposed as bad. A child carrying betrayal may become suspicious, controlling, guarded, angry or unwilling to rely on adults, because trust feels dangerous. A child carrying abandonment may become clingy, peer-dependent, parentified, hyper-independent or desperate for approval, because disconnection feels like a survival threat.

These wounds often hide beneath behaviour that adults find difficult. A child who mocks others may be trying to outrun their own shame. A child who controls everything may be trying to avoid feeling powerless. A child who lies may be trying to avoid the terror of disappointing someone. A child who bullies may be discharging pain they cannot tolerate inside themselves. A child who follows a harmful peer may be choosing belonging over self-respect because abandonment feels worse than self-betrayal. A child who becomes the perfect sibling may be trying to guarantee love by never becoming a burden. A child who becomes numb may have learned that feeling is too dangerous.

Behaviour is often the visible strategy. Shame, betrayal and abandonment are often the hidden wounds. This lens changes how we respond. Instead of asking only, "How do I stop this?" we also ask: what wound is this behaviour protecting, what need is it trying to meet, and what pain is this child trying not to feel?

These questions do not remove accountability. They make accountability more effective. A child cannot grow from a behaviour they are too ashamed to look at. A child cannot repair harm if they believe they are the harm. A child cannot develop self-control if the adults around them only see defiance and never see distress.

All Feelings Are Welcome. All Behaviours Are Not.

This principle may be the most important in the book.

All feelings are welcome. All behaviours are not.

In practical terms, that means a child is allowed to feel angry but not allowed to hit. They are allowed to feel jealous but not allowed to humiliate a sibling. They are allowed to feel rejected but not allowed to bully someone else to regain power. They are allowed to feel embarrassed but not allowed to lie in a way that harms others. A teenager is allowed to feel frustrated by a boundary but not allowed to threaten, intimidate or manipulate to escape it.

This principle protects two things at once: the child's inner world from shame, and the outer world from harm. Many parents accidentally choose one side. Some validate feelings but struggle to hold boundaries; the child may feel understood, but the family may not feel safe. Others enforce behaviour but dismiss feelings; the child may comply in the short term, but shame, resentment and disconnection grow underneath. Children need both. They need to know that their feelings are safe with their parent, and that their parent will not let their feelings run the whole home.

This is the essence of calm authority. It is not permissive, and it is not punitive. It is loving leadership.

Compassion Is Not the Same as Excusing

Some parents worry that if they understand the behaviour, they are excusing it. They may think, "If I say he was dysregulated, does that mean he gets away with it?" The answer is no. Understanding is not the same as excusing. Compassion is not the same as enabling.

A trauma-informed parent does not say, "You hit your sister because you were upset, so it does not matter." A trauma-informed parent says, "You were very upset, and I want to understand what happened. It is still not okay to hit your sister. We need to repair this, and we need a plan for next time."

A compassionate parent does not say, "You lied because you were scared, so lying is fine." A compassionate parent says, "I understand that telling the truth felt scary. We still need honesty in this family. Let us work out how to make the truth safer."

A wise parent does not say, "You bullied that child because your friends pressured you, so it was not your fault." A wise parent says, "It makes sense that you wanted to belong. But belonging cannot come at the cost of someone else's dignity. We need to make this right."

This is the difference between shame-free accountability and permissiveness. Children need to learn that their inner experience matters, and they also need to learn that their impact on others matters. One without the other creates imbalance.

The Problem With "Bad Kid" Thinking

When adults label a child as bad, difficult, manipulative or attention-seeking, they often stop being curious. The label becomes the explanation. Why did he hit? Because he is aggressive. Why did she lie? Because she is manipulative. Why did he refuse school? Because he is lazy. Why did she melt down? Because she wants attention. But labels often describe the behaviour without explaining the need underneath it.

A child who wants attention may need connection. A child who is aggressive may be stuck in a fight response. A child who is manipulative may have learned indirect strategies because direct needs were ignored or punished. A child who is lazy may be depressed, ashamed, overwhelmed, sleep-deprived, anxious, neurodivergent or afraid of failure. A child who is defiant may be trying to protect autonomy in a relationship where they feel controlled. A child who is dramatic may have no other way to get adults to recognise the intensity of their inner world.

This does not mean every behaviour has a deep trauma explanation. Sometimes children test limits. Sometimes they seek power. Sometimes they copy peers. Sometimes they make poor choices because they are immature. But even then, "bad kid" thinking rarely helps. It creates distance between the adult and the child, invites shame, reduces the adult's ability to lead, and makes repair harder. A more useful question is, "What is the pattern, and what does this child still need to learn?" That question keeps the parent in leadership.

The Child Who Causes Harm Also Needs Help

This is hard for families, especially when siblings have been hurt. When one child repeatedly causes harm, parents often swing between two extremes. They may over-identify with the child causing harm and minimise the impact on siblings, or they may become so protective of the harmed child that they see the child causing harm only as the problem. Both extremes miss something important.

The harmed child needs protection, validation and repair. The child causing harm also needs help. They may need boundaries, consequences, treatment, assessment and supervision. They may need reduced access to certain peers, devices or situations. At times they may need to be separated from siblings when the situation is unsafe. But they also need to know they are not beyond love.

A child who causes harm and is then defined by that harm may harden into the role. They may begin to believe, "This is who I am." Once that happens, change becomes harder. The task is to hold the line without cutting the child off from their own goodness. The message is: "I will not let you hurt people," and, "I will not give up on you." Both are necessary.

Seeing the Whole Child

Every child is more than the behaviour that worries us. The child who bullies may also be lonely. The child who lies may also be terrified. The child who refuses school may also be overwhelmed. The child who controls may also be anxious. The child who hits may also be ashamed. The child who copies a harmful peer may also be desperate to belong. The child who withdraws may also be grieving. The child who becomes perfect may also be exhausted. The child who seems fine may also be invisible.

Seeing the whole child does not mean ignoring the behaviour. It means refusing to let the behaviour become the only thing we see. Parents can ask: what is strong in this child, what is sensitive, what is frightened, what is unmet? What is overdeveloped because they had to grow up too soon, and what is underdeveloped because no one has taught it yet? What does this child need to practise, what do they need to repair, and what do they need from me that they cannot yet ask for well?

This is how compassion becomes practical.

Accountability Without Shame

Accountability is essential. Children need to learn that they have an impact on others. They need to learn that words can wound, bodies can harm, lies can break trust, cruelty can leave marks, and silence can abandon. But accountability must be delivered in a way the child can metabolise. A later chapter returns to this in much more detail; here it is enough to name the principle.

If accountability becomes humiliation, the child will defend. If it becomes rejection, the child will hide. If it becomes an attack on identity, the child will collapse into shame or fight back. Researchers June Tangney and Ronda Dearing have spent decades distinguishing shame from guilt, and the difference matters here.[1] Guilt focuses on the behaviour: I did something bad. Shame focuses on the self: I am bad. Guilt motivates repair. Shame motivates concealment, defensiveness and, in children, often more of the very behaviour we are trying to address. The same distinction has been popularised in the parenting and leadership literature by Brené Brown.[2]

The contrast in language is clear. Shame says, "You are bad." Accountability says, "This behaviour caused harm, and you are capable of repairing it." Shame says, "What is wrong with you?" Accountability says, "What happened, what did it affect, and what needs to happen next?" Shame says, "I cannot believe you would do that." Accountability says, "I love you, and I will help you face this."

The goal of accountability is not to make the child feel terrible. The goal is to help the child become responsible. Those are not the same thing.

The Parent's Inner Work

Seeing children compassionately requires parents to notice their own reactions, because a child's behaviour can trigger old wounds in the parent. A defiant child may trigger a parent's fear of disrespect. A clingy child may trigger discomfort with need. An angry child may trigger memories of violence or chaos. A crying child may trigger helplessness. A lying child may trigger betrayal. A child refusing school may trigger parental shame. A child bullying a sibling may trigger rage, fear or disgust.

When parents are triggered, they may stop seeing the whole child. They may see only danger, disrespect, failure or threat. This is why the parent's nervous system matters. A regulated parent can ask, "What is happening underneath this?" A dysregulated parent often asks, "How do I make this stop right now?" Both questions matter, but if the second is the only one, parenting becomes reactive.

The work is not to be calm all the time. The work is to notice when you are no longer calm enough to lead. Sometimes the most powerful parenting move is a pause: a breath, a hand on the chest, a moment of stepping back, a repair after getting it wrong, a willingness to say, "I need a minute so I do not respond in a way that makes this worse." This is not weakness. It is leadership.

From Bad Child to Unfinished Skill

A compassionate parenting lens often asks, "What skill is missing?" This is the central premise of clinical psychologist Ross Greene's Collaborative and Proactive Solutions model. Greene's starting point, kids do well if they can, argues that challenging behaviour is best understood not as wilful misbehaviour but as the predictable by-product of lagging skills in areas like flexibility, frustration tolerance, problem solving and emotion regulation.[3] When the demands of a moment outstrip a child's skills, behaviour breaks down. The behaviour is not the problem. The skill gap is. We will return to Greene's framework in much more detail in Chapter 21.

For now, the practical reframe is simple. A child who hits may be missing frustration tolerance. A child who lies may be missing safe truth-telling. A child who dominates may be missing flexibility. A child who mocks may be missing empathy and shame tolerance. A child who clings may be missing felt security. A child who withdraws may be missing trust in repair. A child who follows harmful peers may be missing internal belonging. A child who explodes may be missing nervous system regulation. A child who refuses responsibility may be missing executive function, hope or confidence.

When we see behaviour as an unfinished skill, we still hold expectations, but we also teach. We do not simply punish a child for not having a skill; we help them build it. This is not the same as removing consequences. Consequences may still be needed, especially when harm has occurred. But consequences alone do not teach the missing skill unless they are paired with reflection, repair, practice and support. The question becomes: what does this child need to learn, and how can I teach it without shaming them?

Key Takeaways

- Children are not bad apples. Harmful patterns, behaviours and environments are the concern.
- Behaviour is not identity. A child can do something harmful without being reduced to that behaviour.
- When children do not have the words, their behaviour often speaks for them.
- Shame, betrayal and abandonment are often hidden wounds beneath difficult behaviour. A later chapter goes deeper into all three.
- All feelings are welcome. All behaviours are not.
- Compassion explains behaviour, but it does not excuse harm.

- Accountability works best when it is firm, clear and free from humiliation. The shame–guilt distinction matters: guilt motivates repair, shame motivates concealment.
- The child who causes harm still needs help, boundaries and a path back to their own goodness.
- Parents need to look beneath behaviour while still protecting the family system.
- Behind most challenging behaviour sits an unfinished skill. The goal is to teach the skill, not to punish its absence.
- The aim is not to raise children who never make mistakes. The aim is to raise children who can take responsibility, repair harm, and stay connected to their worth while they grow.

References

1. Tangney, J. P., & Dearing, R. L. (2002). Shame and Guilt. New York: Guilford Press.
2. Brown, B. (2012). Daring Greatly: How the Courage to Be Vulnerable Transforms the Way We Live, Love, Parent, and Lead. New York: Gotham Books.
3. Greene, R. W. (2014). The Explosive Child: A New Approach for Understanding and Parenting Easily Frustrated, Chronically Inflexible Children (5th ed.). New York: Harper. (Originally published 1998.)

CHAPTER 3

How Harmful Behaviour Spreads: The Neurobiology of Contagion

Why "Just Ignore Them" Does Not Work

Most parents have said it at some point.

"Just ignore him."

"Don't let it get to you."

"Walk away."

"Don't give them the reaction they want."

It is reasonable advice. It is also, at the level of a child's nervous system, not entirely possible.

Children do not absorb the behaviour of others through conscious choice. They absorb it through biology. A sibling who is screaming, a peer who is sneering, a friend who is making cruel jokes about another classmate, these are not neutral inputs that the child can decide whether to let in. The child's brain and body are already responding before any decision arrives.

Telling a dysregulated child to ignore a dysregulated other is a little like telling someone in cold water to stop feeling cold. The instruction does not reach the level at which the experience is happening.

This chapter is about that level. It is about why one person's behaviour spreads so efficiently through a group, why negative behaviour spreads more efficiently than positive behaviour, and why families and classrooms are particularly vulnerable to a single dysregulated member.

It is not a chapter of biology for its own sake. The biology is the reason your child cannot simply choose not to be affected. Once you can see that, the practical work of the rest of the book becomes much clearer.

Emotional Contagion

In 1994, the social psychologists Elaine Hatfield, John Cacioppo and Richard Rapson published a book called Emotional Contagion. The book pulled together evidence from social, developmental, cross-cultural and experimental psychology and made a startling claim: emotion routinely spreads from one person to another, often without either of them noticing it has happened.[1]

Their argument was that we tend to automatically and unconsciously mimic the facial expressions, vocal tone, posture and movement of the people around us. That mimicry is not just an external performance. The act of unconsciously matching another person's expression triggers, in our own bodies, a faint version of the emotional state that produced it. We feel, in a small way, what they are feeling. Emotion travels.

Most of the time, this is the engine of empathy and connection. It is how a baby tunes into a parent. It is how friends arrive at the same mood. It is how a great teacher fills a room. It is also why a tense workplace meeting leaves everyone exhausted, why a partner's bad day arrives home before they do, and why a single dysregulated person can shift the climate of a household.

Empathy and emotional contagion are related but not the same. Empathy is the cognitive capacity to understand and respond to another person's experience while keeping a clear sense of where you end and they begin. Contagion does not maintain that boundary. In contagion, the other person's state becomes your state. There is no negotiation, and often no awareness that anything has happened.

For an adult with a developed nervous system, this is usually manageable. We catch the mood, but we have practice in stepping back, naming what has happened, and recovering.

For a child, the boundary between contagion and self is much thinner. A young child does not yet have the regulatory architecture to hold themselves separate from another's state. They take it in. The smaller the child, the more this is true.

The Mechanism: Mimicry and Mirroring

How does emotion actually move from one person to another?

Part of the answer is what neuroscientists call the mirror system. In the early 1990s, researchers in Italy, working with macaque monkeys, noticed something unexpected. Certain neurons in the monkey's brain fired both when the monkey performed a specific action, reaching for a piece of fruit, for example, and when the monkey simply watched another monkey perform the same action. The brain was, in effect, mirroring the observed behaviour internally.

Subsequent research in humans, summarised for general readers by neuroscientist Marco Iacoboni in his book Mirroring People, has shown that similar circuitry underpins much of how we read, learn from, and emotionally tune to other people.[2] When you watch someone wince, parts of your own pain network activate. When you watch someone smile, the muscles around your own mouth quietly prepare a smile. When you watch someone shout, your nervous system begins to shift toward fight, flight or freeze before any thinking has occurred.

Mirror-system research is still being refined. Not every claim made about mirror neurons in the popular press has held up under careful study. But the broader principle is well supported across many areas of social and developmental neuroscience: the human brain is built to simulate the behaviour and inner states of the people it observes.

For children, this is not a side feature. It is the main mechanism of learning. Children rehearse emotional and behavioural patterns by watching them. They imitate what they see, and they imitate it most strongly when it carries emotional weight, when it is repeated, and when it is performed by someone they are attached to or admire.

This is why a sibling's outburst affects another sibling's body before any words are spoken. It is why a parent's tone, when they think the child is not listening, is doing more teaching than the lecture that comes after. It is why a peer group that mocks one classmate teaches every child in the room something about what the social environment will reward. It is why the cruelty performed by an online personality lands more powerfully than a parent's warning about that personality.

Children are not bad at filtering. They are uniquely good at absorbing.

Bad Is Stronger Than Good

There is one more piece of the picture that matters here, and it is the most uncomfortable one. Negative emotion does not spread through a group at the same speed as positive emotion. It spreads faster.

In a 2001 review article called Bad Is Stronger Than Good, the social psychologists Roy Baumeister, Ellen Bratslavsky, Catrin Finkenauer and Kathleen Vohs synthesised hundreds of studies across psychology, neuroscience and behavioural economics, and arrived at a striking general conclusion. Across an unusually wide range of human experience, emotion, learning, memory, relationships, parenting, social impressions and decision making, bad events have a larger and more persistent psychological effect than good events of equivalent size.[3]

A criticism is felt more deeply than a compliment. A betrayal is remembered for longer than an act of generosity. A frightening encounter writes itself into memory more durably than a pleasant one. A single act of contempt in a friendship can erase weeks of warmth. Negative impressions form faster and resist disconfirmation more stubbornly than positive ones.

There is an evolutionary logic to this asymmetry. Missing a good thing has rarely killed anyone. Missing a bad thing, a predator, an aggressor, a poisonous plant, could end the line. The brain evolved to weigh threat heavily and to spread alarm quickly.

Inside a family, this asymmetry has a particular shape. A regulated parent reading bedtime stories may move a child a small distance toward calm. A parent shouting in the kitchen may move that same child a much larger distance toward fear. One outburst can outweigh many quiet kindnesses, not because the kindnesses are unimportant, but because the brain is calibrated to register threat with more force.

It is not that good does not register. It does. It is that good has to be repeated, consistent and sustained to do the work that bad accomplishes in a single moment.

This is one of the reasons repair matters so much in this book. A single repaired rupture is not just a course correction. It is a deliberate counterweight to the asymmetric pull of negative emotion. It is a parent saying, with the weight of action, that the negative moment is not the last word.

Contagion in Children: Evidence From the Classroom

If contagion is biological and asymmetric, what does that look like in real children?

One of the clearest empirical illustrations comes from a study published in the journal Education Economics in 2019, by economists Kien Le and My Nguyen.[4] Their question was simple. If a child is being treated harshly at home, in this case, exposed to corporal punishment, does that harshness affect only the child themselves, or does it ripple outward into the classroom around them?

Working with a large dataset of Vietnamese fifth graders, and using the random allocation of children to classrooms within a school as a natural experiment, the authors built what they called a Peers' Violence Index for each child: a measure of how much corporal punishment the rest of the child's classmates were experiencing at home.

The result was sobering. As the Peers' Violence Index rose, the academic performance of the surrounding children dropped. A one standard-deviation increase in the violence in a classmate's home was associated with a measurable fall in maths and language test scores for the children sitting next to them. The effect was not on the directly punished children alone, the spillover reached their peers.

When the authors looked at why, the picture sharpened further. Children sitting next to peers who were being treated harshly at home reported lower academic aspirations, reduced learning effort and an increased incidence of physical bullying at school. The dysregulation imported from the home was reshaping the social and emotional environment of the classroom.

This is the bad apple effect, in real children, in real schools, with measurable consequences for the children who never went home to a violent house.

It is not, of course, that the harshly treated children were the cause. They were the visible carriers of a wider system that was harming everyone. The point of the study is not to blame any child. It is to show, with data, that harmful behaviour does not stay where it begins. It moves through groups. It costs the people around it. And it does so even when those around it are doing nothing wrong.

What This Means for Families

If contagion is automatic, asymmetric and measurable, what is a parent supposed to do?

First, take seriously what your child is being exposed to.

If a child is regularly in close emotional proximity to a sibling, peer, coach or adult who is chronically dysregulated, hostile, contemptuous or cruel, the child will absorb some of it. They cannot help it. The advice to "just ignore it" underestimates the biology. This is not the same as saying every difficult relationship must be removed; it is saying the cost of long-term exposure is real and should be weighed honestly.

Second, do not assume that loud good behaviour from you cancels quiet bad behaviour from elsewhere.

It does not, at least not on its own. Bad is stronger than good. A parent who is warm at bedtime but reactive at the dinner table is teaching the child that warmth is conditional on the parent's mood. A family that is loving on weekends but tense on weeknights is teaching the child that the steady weekday tone is the truer signal. The work is to make the consistent climate match the moments of warmth, not to compensate for the climate with occasional kindness.

Third, repair carries weight that explanation cannot.

When something has gone wrong, a parent has yelled, a sibling has been cruel, an external influence has shifted a child's mood, the corrective is not a lecture. It is a deliberate, named, embodied repair. We will give repair a chapter of its own later in the book, but the principle starts here. Repair is not optional, and it is not a sign of weakness. It is the antidote to the asymmetric stickiness of negative experience.

Fourth, recognise that the household is the room with the highest stakes.

An adult who works in a difficult workplace can decompress at home. A child whose home is the difficult workplace has nowhere else to go. Whatever spreads inside the family system is happening to a developing nervous system that is using that environment as the template for what relationships are. This does not mean parents must be perfect. It does mean the family climate carries weight that no other climate carries, and a parent who can hold that climate steady, even imperfectly, is doing real, measurable, biological work for their child.

Key Takeaways

Emotional contagion is not a metaphor. It is a measurable phenomenon, documented across decades of social and developmental psychology.

Children do not choose to absorb the emotional and behavioural states of those around them. The mirror system and automatic mimicry do most of the work below conscious awareness.

Negative emotion spreads more efficiently than positive emotion. Bad is stronger than good. Good has to be repeated, consistent and sustained to keep up.

The cost of harmful behaviour does not stay with the child who carries it. Empirical evidence, including a large study of Vietnamese fifth graders, shows that exposure to a dysregulated peer measurably depresses the academic performance, aspirations and social environment of surrounding children.

"Just ignore them" underestimates the biology. The child is not failing to filter; they are succeeding at absorbing.

Repair is the deliberate counterweight to the asymmetric pull of negative emotion, and the family climate is the highest-stakes room in a child's life.

References

1. Hatfield, E., Cacioppo, J. T., & Rapson, R. L. (1994). Emotional Contagion. Cambridge: Cambridge University Press.

2. Iacoboni, M. (2008). Mirroring People: The New Science of How We Connect with Others. New York: Farrar, Straus and Giroux.

3. Baumeister, R. F., Bratslavsky, E., Finkenauer, C., & Vohs, K. D. (2001). Bad is stronger than good. Review of General Psychology, 5(4), 323–370. https://doi.org/10.1037/1089-2680.5.4.323

4. Le, K., & Nguyen, M. (2019). 'Bad Apple' peer effects in elementary classrooms: The case of corporal punishment in the home. Education Economics, 27(6), 557–572. https://doi.org/10.1080/09645292.2019.1667306

CHAPTER 4
The Family Is a System

The Family as One Emotional Unit

Most of us were raised to think of a family as a set of individuals who happen to live together. Each person has their own personality, their own choices, their own behaviour. When something goes wrong, the natural instinct is to ask: who is causing it?

Family systems theory turns this around.

In the late 1950s, an American psychiatrist named Murray Bowen began studying entire families admitted to live together on hospital wards while one member was being treated for severe mental illness. What he found, watching them day after day, changed the field.[1]

He found that the symptoms of the identified person could not be understood without watching the whole family. Tension that built up in one part of the family seemed to migrate into another. A father's anxiety would settle into a mother's body. A mother's unspoken grief would settle into a child's behaviour. The family did not behave like a collection of separate people. It behaved like a single emotional unit with several bodies in it.

Bowen called this the family emotional system.

It is one of the most useful ideas a parent can carry. A family is not just the people in the room. It is the climate between them. It is the way tension moves, the way relief moves, the way warmth and contempt and silence and laughter pass between bodies. Each family has its own emotional weather. A child arrives into that weather and grows up inside it.

This is not a metaphor.

Children read the climate of a household constantly, accurately, and from a much earlier age than most adults realise. They read it through facial expression, posture, breath, vocal tone, the spacing between sentences, who looks at whom, what gets noticed and what gets ignored. They are reading it before they have words. They are reading it when the adults think nothing is happening. They are reading it now.

And what they are reading is the system, not just the people inside it.

Circular Causality: Why "Who Started It?" Misses the Point

When something goes wrong in a family, the most natural question, and the one that fuels most of the arguments in most of the world's households, is, "Who started it?"

It is the wrong question.

Family systems theorists describe two ways of thinking about cause. The first is linear causality. A causes B. The car runs out of fuel because no one filled it. The cake burns because the oven was left on. Linear causality is how engineers think about machines.

The second is circular causality. A and B cause each other. Each is shaping the other in real time. There is no first mover, only a pattern that has been turning for so long that it now looks like single events.

Most of what happens between people inside a family runs on circular causality.

Consider a simple example. A teenager comes home and slumps on the couch without speaking. Her mother feels worried and a little dismissed, so she asks, sharply, "How was school?" The teenager hears the sharpness, takes it as criticism, mutters "fine" and leaves the room. The mother feels rejected and tells her partner the teenager is becoming impossible to talk to. The teenager hears the conversation through the wall, decides that nothing she says will land well, and resolves to volunteer less next time.

Who started it?

It is impossible to answer. The mother could equally say the teenager started it by walking past her without speaking. The teenager could equally say the mother started it by snapping. Both of them are correct, in the sense that each is responding to the other. Both of them are wrong, in the sense that there is no first cause to find.

What there is is a pattern. A pattern that has been turning for some time. A pattern in which both of them have a part.

This is one of the most freeing ideas a parent can take from family systems work. It does not say the parent is to blame. It does not say the child is to blame. It says: the pattern is the thing to look at, and the pattern is something both of you can change.

The question shifts. From, "Who is the problem?" to, "What is the pattern, and who needs to change their part of it?"

Most of the time, the parent is the part of the pattern that can change first. Not because the parent is at fault, but because the parent has the more developed nervous system, the longer view, and the social authority to alter the family's emotional weather.

When the parent shifts their step, the dance changes. The child cannot help responding to the new music.

Subsystems: The Architecture Underneath the Roof

If the family is one emotional unit, it is also an emotional unit with an internal architecture. Some relationships are closer than others. Some carry more authority than others. Some carry more vulnerability than others.

The Argentinian psychiatrist Salvador Minuchin, working in New York with families in poverty, named these patterns of internal architecture clearly and famously. In his 1974 book Families and Family Therapy, he described a family as a web of overlapping subsystems, each with its own task and its own boundary.[2]

There is the marital subsystem, the relationship between the partners, where the work is intimacy, repair and shared decision making.

There is the parental subsystem, the way the partners function together when they are leading the children. This may include grandparents, step-parents, ex-partners, foster carers, kin.

There is the sibling subsystem, the relationships between the children, where they learn how to share, compete, cooperate, defend, repair and form their first peer experiences.

Each subsystem has a job. And each subsystem has a boundary, not a wall, but a permeable membrane that says what crosses in and what does not.

Trouble in a family often shows up where boundaries are unclear. A child who is drawn into the parents' marital conflict and asked to take sides is being pulled across the marital boundary. A parent who relies on a child as their main emotional support, sharing adult worries, turning to the child to feel less alone, is reaching across the parental boundary into territory that does not belong to a child. A sibling subsystem in which one child is given parental authority over another, beyond ordinary helpfulness, is one in which the sibling boundary has been crossed.

These crossings are usually not deliberate. They happen because adults are tired, lonely, traumatised, distracted, or trying to manage a child's behaviour the only way they know how. Naming them is not blaming. It is just naming, which is the start of changing.

When the subsystems do their own jobs, the family climate stabilises. Children carry only what is theirs to carry. Parents carry only what is theirs to carry. The marriage is held by the partners, not by the children. The children get to be children.

Triangulation: When Two Become Three

There is one specific subsystem-crossing that comes up often enough in family work to warrant its own name: triangulation.

Bowen observed that when tension between two people in a family becomes uncomfortable, one of them will often pull a third person into the relationship to relieve the pressure.[1]

A couple is fighting. Rather than face the conflict, one parent begins focusing intensely on the difficult child. The child becomes the topic of the relationship. The conflict between the partners cools down because they now have a shared problem to discuss. The original tension has been displaced into a triangle.

A parent is angry with the other parent and quietly enlists a child as their confidant: "Your father is so unreasonable. Don't tell him I said anything." The child is now carrying weight that does not belong to them, in a relationship structure that requires them to keep secrets from one parent in order to belong to the other.

A child is anxious about a friendship, and the parent feels the anxiety as their own. The parent begins managing the friendship from the outside, coaching, intervening, contacting the other parent, because their own discomfort has been displaced through the child.

Triangles are not always destructive. A baby is, in a real sense, a triangle: a third person who relieves and complicates a couple's relationship at the same time. A trusted aunt, a wise grandparent, a good therapist can be welcome triangulators, third points that steady the system rather than capture its tension.

But chronically captured triangles cost children dearly. A child who has been pulled in to manage a parent's loneliness, distract a parent's anger, or carry a parent's anxiety has been given a job that does not belong to them. They will often perform the job well, because children are loyal and clever. The cost is paid in the rest of their development.

Watching for triangles is one of the most useful things a parent can do, especially in the moments when family tension is highest. The question to ask is: who is being asked to carry what? And who is the relief in this triangle costing?

Why Focusing Only on the Identified Child Usually Fails

Most families come to clinical attention because of one child.

It is the child who is melting down. The child who has refused school. The child who is hitting siblings, lying, withdrawing, stealing, being bullied or doing the bullying, exploding at bedtime, quietly cutting, vomiting after meals, or texting the parent from school to be picked up before lunch.

From the outside, the child looks like the problem.

From a family systems perspective, the child is more often the symptom carrier.

This is not a soft, vague claim. It is a clinically observed pattern. When a family system is under sustained strain, through marital conflict, parental trauma, financial crisis, illness, intergenerational pain, secrecy, addiction, a recent loss, or a chronic mismatch between household demands and household capacity, the strain does not stay evenly distributed. It tends to settle into the most sensitive member, the one whose nervous system is least armoured.

Often that is a child. Sometimes it is the youngest. Sometimes it is the most temperamentally reactive. Sometimes it is the one whose particular wiring, high sensitivity, neurodivergence, an early history of disruption, an attachment injury, makes them the place where the family's unfelt feelings find their first expression.

The behaviour that follows is real. It is not theatre, and it is not the child's fault. The child is struggling. They may need their own assessment, their own therapy, their own boundaries, their own skill-building. None of that is wrong.

What is wrong is the shorter version of the story: that this child is the family's problem.

When parents arrive at family work with that belief intact, the most common pattern is that everyone's effort is poured into changing the child while the system around them stays exactly as it was. The child becomes the project. The household climate is unexamined. The marital tension is unaddressed. The parent's own dysregulation is not named. The sibling subsystem keeps its existing roles. The triangle stays captured.

And then, even with the best therapist and the most diligent child, change is partial and slow. The child improves a little, regresses, improves again. Everyone is exhausted. The family wonders if it is, in the end, just the way the child is.

It usually is not just the way the child is.

It is usually the way the system is, expressed through the child.

If the family system can shape the dysregulation, the family system can also shape the healing. That is the entire promise of working with the system instead of working only with the child.

The System Already Has the Tools to Heal

The good news is that families are not fragile. The same circular causality that creates a stuck pattern can also create a healthy one.

When one parent shifts from reactive to regulated, the other parent's response often softens. When the marital subsystem is repaired, the children's symptoms frequently ease without anyone targeting them directly. When triangles are dissolved and each subsystem is asked to do only its own work, children stop carrying weight that was never theirs.

This is not about perfection. It is about direction. A family that begins, in small ways, to ask, "What is the pattern?" instead of, "Who is the problem?" has already changed the system.

The next two chapters narrow the lens in particular places where this matters most. Chapter 5 takes on the most important diagnostic distinction in this book: between a child who is unconsciously carrying the family's pain (the Identified Patient) and a person whose own sustained harmful behaviour is destabilising an otherwise sound system. Confusing these two is one of the most expensive mistakes a family can make. Chapter 6 returns to the three hidden wounds, shame, betrayal and abandonment, and shows how each one can shape the behaviour we then describe as a problem.

But the larger frame begins here. The family is a system. The behaviour we are watching is rarely the whole story. And the place to look first is not at the child but at the climate around the child.

Key Takeaways

A family is not a set of separate individuals. It is a single emotional system with several bodies in it.

Most of what happens between people in a family runs on circular causality, not linear cause and effect. The useful question is, "What is the pattern?" not, "Who started it?"

Inside the system there are subsystems, marital, parental, sibling, each with its own task and boundary. Trouble often shows up where the boundaries blur.

Triangulation occurs when tension between two people is relieved by pulling in a third. Children are common triangulation points and pay a real developmental cost when chronically captured.

When a family is under strain, the strain tends to settle into the most sensitive member. That child is often the symptom carrier, not the source.

The same circular causality that creates a stuck pattern can create a healthy one. Small shifts in parental regulation, marital repair, and the integrity of subsystems often ease the child's presenting behaviour without targeting it directly.

References

1. Bowen, M. (1978). Family Therapy in Clinical Practice. Northvale, NJ: Jason Aronson.

2. Minuchin, S. (1974). Families and Family Therapy. Cambridge, MA: Harvard University Press.

3. Kerr, M. E., & Bowen, M. (1988). Family Evaluation: An Approach Based on Bowen Theory. New York: W. W. Norton.

CHAPTER 5

The Identified Patient and the True Bad Apple

The Most Important Distinction in This Book

Of all the chapters in this book, this is the one most likely to be misused if read alone.

Everything until now has been laying the ground. The bad apple effect is real. Behaviour is contagious. Systems carry strain. A child who appears to be the problem is often the symptom carrier, not the source. These are useful ideas. They are also dangerous if applied bluntly.

Because there is a difference, a clinical, life-altering difference, between two situations that can look almost identical from the outside.

In the first situation, a family is under sustained strain, and the strain has settled into one child. That child is now carrying the visible cost of a much larger pattern: parental dysregulation, marital conflict, intergenerational pain, secrecy, exhaustion, untreated trauma, or a household whose demands quietly outstrip its capacity. Their behaviour is real. Their distress is real. But the centre of gravity is not in the child. It is in the system around them.

In the second situation, an otherwise sound family is being destabilised by one member whose behaviour is harmful, a child with serious neurodevelopmental, behavioural or psychiatric needs that the family cannot manage on goodwill alone, or an external influence (a peer, a coach, an adult, an online community) whose harmful patterns are being imported into the home. The behaviour is real. The harm is real. The centre of gravity is in the person, or in the influence, not in the family climate.

The first situation is what family therapists have long called the Identified Patient. The second is what we have been calling the true bad apple.

These two situations look similar at first glance because they share a surface feature: the family is organising itself around one child whose behaviour is causing distress. But the underlying physics is different, and the right response is different.

Confusing the two is one of the most expensive mistakes a family can make. Treating an Identified Patient as if they are a true bad apple intensifies the family's pain, deepens the child's trauma, and pushes the underlying problem somewhere else where it will eventually erupt. Treating a true bad apple as if they are an Identified Patient leaves the harm unchecked, leaves siblings exposed, and leaves the harming child without the firm, contained, structured help they need.

Getting this distinction right is the most important diagnostic work a parent can do.

The Identified Patient: A Child Carrying the System's Pain

The phrase Identified Patient was first used in family-systems literature in the late 1950s and 1960s, by clinicians who had begun watching whole families instead of single members. They noticed that the person formally bearing the diagnosis was rarely the only one in distress. The whole family was struggling. But by an unspoken agreement, no one named that. Instead, the family pointed at one of its members and said, in effect, "If only this person were well, we would be fine."

Murray Bowen described this as the family projection process: the unconscious collective decision to locate a family's unprocessed tension inside one member, usually the most vulnerable one.[1] Salvador Minuchin saw the same pattern in the families he worked with in New York and described it as a structural defence, a way for a stressed system to hide the wider dysfunction by concentrating its visibility in one person.[2]

The Identified Patient does not volunteer for the role and does not know they have it. They are simply the family member whose nervous system, temperament, life circumstances or sensitivity makes them the first to break under the weight everyone is carrying. Their symptoms are real. Their suffering is genuine. They are not pretending. They are not strategising.

But the symptoms are also serving the system. They give the family a place to put its pain. They allow the marital conflict to be displaced into a parenting problem. They allow the parents' own grief, trauma or exhaustion to remain unspoken because everyone is busy worrying about the child. They allow the wider story to stay hidden under one visible story.

In contemporary popular writing, this dynamic has been reframed for adult readers as family scapegoating, including in the work of marriage and family therapist Rebecca Mandeville.[3] The clinical phenomenon and the popular phenomenon are the same thing seen from different angles.

What does an Identified Patient look like in practice?

Often they are the child who has been called difficult since they were a toddler.

Often they are the child whose anxiety, depression, anger or refusal seems out of proportion to anything visible in their immediate life.

Often they are the child who reacts most strongly to changes in the household climate, a parental argument, a job loss, a grandparent's illness, an unspoken grief.

Often, when one parent describes them, the descriptions skew negative even as the parent insists they love the child.

Often the family treats them as the puzzle to be solved.

And often, when the wider system shifts, when the marriage is repaired, when a parent gets their own help, when the household becomes less chaotic, the child's symptoms ease without anyone working on the child directly. That is one of the clearest signs, in retrospect, that the child was carrying the system's pain.

Bateson's Double Bind

One of the most useful descriptions of how an Identified Patient gets caught comes from a paper published in 1956 by anthropologist Gregory Bateson and his colleagues Donald Jackson, Jay Haley and John Weakland. Their paper was titled Toward a Theory of Schizophrenia, and although the schizophrenia hypothesis they made has not held up over time, the broader concept they introduced has been one of the most influential ideas in family therapy ever since: the double bind.[4]

A double bind is a situation in which a person is given two contradictory messages, told that they cannot escape, and not allowed to comment on the contradiction. Whatever they do, they are wrong. If they obey the first message, they violate the second. If they obey the second, they violate the first. If they try to point out the impossibility, they are punished or dismissed for the attempt.

Children inside families under strain often live in low-grade double binds.

"Tell me how you really feel," a parent says, and reacts with hurt, withdrawal or rage when the child does.

"Be more independent," a parent says, and treats the child's independence as a betrayal of closeness.

"It's fine to disagree with me," a parent says, and lengthens every disagreement until the child gives in for peace.

"We are a happy family," the household says, and punishes any expression of unhappiness.

A child caught in a chronic double bind cannot win, cannot escape, and cannot name the trap. So the trap shows up in their body. It comes out as anxiety, anger, withdrawal, refusal, somatic illness, or symptoms that the family then labels as the child's problem.

The point of naming the double bind is not to assign blame to the parents. Most parents who set up double binds are not doing it deliberately. They are usually replicating the binds they themselves grew up inside, often with great love and great unawareness. The point is to recognise the pattern, so the bind can be loosened, by the parent, with adult help if needed.

An Identified Patient often becomes more themselves the moment the bind is broken. The work, then, is on the bind, not on the child.

The True Bad Apple: A Person Destabilising an Otherwise Sound System

Now consider the other situation.

Some families are not running on chronic strain. The marital subsystem is reasonably steady. The parents are mostly regulated. There is room in the household for a range of feelings. There are repairs after rupture. There are clear, fair expectations. There is laughter as well as discipline.

And inside that family, one member's behaviour is harming the others.

It might be a child whose serious neurodevelopmental needs, an externalising behavioural condition, severe trauma history before joining the family, a co-occurring psychiatric difficulty, are larger than the family can manage on warmth and patience alone. It might be an older sibling who has begun bullying, intimidating or sexually coercing a younger sibling. It might be a teenager whose behaviour has shifted under the influence of a peer group, an online community, or a substance, and who is now bringing those imported patterns home. It might be an adult, a step-parent, an extended family member, a coach, a friend's parent, whose contempt, manipulation or volatility is reshaping the family's climate.

In all of these cases, the family system is not the source of the dysregulation. It is the receiver of it.

The behaviour does not need to be explained as a symptom carried for the family. It is what it appears to be: a sustained pattern of harm, originating in one person or one external influence, that the family is now adapting around at real cost to its other members.

This situation calls for a different kind of response. Not less compassion, the harming child is still a person, still loved, still deserving of help. But the centre of gravity sits with them and with the harm, not with the family's climate. The response is structured, often clinical, and may involve assessment, specialist treatment, behavioural intervention, parental monitoring, careful gatekeeping, restorative repair, and, in some situations, the kind of structured supervision that protects siblings while everyone gets help.

Most importantly, this situation calls for parents who can stop searching for the family-systems explanation that would let everyone off the hook, and accept that what is in front of them is real, sustained, harmful behaviour that needs to be contained.

Some children are Identified Patients. Some children are not. Some adults are. Some adults are not. The honest work is figuring out which is which.

How to Tell Which Is Which

There is no single test. The distinction between an Identified Patient and a true bad apple is a clinical judgement, often one that benefits from outside help. But several questions tend to clarify the picture.

Where is the strain coming from?

If you map the family honestly, the marriage, the parents' own histories, the household pace, financial pressure, work demands, recent losses, intergenerational patterns, does the strain look like it is generating itself somewhere upstream of the child? Or does the family climate appear stable, with one member's behaviour pulling everyone else off course?

What does the child's behaviour do for the system?

An Identified Patient's symptoms tend to relieve a tension somewhere else in the family. Marital arguments cool down because the child needs attention. Difficult feelings stay unspoken because everyone is busy worrying about the child. Notice what the behaviour is enabling the rest of the system to avoid. A true bad apple's behaviour tends to do the opposite: it generates new tension across the family that wasn't there before.

Has the child changed under sustained, well-resourced support?

An Identified Patient often improves dramatically when the system shifts, even when no one has worked directly with them. A true bad apple's behaviour tends to remain stable, escalate, or briefly improve and then return when the family lowers its supervision.

Is there genuine harm to others, and is it sustained?

Identified Patients often appear to harm others, but the harm is usually diffuse, anxiety leaking into the household, mood ruining a dinner, a sibling crying because their brother won't talk. A true bad apple's harm is usually more pointed and more sustained: targeted aggression, deliberate cruelty, manipulation, intimidation, sexualised behaviour toward a younger sibling, prolonged campaigns of control, persistent dishonesty that erodes the family's trust.

What does the child say about themselves when they are calm?

An Identified Patient, in calmer moments, often expresses confusion, sadness, shame or grief. They may say things like, "I don't know why I'm like this," or, "I feel like I ruin everything," or, "I just want everyone to be okay." A child caught in a more deliberate harmful pattern, particularly one shaped by external influence or by an entrenched personality structure, tends to express less of that. They may rationalise, blame the victim, minimise, or insist on their right to act as they did.

And finally, what does an outside professional see?

The most reliable answer here is rarely the one a parent reaches alone. A trauma-informed family therapist, child psychologist, or psychiatrist who can sit with the whole family, not just the child, can usually see the pattern within a few sessions. Australian families have access to a number of clinical pathways through GPs, the Better Access initiative, perinatal and family services, and child and adolescent mental health services (CAMHS); the international equivalents apply in other countries. If the cost of the wrong answer is high, and it almost always is, outside help is not optional.

Why Getting It Wrong Amplifies Harm

If a true bad apple pattern is treated as if the child is an Identified Patient, the family is, in effect, told that the harming behaviour is a symptom of something else and will resolve once the system is healthier. Siblings are asked to be patient. Limits are softened. Specialist help is delayed. Meanwhile, the harm continues, and the harmed children learn that the family is not a place where they will be reliably protected.

If an Identified Patient is treated as if they are a true bad apple, the family doubles down on the child as the problem. The child is sent to therapy alone. They are punished, medicated, contained, monitored, possibly excluded from school, and often slowly written off as the difficult one. The wider strain that produced their symptoms is left untouched. The family achieves a temporary peace at the cost of one child's identity. Years later, that child often arrives in adult therapy with the wound of having been the family's designated problem.

Both errors have a common cost: a child being asked to carry a story that is not theirs to carry.

This is why the chapter on the bad apple effect needs the chapter on the Identified Patient sitting beside it. The same word, pattern, has to be applied honestly. Sometimes the pattern is a system pulling on a child. Sometimes the pattern is one person's behaviour pulling on a system. Both are real. Confusing them costs everyone.

Holding the Both/And

these two situations are not always cleanly separable. Real families are messy. A child can be partly an Identified Patient and partly the source of harmful behaviour. A teenager can be carrying intergenerational pain and be importing harmful peer behaviour. A parent can be both a long-suffering victim of someone else's patterns and a contributor to the household's dysregulation.

The point of the distinction is not to force every family into one category. It is to keep both questions alive at the same time:

Is the centre of gravity in the system or in the person?

And is the family asking the right one of those questions, given what is in front of it?

When parents can hold both questions, without collapsing into either blame or denial, the family begins to find more accurate responses. The child who is mostly an Identified Patient gets the system change they need, and lighter, kinder direct work. The child who is mostly a true bad apple gets the structured, contained, often clinical help they need, and the family gets the protection and clarity it needs.

Most of the time, both will be partly true. Most of the time, the work is to do enough of the system repair, and enough of the structured response, that no one has to be reduced to a single label.

Key Takeaways

There is a clinically critical difference between an Identified Patient, a child carrying the system's pain, and a true bad apple, a person or external influence destabilising an otherwise sound family.

The two situations look similar from the outside. Both feature a family organising around one child. The underlying physics, and the right response, are different.

Identified Patients are often produced by chronic family strain, including the kinds of double binds Bateson and his colleagues described in 1956: contradictory messages a child cannot win, escape or comment on.

A true bad apple pattern is sustained, pointed harm coming from one source, in a family that is otherwise mostly stable. It calls for structured, often clinical responses, not just family-systems work.

Useful diagnostic questions: Where is the strain coming from? What does the behaviour do for the system? Has the child changed under sustained system support? Is the harm sustained and pointed? What does the child say about themselves when calm? What does an outside professional see?

Treating one situation as if it is the other amplifies harm in both directions. The honest work is to keep both questions alive, often with outside help, and to allow that real families usually contain a mixture of both.

References

1. Bowen, M. (1978). Family Therapy in Clinical Practice. Northvale, NJ: Jason Aronson.
2. Minuchin, S. (1974). Families and Family Therapy. Cambridge, MA: Harvard University Press.
3. Mandeville, R. C. (2020). Rejected, Shamed, and Blamed: Help and Hope for Adults in the Family Scapegoat Role. Independently published.
4. Bateson, G., Jackson, D. D., Haley, J., & Weakland, J. (1956). Toward a theory of schizophrenia. Behavioral Science, 1(4), 251–264. https://doi.org/10.1002/bs.3830010402

CHAPTER 6

The Three Hidden Wounds: Shame, Betrayal, Abandonment

Why the Wounds Are Hidden

Most of the difficult behaviour we see in children is the visible top layer of something the child cannot yet see, name or describe.

Underneath, in many children, sits one of three wounds, sometimes one alone, more often a tangle of all three.

Shame is the wound that says, "There is something wrong with me."

Betrayal is the wound that says, "The people I trusted were not safe."

Abandonment is the wound that says, "I am on my own."

These are not just uncomfortable feelings. At the level a child usually carries them, they are organising principles. They quietly shape what a child believes about themselves, what they expect from other people, and what their nervous system does when relationships become close, important or unstable. They turn up in behaviour because they have to. The child does not yet have the language, the concept maps, or the developmental capacity to think them through. The body and the behaviour speak first.

If you only see the behaviour, you will keep responding to the wrong layer. You will keep treating the visible smoke as if it were the fire. You will keep changing strategies that do not work, because none of them are addressing the wound underneath.

If, on the other hand, you can see what the behaviour is protecting, accountability becomes more effective, not less. The child does not get to escape responsibility because they are wounded, that is not what this chapter argues. They get to be addressed at the level where change is possible.

This chapter takes each of the three wounds in turn, looks at the inner experience, traces the behavioural signature, and ends with what is useful for parents at home.

Shame: I Am Bad

The first wound, and the one most likely to be inside any of the others, is shame.

Shame is not the same as guilt. The distinction was already introduced in Chapter 2 and is central to how parents respond to harm. Guilt focuses on the behaviour: I did something bad. Shame focuses on the self: I am bad. Decades of research by social psychologists June Tangney and Ronda Dearing, and the popular work of Brené Brown, both find the same thing: guilt motivates repair, while shame motivates concealment, defensiveness and, in children, often more of the very behaviour we are trying to change.[1]

What does shame actually feel like inside a child?

It is closer to a body experience than a thought. A flush rising in the face. A sudden urge to disappear. A drop in the gut. A heat behind the eyes. A wish for the floor to open. For some children, shame arrives almost without content, the child cannot tell you what they did wrong, only that something has gone wrong with them.

Because shame is so unbearable to sit with, most children do not. They move. They displace it. They get rid of it as fast as they can.

Psychiatrist Donald Nathanson, building on the affect research of Silvan Tomkins, mapped four common ways human beings move shame out of the body. He called it the Compass of Shame.[2] A child caught in shame typically responds in one of four directions:

Attack self. The child turns the shame inward. They become harshly self-critical, perfectionistic, anxious, sometimes self-harming. They get there first: if they hate themselves more than anyone else can, no one can hurt them with criticism. Outwardly, this child often looks high-achieving, careful, even excessively responsible. Inside, they are fighting a constant private war.

Withdrawal. The child collapses inward. They go quiet. They hide in their room. They stop trying. They become invisible. They may say very little when corrected, while the storm inside them is enormous. Withdrawal can look, from the outside, like compliance. It is not. It is collapse.

Attack other. The child gets rid of the shame by putting it onto someone else. They mock a sibling. They pick on a peer. They humiliate a younger child. They become the bully, not because they enjoy cruelty, but because the cruelty empties the shame out of their own body for a moment. This is one of the most painful patterns to see in a child, and one of the most misunderstood.

Avoidance. The child runs. They distract. They lie. They refuse to talk about what happened. They scroll, game, change the subject, deny outright. Avoidance can become a lifelong style: anything to keep the shame from being looked at.

Most children do not stay on one point of the compass. They cycle. The same child may attack a sibling on Monday, withdraw into their bedroom on Tuesday, and present a perfect, anxious façade on Wednesday. The needle is moving because the shame underneath is unbearable and is searching for relief.

Knowing this changes how a parent responds.

When you see attack-other, you are not only seeing aggression. You are seeing a child trying to evict shame from their own body.

When you see withdrawal, you are not only seeing avoidance. You are seeing a child whose system has chosen disappearing over rupture.

When you see attack-self, you are not only seeing perfectionism. You are seeing a child who has decided that pre-emptive self-criticism is safer than being criticised by anyone else.

When you see avoidance, you are not only seeing dishonesty or distraction. You are seeing a child for whom looking at what happened is, for now, intolerable.

The work, in each case, is the same in shape and different in detail: bring the shame down to a size the child can be near, without the child being humiliated for having it. That work is the heart of the accountability-without-shame chapter later in the book.

Betrayal: The People I Trusted Were Not Safe

The second wound is betrayal.

Betrayal is what happens when someone a child needs to trust, a parent, a sibling, an adult relative, a coach, a teacher, a close friend, uses that trust against the child or fails to protect them when the child reasonably expected they would.

It does not require dramatic, named abuse, although it can include it. It can be much smaller and more chronic. It can be a parent who promises and then does not follow through, repeatedly. It can be a sibling who exposes a younger child's vulnerability for laughs. It can be an adult who agrees to keep a confidence and then shares it with another adult while the child overhears. It can be a parent who, in moments of stress, mocks a child's body, fears or interests. It can be a friend who, having been let into the child's inner world, weaponises what they were told.

Betrayal stings differently from other forms of pain because it cannot be filed under impersonal misfortune. It comes from the people who were supposed to be the safer side of the world.

Psychologist Jennifer Freyd has written some of the most rigorous work on this wound. In her 1996 book Betrayal Trauma, she argued that betrayal by an attachment figure imposes a particular cognitive burden on a child: the child has to remain attached to the very person who has hurt them, because the child cannot survive without that attachment.[3] The child's mind manages this impossible situation by suppressing, fragmenting or reorganising the betrayal. The cost of that suppression turns up later, as anxiety, hypervigilance, controlling behaviour, difficulty trusting peers, difficulty trusting authority, difficulty believing one's own perceptions.

What does betrayal look like in a child's behaviour?

It often looks like suspicion, even toward people who have done nothing wrong. The child who has been betrayed pre-emptively reads relationships for the next betrayal. They may test friendships and then leave the moment a small letdown occurs. They may keep their parents at a careful distance after a pattern of broken promises. They may resist asking for help, because asking for help is what got them hurt before.

It often looks like control. The betrayed child cannot rely on the world to be safe, so they try to make it predictable. They become the child who plans, who organises, who sets the rules of every game, who refuses surprises, who needs to know exactly what will happen and when.

It often looks like self-protective dishonesty. The child does not lie because they are dishonest. They lie because the truth, in the past, was used against them. Telling the truth and then being mocked, betrayed, or punished trains a child to keep the truth back. Their lying is a residue of the original wound.

And it sometimes looks like preemptive cruelty. The child who has been betrayed may strike first, especially in friendships and sibling relationships, because being the one who breaks the connection is less terrifying than waiting to be broken.

The most important thing for parents to understand about a betrayed child is that they are not refusing to trust. They have learned not to trust. Reaching them takes time, consistency and the dull, repeated, unglamorous work of being someone who keeps small promises.

betrayal can come from any direction in a family system. Sometimes it comes from a parent. Sometimes it comes from a sibling. Sometimes it comes from a member of the extended family. Recognising betrayal is not a project of finding the villain. It is a project of believing the child's body when it tells you, through their behaviour, that something at some point was not safe.

Abandonment: I Am on My Own

The third wound is abandonment.

Abandonment is what happens to a child when the people they need do not arrive, physically, emotionally, or both. It can be the dramatic version: a parent who left, a death, a placement disruption, a divorce that took most of one parent out of a child's life. It can also be the quiet version: a parent who was physically present but emotionally somewhere else, lost in their own depression, addiction, work, trauma, screen, or simply the chronic exhaustion of survival.

It can be the version that comes through illness, through caregiver overwhelm, through a sibling whose needs absorbed everything, through a household in which the adults loved the child but were not actually available to them.

John Bowlby, the British psychiatrist who founded attachment theory, spent his life mapping what happens when a child cannot reliably reach the people they depend on.[4] His work, and the decades of attachment research that followed, made one of the most important findings in modern child development clear: a child does not simply need to be near a caregiver. A child needs to be able to count on returning to a caregiver, again and again, especially when frightened or distressed. When that return is uncertain, repeatedly broken, or never quite available, the child's nervous system adapts.

Those adaptations are not random. They show up in three broad shapes that parents will recognise.

Some children become clingy and pre-emptively distressed. They protest separations loudly. They will not let the parent out of sight. They check in constantly. They are not attention-seeking.

They are connection-seeking, in the only way their nervous system has learned reliably works.

Some children become hyper-independent. They stop asking. They stop expecting. They begin to handle things themselves, often very early, often very competently. Outwardly, they look mature. Inwardly, they have made a decision a child should never have to make: that they are on their own. These children are often praised for being "easy". Easy is rarely the right word.

Some children become parentified. They begin to care for the adults around them. They notice when mum is sad and try to cheer her up. They ask the angry parent if they are okay. They run interference between their parents. They mediate sibling conflict. They become, in effect, small managers of the household's emotional weather. Parentification can look like sweet maturity from the outside. From the inside, it is a child who has learned that their needs are inconvenient and that being useful is the safest way to be loved.

Abandonment is also one of the wounds that most reliably drives a child toward harmful peer influence. A child who feels unmet at home will often work harder to belong somewhere, anywhere, that feels like it has a place for them. If the only group that has a place for them is one that rewards cruelty, contempt or risk, the child may take the place anyway, because abandonment feels worse than self-betrayal. Belonging at any cost is a survival decision before it is a moral one.

Bessel van der Kolk's widely read work on trauma, while not without recent academic debate, sits with this picture clinically: when a child cannot rely on relational return, the body keeps the cost, in vigilance, in over-arousal, in numbed disconnection.[5]

The repair for abandonment is not a single moment of reassurance. It is the slow, repeated experience of return. A parent who is reliably available, again and again, in small moments, over years, is doing the actual neurological work of correcting the wound. There are no shortcuts here. There is also no need to be perfect. What matters is the pattern: that the child can count on the parent coming back.

How the Wounds Interact

Most children do not carry only one of these wounds. They carry a tangle.

A child who has been chronically betrayed often also feels deeply ashamed, "there must be something about me that made the people I trusted treat me this way."

A child who has been emotionally abandoned often feels both alone and ashamed of their own need, "if I needed less, someone might have been there."

A child who is steeped in shame may eventually, with the wrong peer group at the wrong moment, begin betraying others, because betraying first is one way to escape the unbearable inside.

When all three are running, you see something most parents recognise without having a name for it: a child who is at once anxious and angry, controlling and collapsed, desperate to belong and cruel to anyone who tries to belong to them. The behaviour is bewildering until you realise it is not a single child making a single decision. It is a child being pulled in three directions by three different injuries at once.

This is also why simple behaviour management approaches so often fail with these children. Behaviour management addresses the visible action. It does not address the wound it is protecting. The child obeys for a while, then erupts in a different shape, because the wound is still there.

The work is not to do trauma therapy at the kitchen table. The work is to recognise what you are looking at, respond at a level the child can reach, and bring in clinical help where the wounds are larger than what a household can hold. There is no shame in needing help here. Most families do.

Why Naming the Wound Makes Accountability More Effective

Some parents worry, reading a chapter like this, that naming the wound will let the child off the hook. If everything is trauma, what about responsibility?

The opposite is true.

A child cannot grow from a behaviour they are too ashamed to look at. Shame, by its nature, makes the child more defensive, not less. A child cannot repair harm if they secretly believe they are the harm. A child cannot develop self-control if the adults around them only see the defiance and never see the distress.

When a parent can say, "I know something hurt before this happened, and I will help you find it. And it is still not okay to hit your sister, and you are going to make this right," the child is being asked to do two things at once: to be honest about the inside and to be responsible for the outside. Most children can do this work, given that frame.

What most children cannot do is hold themselves accountable for behaviour that has been treated as proof that they are bad. That move collapses the project. It produces either submission without learning, or rebellion without repair. Neither is what we are after.

Accountability without shame is not soft. It is precise. It says: the wound is real, the harm is real, and you are capable of facing both.

That sentence is the hinge of the rest of this book.

What Helps, Briefly

Each wound has a corresponding repair, which the practical chapters later in this book will return to in detail. For now, in summary:

Shame heals through being seen without being humiliated. The corrective experience is being known by an adult, clearly, including the parts the child finds unbearable, and being met with care rather than contempt. Repair after rupture, named and embodied, does this work.

Betrayal heals through small, repeated, kept promises. Not grand declarations of trustworthiness. Not heart-to-hearts that demand the child immediately re-trust. Just the dull, faithful, accumulating evidence that the adult shows up, follows through, does not weaponise the child's vulnerabilities, and apologises clearly when they slip.

Abandonment heals through reliable return. The parent does not have to be present every minute. The parent has to be reachable, recoverable and consistent. Routines help. Predictable rhythms help. A parent who can name leaving and arrival, "I am going now, I will be back at this time, here is who is with you, I love you", helps. So does, simply, a parent who keeps coming back.

None of this is fast. None of it is dramatic. All of it is the actual mechanism.

The bad apple effect runs more easily through children carrying these wounds, because the wounds make them more vulnerable to harmful belonging, more reactive to negative emotional contagion, and more likely to be drawn toward influences that promise relief. The strongest protection a parent can offer, beyond gatekeeping and monitoring, is the slow, deep, daily work of healing the wounds underneath.

A child who is loved into safety from these three wounds is not a child who never has hard moments. They are a child who has a place to come back to.

That place is the family the parent is building.

Key Takeaways

Most difficult behaviour in children sits on top of one or more of three hidden wounds: shame ("I am bad"), betrayal ("the people I trusted were not safe"), abandonment ("I am on my own").

These wounds are not just feelings. They are organising principles that shape what a child expects of themselves, of others, and of the world.

Shame typically moves in one of four directions, attack self, withdrawal, attack other, avoidance, and a single child can cycle through all four. Each is a strategy for evicting unbearable shame from the body.

Betrayal teaches a child that trust is dangerous. It often shows up as suspicion, control, self-protective dishonesty and pre-emptive cruelty. Repair is dull, repeated, unglamorous reliability.

Abandonment shapes the nervous system into clinginess, hyper-independence or parentification. It also drives a child toward harmful peer belonging when home does not feel like a place for them. Repair is reliable return, again and again, over time.

Most children carry a tangle of all three wounds. Behaviour management alone rarely reaches them. The right work is to respond at the level of the wound while still holding accountability for the behaviour.

Naming the wound underneath behaviour makes accountability more effective, not less. It is the only way a child can do the inside-outside work that real responsibility requires.

References

1. Tangney, J. P., & Dearing, R. L. (2002). Shame and Guilt. New York: Guilford Press. (See also Chapter 2.)

2. Nathanson, D. L. (1992). Shame and Pride: Affect, Sex, and the Birth of the Self. New York: W. W. Norton.

3. Freyd, J. J. (1996). Betrayal Trauma: The Logic of Forgetting Childhood Abuse. Cambridge, MA: Harvard University Press.

4. Bowlby, J. (1969). Attachment and Loss, Vol. 1: Attachment. New York: Basic Books.

5. van der Kolk, B. (2014). The Body Keeps the Score: Brain, Mind, and Body in the Healing of Trauma. New York: Viking Penguin. (Note: while widely influential, some claims in this book have been contested in the recent academic literature; the broad point that trauma is held somatically remains well supported.)

CHAPTER 7

Sibling Dynamics: When the System Adapts to the Loudest

The Sibling Subsystem: The First Peer Group

For most children, brothers and sisters are the first peer group, the first audience, the first rivals, the first long-term cooperators and the first long-term combatants. Long before any classroom culture takes shape, the sibling subsystem is teaching a child what closeness costs, what conflict feels like, what repair looks like, and what it means to lose and recover an important relationship.

Developmental psychologist Judy Dunn, working with very young children in their own homes, was one of the first researchers to take this subsystem seriously on its own terms. In her 1985 book Sisters and Brothers, and in the decades of research that followed, she showed something that surprised the field at the time but is obvious to anyone who has watched two small siblings: the sheer volume, intimacy and frequency of sibling interaction makes this relationship one of the most powerful developmental laboratories a child has access to.[1]

More striking still, Dunn's work showed how early children begin reading their siblings socially, registering jealousy, comforting distress, exploiting vulnerability, sharing humour, taking sides, long before adults assumed children were capable of such things. By the time a child is two or three, the sibling subsystem is already shaping their understanding of human relationships.

All of this means that what happens between siblings is not a side story. It is one of the central engines of a child's emotional development. And because of the volume of the contact, the sibling subsystem is also one of the places where the bad apple effect spreads most efficiently, and most invisibly.

Most parents underestimate how much a sibling pattern is teaching their children. We notice the loud explosions. We rarely notice the quiet, repeated micro-interactions that make up most of a sibling relationship. Those micro-interactions are doing the real teaching.

The Matching Response: How Conflict Escalates

Watch two siblings argue and you will see, in miniature, one of the most powerful patterns in human relating. They tend to match each other's emotional intensity, beat for beat. A small complaint is met with a small protest. A raised voice is met with a louder one. A push is met with a shove. A shove is met with a slap. The two children are not, in any conscious way, deciding to escalate. Their nervous systems are pulling each other up the ladder.

This is the matching response, and it is older and faster than any moral choice the children might make.

It is the same biological machinery we met in Chapter 3, applied to a relationship that is already extraordinarily close. Each child reads the other's face, voice and body, and adjusts their own to match. When the affect being matched is positive, the result is laughter, play, shared invention. When the affect is negative, the result is escalation.

The escalation does not stop on its own. Two children at the same level of arousal are unlikely to spontaneously calm down without an external regulator stepping in. That regulator is, almost always, an adult. A parent who can hold their own state steady, and who can step in early enough, can interrupt the climb. A parent who is themselves dysregulated tends to add a third voice to the same key, and the conflict gets louder.

This is one of the harder parts of parenting siblings honestly. Many sibling fights are not really resolved by clever discipline strategies. They are resolved by an adult who is regulated enough to be the third nervous system in the room, the one who breaks the matching loop by introducing a different rhythm.

Where the adult cannot do this, because they are exhausted, dysregulated themselves, distracted, or chronically absent, the matching loop runs uninterrupted. Over time, the children stop expecting it to be interrupted. They begin to settle their conflicts the only way they know how, which is by going up the ladder until someone breaks first.

This is how households arrive at the situation in which one child reliably wins by escalating hardest, and the other reliably loses by retreating earliest, and the parents start describing the older sibling as “the difficult one” and the younger as “the easy one” without recognising what they are watching.

Inertia: The Older Sibling Who Will Not De-Escalate

There is a particular sibling pattern that hides inside many of these escalations. Researchers in family interaction sometimes call it inertia: the tendency for one person to remain stuck in an aggressive or hostile state once they have entered it, regardless of what the other person does to repair the moment.

In a sibling dyad, inertia often shows up as the older child refusing to climb back down.

A small disagreement starts. The younger sibling, perhaps having matched the early escalation, then tries to repair, backs off, apologises, offers a peace offering, hands over the toy, walks away. The older sibling does not match the de-escalation. They remain in the activated state. They keep pressing. They keep punishing. They keep finding new reasons the conflict is not yet over.

From the outside, this looks like the older child being unreasonable, controlling or cruel. From the inside, the older child often cannot tell you what they want. They are caught in a state, and the state has not finished moving through their body. The de-escalation cues from the younger child are not reaching them.

What inertia teaches a younger sibling is corrosive. It teaches them that repair does not work. That backing down does not protect them. That the only options are to fight harder or disappear. Children who grow up with high-inertia siblings often develop one of two adaptations. They either learn to escalate first, pre-emptively, to control the start of every conflict, or they learn to disappear before any conflict can begin, suppressing their own needs in advance.

Both adaptations cost.

If you are watching a sibling pattern that has this shape, the work is not primarily on the younger child's response. It is on the older child's capacity to come back down, and on the adults' capacity to be the regulating presence that helps them do it. Inertia is rarely a moral failure. It is more often a regulation gap that has not yet been taught around.

Specific Risks: Boy-Boy Dyads and Normalised Aggression

Sibling research has consistently found that not all sibling pairs are equally vulnerable to escalating conflict. Dyad composition matters.

Boy-boy sibling pairs, on average, exhibit higher rates of inter-sibling conflict and physical aggression than mixed or girl-girl pairs. This is not an iron rule, and it does not predict any individual family. But it is a robust pattern, and parents of two or more boys deserve a clear-eyed conversation about it rather than the well-meaning shrug of, "Boys will be boys."

The phrase "boys will be boys" has, in recent decades, done a great deal of damage. It is often used to dismiss escalation that, if performed by adults, would be recognised as physical assault. It allows aggression to be normalised as developmental. It allows the older brother who reliably hurts the younger brother to be recoded as a personality, rather than recognised as a sustained pattern that the family is paying for.

What is true about boy-boy dyads is more useful than the cliché. Boys, on average, mature in regulation skills slightly later than girls. They tend to play in modes that include more rough-and-tumble. They are, at the population level, more likely to express distress through externalising behaviour, including aggression, than through internalising behaviour. None of this excuses harm. All of it matters for parenting.

It means that boy-boy dyads need more, not less, of three things: explicit teaching of the regulation skills the boys are still building, more visible adult presence during the high-risk periods of the day (after school, weekends, transitions), and earlier intervention when a pattern of intimidation begins to set in. The cost of leaving a boy-boy dyad to "sort itself out" is often paid by the younger brother, in losses to his sense of safety, his self-image, and sometimes his body.

Girl-girl and mixed-sex dyads have their own characteristic patterns, more relational and verbal aggression, more strategic exclusion, more sustained social manoeuvring. None of these are softer than physical aggression in their effect on a child. The point of naming dyad composition is not to rank harms. It is to help parents see what their particular sibling subsystem is most likely to need.

The Coercive Cycle

One of the most important pieces of research on how aggressive sibling and family patterns become entrenched comes from a long line of work led by the American developmental psychologist Gerald Patterson, working at the Oregon Social Learning Center.

In their 1992 volume Antisocial Boys, Patterson, John Reid and Thomas Dishion described what they called the coercive cycle: a moment-by-moment interactional pattern in which aggressive behaviour is reliably reinforced by getting the aggressor what they want.[2]

It works like this. A child wants something, a toy, attention, the end of a demand they do not want to meet. They escalate to get it: whining, then yelling, then hitting, then a tantrum, then aggression toward a sibling. The parent (or sibling, or other adult), worn down by the intensity and wanting peace, gives in. The aggression is rewarded. The child has just learned, in the most direct way possible, that escalation works.

The cycle is reinforced from both sides. The parent has also learned something: that giving in produces immediate (if temporary) calm. The child's aggression and the parent's capitulation now train each other. Over time, the child needs to escalate further to achieve the same effect. The parent gives in faster to avoid the highest-intensity behaviours. The cycle deepens.

Inside a sibling subsystem, the coercive cycle has another layer. The siblings are also training each other. The younger child learns that crying loudly enough, or claiming victimhood quickly enough, mobilises adult intervention in their favour. The older child learns that escalating physically pre-empts the younger child's claim. Both children become technicians of escalation, because escalation has been the most reliably effective strategy in the household.

Breaking a coercive cycle is one of the harder pieces of parenting work, and it is difficult to do without outside help when the cycle is well-established. The general direction is clear, even when the practice is slow:

Aggression has to stop being effective. The thing the child is trying to get by escalating cannot be delivered when they escalate.

Calm, cooperative behaviour has to start being more effective. The same thing the child wants needs to be available, reliably, when they ask for it without escalating.

Adults have to step in early, before the cycle reaches the highest-intensity behaviour, while everyone's nervous system can still hear an alternative.

And the children have to be helped to build the regulation and problem-solving skills the cycle has been substituting for. We will return to that part in Chapter 21, on Ross Greene's collaborative and proactive solutions model.

Gottman's Four Horsemen, Translated to Siblings

John Gottman's research on marital conflict is one of the most-cited bodies of work in twentieth-century psychology, and the heart of it is a simple finding: it is not the presence of conflict that predicts whether a marriage will fail. It is the kind of conflict.

From observing thousands of couples in his Seattle laboratory, Gottman identified four communication patterns that, when chronic, reliably predicted relational failure. He called them the Four Horsemen of the Apocalypse.[3]

Criticism, attacking the partner's character rather than naming a specific behaviour: "You are so selfish," instead of, "When you came home late without telling me, I felt forgotten."

Contempt, communicating disgust at the partner: eye-rolling, sneering, sarcasm, mockery, name-calling. Gottman found contempt to be the single strongest predictor of divorce.

Defensiveness, refusing to take responsibility for any part of the conflict, treating any feedback as an attack, counter-blaming.

Stonewalling, withdrawing from interaction, going silent, leaving the room, refusing to engage. Often a flooded nervous system that has shut down.

Apply the same framework to a sibling relationship and the picture becomes uncomfortably familiar.

Criticism: "You are such an idiot." "You are so weird." "No one likes you."

Contempt: the eye-roll across the dinner table, the imitation of a younger sibling's voice, the sneering nickname, the laughter at a sibling's tears.

Defensiveness: blaming a sibling for every conflict the harming child is part of. Refusing to ever acknowledge a contribution. Insisting they were the one who was hurt.

Stonewalling: silence. The older sibling who simply will not speak to the younger one for three days. The teenager who walks past their younger brother as if he does not exist.

Gottman's research was conducted on adult marriages, and he was clear that adult intimate relationships are not the same as sibling relationships. But the underlying pattern, that contempt, in particular, is corrosive in a way that ordinary disagreement is not, translates well to the sibling subsystem. A sibling subsystem in which contempt is normalised is one in which one child is being slowly taught to treat another with disgust, and one in which the receiving child is being slowly taught that they are someone disgust is appropriately directed at.

Both lessons stay.

When parents intervene in sibling conflict, the most useful diagnostic question is not, "Who started it?" It is closer to, "Which of the four horsemen is loose in this relationship right now?" That question changes what the parent says when they step in.

Criticism gets answered by helping the children name behaviour, not character.

Contempt gets named explicitly and refused. "We do not speak about each other in this family in that tone."

Defensiveness gets met with curiosity. "I am not asking you to take all the blame. I am asking you to look at your part."

Stonewalling gets met with patience and structured re-engagement, not punishment, because the stonewalling child is usually flooded, not coldly defiant.

These are slow corrections. They make sense over years, not days. They are also, over years, what changes a sibling subsystem from a place of mutual erosion to a place of mutual support.

What Helps

Most of the practical work for sibling subsystems lives in the practical chapters later in this book. The headlines, in summary, are these.

Be the regulating third nervous system. Most sibling escalations are interrupted, not solved, in the moment. The parent who can stay steady, or at least more steady than the children, is the actual mechanism that breaks the matching loop. Your state matters more than your script.

Step in early. Inertia is harder to interrupt than escalation, and escalation is harder to interrupt than the first match. The parent who notices the first eye-roll has a much easier job than the parent who arrives at the slap.

Refuse contempt explicitly. The single most worthwhile sibling rule, modelled by the parents and enforced consistently, is the rule that no one in the family speaks to or about another family member with contempt. The behaviours can be stopped. The mockery can be named. The eye-rolls can be returned. This is harder than it sounds and more important than it appears.

Treat sibling repair as a teachable skill, not an automatic outcome. After a rupture, the children are often not capable of repairing on their own, especially when one of them is younger or less regulated. The adult walks the repair through, with both children, in slow steps. We will return to repair in Chapter 25.

Watch the patterns, not just the events. A single bad afternoon between siblings is not the bad apple effect. A pattern, repeating across months, is. The question to keep asking is, "What is this relationship teaching each of these two children about themselves?"

Get help when the pattern is bigger than the household can hold. Coercive cycles, sustained sibling intimidation, sexualised behaviour between siblings, or violence that is repeating regardless of intervention all warrant professional family therapy or specialist clinical support, not just better parenting strategies.

Key Takeaways

The sibling subsystem is one of the most powerful developmental laboratories a child has, and one of the places where the bad apple effect spreads most efficiently and most invisibly.

Sibling conflict tends to escalate via the matching response, children pulling each other up the ladder of arousal until an external regulator (an adult) breaks the loop.

Inertia is the tendency for one child, usually the older, to remain stuck in an activated state and refuse to de-escalate even when the other backs down. It teaches the other child that repair does not work.

Boy-boy dyads, on average, carry a higher base rate of physical aggression than other compositions and need more, not less, explicit teaching, adult presence at high-risk transitions and early intervention.

The coercive cycle (Patterson, Reid and Dishion) describes how aggressive behaviour gets reinforced when it reliably produces what the child wants. Breaking it requires aggression to stop being effective and calm cooperation to become more effective.

Gottman's Four Horsemen, criticism, contempt, defensiveness, stonewalling, translate intact from marital conflict to sibling relationships. Contempt is the single most corrosive of the four.

The parent's job in sibling work is less to be a judge than to be a regulating third presence, naming patterns, refusing contempt, and walking children through slow, structured repair.

References

1. Dunn, J. (1985). Sisters and Brothers. Cambridge, MA: Harvard University Press.
2. Patterson, G. R., Reid, J. B., & Dishion, T. J. (1992). Antisocial Boys (A Social Learning Approach, Vol. 4). Eugene, OR: Castalia Publishing.
3. Gottman, J. M. (1994). Why Marriages Succeed or Fail: And How You Can Make Yours Last. New York: Simon & Schuster.
4. Gottman, J. M., & Levenson, R. W. (1992). Marital processes predictive of later dissolution: Behavior, physiology, and health. Journal of Personality and Social Psychology, 63(2), 221–233. https://doi.org/10.1037/0022-3514.63.2.221

CHAPTER 8

The Quiet Child: When the Cost Is Carried Silently

The Child Who Stopped Asking

There is a child in many families who almost never appears in the chapters of a parenting book. This is the chapter for that child.

They are not the child who is hitting, refusing school, exploding at bedtime, or sliding into a peer group that frightens you. They are the other child. The one who, while everyone else has been worrying about a sibling, has quietly become the easy one.

They go to school. They do their homework. They brush their teeth. They have friends, mostly. They do not complain. They do not ask for much. They are described, often with relief, with adjectives like mature, sensible, helpful, calm. They are sometimes even described, in private moments between exhausted parents, as the only thing keeping the household functional.

And they may be in trouble.

Not loud trouble. Not visible trouble. Trouble of a kind that does not show up at school meetings, GP appointments or therapy referrals. Trouble that sits inside the body, builds slowly over years, and arrives, often, in adolescence or early adulthood as anxiety, perfectionism, depression, eating-disordered behaviour, identity collapse or a profound exhaustion that the rest of the family did not see coming.

Because while the dysregulated child has been pulling the household toward them, this child has been adapting in the opposite direction. They have been learning to take up less space, ask for less, need less, feel less. They have been learning to be useful. They have been learning that their job is to keep the system running.

This is the quiet child. And the quiet child is paying for the bad apple effect, in their own way, just as much as the loud one.

Parentification: The Child Who Cares for the Adults

One of the most clinically described patterns in the quiet-child story is parentification.

The term was introduced into family therapy by Hungarian-American psychiatrist Ivan Boszormenyi-Nagy and his colleague Geraldine Spark in their 1973 book Invisible Loyalties, where they used it to describe a structural inversion of the family hierarchy: a child taking on developmentally inappropriate responsibility for the emotional or practical needs of a parent or sibling.[1] More recently, family-systems researcher Lisa Hooper and colleagues have rebuilt the concept on attachment-theory foundations and produced empirical instruments to measure it, mapping its long-term effects on adult mental health.[2] A 2011 meta-analysis of twelve studies found a small but reliable association between childhood parentification and adult psychopathology.[3]

The everyday version of parentification is more common than the clinical literature might suggest. It does not require an absent parent or a household in crisis. It can happen in a stable home, run by loving parents, where one child has simply learned earlier than the others to read the adults' moods and adjust accordingly.

Parentification has two main forms.

The first is instrumental parentification. The child takes on practical adult responsibilities, running the household, looking after younger siblings, preparing meals, managing logistics, often when illness, disability, addiction, single parenthood or sheer overwhelm has stretched the adults' capacity. Some versions of instrumental parentification are unavoidable in particular family circumstances; what matters is whether the child is recognised, supported and given relief, or whether the role is invisibly assumed and never named.

The second is emotional parentification, which is the form most relevant to this chapter. The child takes on responsibility for the emotional weather of the household. They notice when their mother is sad and try to cheer her up. They ask their father if he is okay. They de-escalate parental arguments. They become the confidant of one parent against the other. They develop a finely tuned radar for parental mood and re-shape their own behaviour to manage it. In adolescence, they may become the one their parents talk to about the marriage, the work stress, the family difficulty. They function, in effect, as a small therapist for the adults.

Children are usually competent at this work. They are also unfit for it. The competence is real. The cost is also real.

What is being lost when a child is emotionally parentified is the experience of being the one who is taken care of. They miss the part of childhood in which an adult holds the weight, makes the calls, regulates the climate, and lets the child simply be a child. That missing is not always visible at the time. It often appears later, in patterns adults bring to therapy: difficulty asking for help, difficulty knowing what they themselves want, difficulty receiving love that is not contingent on usefulness, an over-developed sense of responsibility for other people's feelings, and a quiet, persistent sense of being alone.

The Good Child as a Survival Strategy

Some quiet children are not parentified in the clinical sense. They have simply read the household correctly and concluded, without ever putting it into words, that being good is the safest way to be loved.

If one sibling is constantly in crisis, taking up most of the parents' attention and emotional bandwidth, the other child often calculates, silently, intelligently, that adding any further demand will tip the household over. So they do not. They become the child who never causes trouble. The child who handles their own problems. The child the parents can stop worrying about.

From the outside, this looks like maturity, even like resilience. From the inside, it can be something else.

The good child often learns:

What that learning consists of accumulates quietly. The good child learns that their needs are inconvenient, that their job is to keep the peace, and that their sadness creates more stress for the adults and is therefore something to manage privately. They learn that praise is more reliable than connection, so getting the grades, performing the helpfulness, being the one teachers love, becomes a way to secure attention without demanding it. They learn that anger is dangerous, because it sounds too much like the sibling who is already exhausting everyone. And they learn that love, in this household, is conditional on functioning.

Each of these is, in its own way, a survival strategy. Each is also a real cost.

The good-child role is one of the places where the bad apple effect is most insidious, because it does not look like dysregulation. It looks, for years, like everything is fine. Parents are often not given any signal that this child needs more attention until the day they suddenly do, by collapsing, by acting unrecognisably, or by leaving home and not coming back the same.

If you have a child who has been the easy one for a long time, the kindest, most useful thing you can do is to begin treating their easiness with the same curiosity you would treat a more difficult child's behaviour. Ask what their internal world is like. Ask what they have been carrying that you have not noticed. Make space for needs that have not, in your household so far, been welcome.

Compliance Is Not Security

One of the most useful distinctions in attachment theory is the difference between a child who is securely attached and a child who has organised their behaviour to look secure while their internal world is anything but.

A securely attached child does well, on the whole, because their nervous system is calm enough to do well. They can ask for help when they need it. They can fall apart and recover. They can disagree with a parent without believing the relationship is now in danger. They can hold their own preferences alongside other people's.

A compliantly organised child often looks similar from the outside. They do well at school, behave well at home, get on with siblings, and rarely make demands. The difference is what happens in the inside, and what happens under stress.

Compliantly organised children tend to:

Become anxious about minor mistakes, because being good is the system that holds up their place in the family.

Have difficulty saying no, because no historically led to disconnection.

Struggle to identify their own preferences, because they have spent so long shaping themselves to other people's.

Become exhausted in adolescence, when the demands of being good begin to outstrip what is sustainable.

Develop somatic symptoms, stomach aches, headaches, insomnia, restricted eating, that the body uses to signal a distress the mind has been trained to suppress.

Compliance and security are not the same thing. They look the same in calm weather. They diverge in the storm. A parent who can tell the difference is a parent who knows to check in with their easy child, especially during transitions, exam pressure, family stress, or social difficulty.

The simplest diagnostic question is this: does this child show me their messy, frustrating, not-easy parts, or have they only ever shown me their useful ones?

If the answer is the second, the household has work to do.

Three Faces of the Quiet Child

Quiet children, in family-systems and clinical practice, often shape themselves into one of three recognisable patterns. Most quiet children carry traces of all three; many sit clearly in one.

The achiever. This is the child who has decided, often very young, that performance is the way to be loved. They get the marks. They make the team. They build the trophy shelf. They are praised and praised and praised. Underneath, there is often a steady, quiet anxiety: a sense that the praise is for the performance, and that the performance must therefore continue. The achiever frequently arrives in late adolescence in burnout, or with an eating disorder, or with a perfectionism so calcified that any failure feels catastrophic.

The caretaker. This is the child who has been parentified, in the small or large sense, and who organises their identity around being useful to other people. They are the one who notices when others need help. They are the one who runs interference between adults. They become, very young, the wise one, the kind one, the responsible one. The caretaker often arrives in adulthood in relationships in which they continue to caretake, often at considerable personal cost, and only slowly recognise that this is not the same as being loved.

The invisible one. This is the child who has decided that needing nothing is the safest position. They retreat into rooms, books, hobbies, devices, music. They stop volunteering information. They become hard to know. From the outside, they look independent. From the inside, they often feel deeply alone. The invisible child is at particular risk in adolescence of finding their first real sense of belonging in an online space or peer group that may not have their best interests at heart, because that space is the first one in which they were noticed.

These three patterns are not personality types. They are adaptations. Adaptations can be unlearned, especially when the family system that produced them shifts. The fact that a child has organised themselves around achievement, caretaking or invisibility does not mean they are stuck there forever. It means they have been working with what was available.

The Long Cost

what the long cost of the quiet-child role can look like, because the cost is often underestimated by parents whose attention has been pulled toward the louder child.

Adults who were quiet children commonly struggle with:

An over-developed sense of responsibility for other people's feelings, including in relationships where this is not appropriate.

Difficulty knowing what they themselves want, because the practice of asking themselves that question was never embedded in childhood.

Anxiety, particularly around making mistakes or disappointing others.

Perfectionism that masquerades as standards but functions as fear.

A pattern of choosing partners, friends or workplaces that recreate the old role: someone who needs caring for, a workplace that exploits their reliability, an environment in which their value is contingent on usefulness.

A dull, persistent loneliness that is not always linked to actual isolation. They can have a partner, friends and a busy life and still feel alone, because the part of themselves that learned to disappear has not been visible in any of those relationships.

A vulnerability to burnout, somatic illness and mid-life depression.

Difficulty receiving help, comfort or unconditional love.

These are real costs. They are also corrigible. Adults who were quiet children can do enormous work to recover their voices, name their needs, and unlearn the old contract. But it is much, much easier to prevent the contract being written in the first place than it is to renegotiate it as an adult.

That preventive work is, in large part, what this chapter is about.

What Helps

Reach for the easy child first. The intuitive instinct is to put attention where the trouble is loudest. The corrective discipline is to put attention, regularly and unconditionally, on the child who is asking for the least. Not as a reward for being easy. As a refusal to confuse easiness with okayness.

Make their needs welcome. A quiet child often does not believe that their needs are okay to bring. The most powerful thing a parent can do is to actively invite the messy parts. "What is something hard you have been carrying that you have not told me?" "What is something you wanted recently and did not ask for?" "What would you tell me, if you knew I would not be too busy or too tired?" These questions need to be asked repeatedly and met with full attention when answered.

Notice the easy parts and ask after the hard ones. When a child performs an act of caretaking, achievement or invisibility, notice it, and gently ask about the inside. "You did such a good job looking after your brother today. What was that like for you?" "You were so quiet when we were arguing, what was happening for you?" "You handled that grade calmly. How did it feel?"

Refuse the temptation to use them as the steady one. A parentified child often becomes the parent's emotional support system. This is not their job, even when they appear willing. Take your adult problems to other adults, your partner, your friends, your therapist, not to the child who has been holding too much already.

Watch the transitions. Quiet children often become visible at transitions: a new school, a sibling's crisis, a family illness, an adolescent shift. These are the moments to lean in, not to be relieved that this child is still doing fine.

Do not be reassured by competence. Competence in a quiet child is not the same as well-being. A child who is functioning well at school, at home, with friends, can still be drowning quietly. Their competence does not mean they do not need you. It often means they have been compensating, and the compensation has a half-life.

Get help when you suspect you are watching one of these patterns settle in. A good child psychologist or family therapist will not tell you the child is fine because they look fine on the outside. They will look at how the child is organising themselves around the family system, and they will know the difference between security and compliance.

If you have been the loud-child parent for a long time and you are realising, reading this chapter, that you have a quiet child you have not been seeing, it is not too late. The bad apple effect runs through families partly because the loud child pulls all the parental bandwidth. Re-balancing that bandwidth is one of the most important things a parent can do, and one of the things this book quietly hopes more parents will do, more often, than they have been.

Key Takeaways

While the dysregulated child pulls parental attention, another child in the same household often adapts in the opposite direction, taking up less space, asking for less, becoming the easy one.

Parentification is a structural inversion of the family hierarchy in which a child takes on developmentally inappropriate responsibility, especially for the emotional needs of adults. It is associated with measurable adult mental-health costs.

The good-child role is often a survival strategy in households where one sibling already absorbs most of the emotional bandwidth. It looks like maturity but functions as a contract.

Compliance is not the same as security. A child who looks like everything is fine may have organised themselves around being fine. The diagnostic question is whether the parent has seen this child's messy and frustrating parts, not just their useful ones.

Quiet children commonly shape themselves into one of three patterns: the achiever, the caretaker or the invisible one. These are adaptations, not personality types, and can be unlearned when the family system shifts.

Adult costs of an unaddressed quiet-child role are real and well documented. Prevention is far easier than later renegotiation.

The corrective discipline is to actively reach for the easy child, invite their needs, watch transitions, and refuse to use them as the household's steady one.

References

1. Boszormenyi-Nagy, I., & Spark, G. M. (1973). Invisible Loyalties: Reciprocity in Intergenerational Family Therapy. Hagerstown, MD: Harper & Row.
2. Hooper, L. M. (2007). The application of attachment theory and family systems theory to the phenomena of parentification. The Family Journal, 15(3), 217–223. https://doi.org/10.1177/1066480707301290
3. Hooper, L. M., DeCoster, J., White, N., & Voltz, M. L. (2011). Characterizing the magnitude of the relation between self-reported childhood parentification and adult psychopathology: A meta-analysis. Journal of Clinical Psychology, 67(10), 1028–1043. https://doi.org/10.1002/jclp.20807

CHAPTER 9

The Parental Subsystem Under Strain

A Note on Language Before We Begin

This chapter began life with the title "The Marital Subsystem Under Strain." I changed it.

The word marriage describes one shape a parental partnership can take. Many of the families this book is for are not in that shape. They may be sole parents raising children alone, by choice or by circumstance. They may be separated or divorced parents co-parenting across two households. They may be same-sex couples, blended families with step-parents, multi-generational households where a grandparent shares the parenting work, kinship carers, foster carers, adoptive parents, or any of the other configurations real Australian families take.

The structural insight in this chapter applies to all of them.

The phrase parental subsystem describes whatever shape your parenting partnership takes, including the shape in which you are doing it on your own, with periodic input from a former partner, an extended family member, or a co-parent across town. What matters is not the shape but the question: how is the strain on the adults travelling into the children?

If you are a sole parent reading this, the chapter is still for you. The parental subsystem can be a single nervous system carrying everything, with all the same vulnerabilities to strain that a partnered subsystem has, plus a few of its own. We will return to that explicitly.

What the Children Are Reading

Children read the parental subsystem the way they read the weather. They register the temperature constantly, often without naming it. They notice when the adults are aligned and when they are not. They notice when there is warmth between the parents and when there is contempt. They notice when the household has a steady centre and when it does not.

Among the most empirically robust findings in modern developmental research is this: the way the adults in a child's home handle conflict has a measurable effect on the child's emotional and behavioural development, often as large as anything more obviously aimed at the child.

The American developmental psychologists E. Mark Cummings and Patrick Davies have spent more than three decades mapping this in detail. Their book Marital Conflict and Children: An Emotional Security Perspective synthesises a long line of research showing that what predicts a child's outcomes is not whether the adults disagree, disagreement is normal and unavoidable, but whether the disagreements are constructive or destructive, whether they get resolved, and whether the child leaves the room with their sense of family security intact.[1]

Constructive conflict, Cummings and Davies found, can strengthen children. Children who watch their parents disagree, work the disagreement through respectfully, and reach a resolution learn something foundational about how human beings repair after rupture. Their nervous systems, watching this play out, calibrate to the truth that conflict is survivable.

Destructive conflict, which they define as conflict marked by hostility, contempt, name-calling, threats, withdrawal that is not eventually repaired, or violence, does the opposite. The child's sense of emotional security in the family is degraded. They become hypervigilant. They scan the adults for the next outburst. They begin to take responsibility for keeping the temperature down. They sleep less well. They behave more reactively at school. Over time, they show measurable increases in anxiety, depression and conduct difficulty.

The mechanism is the one we met in Chapter 3. Children are not separate observers of their parents' relationship. They are inside its emotional weather, with the same nervous system mimicry and contagion that runs everywhere else in human life. When the adults are activated, the children are activated. When the adults stay activated, the children stay activated.

This is not a chapter telling you to stop fighting. Disagreement is part of any honest partnership. It is a chapter telling you that what your children are reading from your conflict, and from your repair, is shaping them.

How a Difficult Child Strains the Adults

There is a particular kind of strain that runs through families when one child is chronically dysregulated, oppositional, anxious, neurodivergent, traumatised, or going through a hard period.

It is the strain of relentlessness.

It is the early-morning waking and the late-night unwinding. The school refusal calls. The public meltdowns. The sibling fights. The phone messages from the school. The therapy appointments. The medication conversations. The constant low-grade negotiation.

It is also, often, the strain of disagreement. One parent thinks the child needs more boundaries. The other thinks they need more compassion. One parent leans in. The other has reached the end of their rope. Each one is, in their own way, correct. And each one is finding it harder, day by day, to see the partner's correctness.

Research on couples raising dysregulated children consistently finds that the disruptive child's behaviour and the parents' relational stress feed each other. The child's behaviour generates strain between the adults. The strain between the adults reduces their capacity to parent the child cohesively. The reduced cohesion further destabilises the child. Around the loop goes.

It is important to name this loop because most parents inside it cannot see it. They feel as though they are simply failing, failing the child, failing each other, failing themselves. What is happening is structural. The system is under load, and the adults are paying for it inside their relationship long before either of them is ready to admit it.

Sole parents experience a version of this loop that does not get spread across two adults. The whole load lands in one nervous system, often after the working day, often after the school logistics, often after a phone conversation with a co-parent who is not pulling their weight. The cost is real. Sole parents reading this need to hear, very clearly, that the chapter is not about how to keep a marriage going under strain. It is about how to keep a parental subsystem, yours, in whatever shape it takes, functioning well enough that the children remain reasonably steady inside it.

The Feedback Loop

If a single line could summarise what the marital and family-systems literature has found over the last forty years, it might be this: a strained parental subsystem produces a less cohesive parenting environment, which produces more difficult child behaviour, which produces a more strained parental subsystem.

Inside this loop, several familiar patterns emerge.

The parents begin to disagree more visibly in front of the children. The disagreements include the children, sometimes by name. "Look what you let her do." "If you actually disciplined him, this wouldn't happen." The children become not the people the disagreement is happening around, but the substance of the disagreement.

Triangulation increases. Each parent, feeling unsupported, may pull a child closer to them as an ally. The child becomes the confidant, the consoler, the one who agrees with this parent against the other. The child has now been recruited into a job they did not apply for.

Discipline becomes inconsistent. One parent overcorrects. The other under-corrects. Children quickly learn which parent to ask, and the parent who is bypassed feels increasingly undermined. Trust between the adults erodes.

Affection retreats. There is no time. There is no inclination. The marriage that began as the foundation of the household becomes the part of the household that is least cared for. The bedroom door closes on a roommate, not a partner. Both of them feel the loss. Neither has the capacity to address it.

Children read all of this. They register it. Some of them, especially the more sensitive or older ones, begin trying to repair it. The good child becomes better. The parentified child takes on more emotional management. The dysregulated child sometimes increases their dysregulation, because intense behaviour is what reliably puts the parents on the same side again, even briefly.

If any of this is recognisable, you are not unusual, and you are not failing. You are inside a structural pattern that almost always intensifies under sustained strain. The loop is not a moral verdict. It is a feedback system. Feedback systems can be changed by changing one part of the loop. That is the project of this chapter.

Sole Parents and Co-Parenting Across Households

If you are parenting alone, or co-parenting across two households after separation, the parental subsystem still exists. It just has a different shape and a different set of pressure points.

For sole parents, the most common pattern is that the strain settles into a single body. There is no second adult to share the moments of escalation, to take the next call from the school, to read the bedtime story when you have nothing left. The same regulating-third-presence work that two parents share, you do alone. This is not impossible. It is also not what the human nervous system is built for.

What helps, in practice, is the deliberate construction of a wider supporting network. A trusted relative who can be the second adult on hard afternoons. A close friend who knows the kids and can step in. A regular routine of adult support that does not depend on romantic partnership. A GP, a psychologist, a parenting helpline, a support group. This is not weakness. It is structural realism. A sole parent who builds in supports does better, on average, than a sole parent who tries to carry it all alone.

For co-parents across households, the parental subsystem now spans two roofs. The work becomes coordinating across them. Children read the temperature of both households and the temperature of the relationship between the parents. Children do best when the adults can keep their own conflict at a low temperature, when the rules across households are at least vaguely consistent, when neither parent disparages the other in front of the child, and when the child does not have to carry messages between the houses.

Australian research and clinical experience are clear: it is the conflict between separated parents, more than the separation itself, that does the lasting damage to children. Parents who can manage their post-separation relationship with civility, even if not warmth, protect their children from much of what makes divorce hard.

If your co-parent is unsafe, abusive, or refuses to engage cooperatively, the picture changes. Then the work becomes minimising the child's exposure to the destructive dynamic, while still preserving the child's right to a relationship with the other parent where that is possible. This is hard, often slow, often legally complicated work, and is one of the situations where outside support, Family Relationship Centres, family law services, child psychologists, is not optional.

What Helps

This is not a marriage book, and the chapter is not going to pretend to be one. There are entire libraries of competent, evidence-informed marriage and co-parenting writing for that work. Several of them, including Gottman's, are referenced at the end of this chapter and at Chapter 7.

What this chapter can offer is the parenting-shaped version of the question: what helps, specifically in service of keeping the children steady inside the parental subsystem?

Disagree away from the children when you can. The point is not to hide all conflict from your children. They need to see disagreement, and they need to see repair. The point is that prolonged, escalating, contemptuous conflict is not good information for a child to process in real time. Take the harder conversations off the floor of the family room.

Repair publicly. When the children have witnessed a rupture, let them see at least part of the repair. They do not need every detail. They need the fact: the adults disagreed, the adults are working it out, the family is not under threat. A short sentence at dinner, with both adults present, is enormously reassuring to a child who has been holding their breath.

Refuse contempt. The Gottman research is unambiguous: contempt is the single most corrosive pattern in adult relationships. It is also one of the things children read most accurately. If contempt has begun creeping into your parental partnership, naming it and pulling it back is one of the most protective things you can do for the household.

Stay aligned on the child, even when you disagree. You can disagree about strategy without breaking ranks in front of the child. "Mum and I are going to talk this through and come back to you with what we've decided," is a perfectly accurate sentence, and it leaves the parental subsystem visible to the child as a unit.

Notice the triangulation creeping in. If you have started using a particular child as your ally, sounding-board or confidant against the other parent, that is information. Take the adult content back to other adults, your partner directly, a friend, a therapist.

Protect some maintenance time for the partnership. Even fifteen minutes, after the children are asleep, of attention to each other rather than to the latest crisis, is structural maintenance. A parental subsystem is the foundation of the household. Foundations need looking after.

Get help when the loop is bigger than you can interrupt yourselves. A short course of couple therapy, or a single skilled family-therapy session, can change the dynamic faster than years of solo effort. Australians can access these through Medicare-rebated psychology pathways, the Better Access initiative for individuals, Family Relationship Centres, Relationships Australia, and most major employee assistance programmes.

When the Strain Is the Marriage Itself

some marriages, and some co-parenting partnerships, are not going to recover, and the children are not best served by a household held together at the cost of everyone's wellbeing.

If your relationship is characterised by sustained contempt, emotional or physical abuse, control, coercion, dishonesty that has not been addressed, or a chronic mismatch in how each of you wants to live, the most child-protective thing you can do may be to end the partnership well, rather than to continue it badly. Children inside a hostile, contemptuous or abusive household do worse, on average, than children inside a respectful post-separation arrangement.

This is not a recommendation either way. This is a clarification: the message of this chapter is not, "Stay together for the children at any cost." The message is, "What the children read from the parental subsystem matters; choose your repair, your ending or your new partnership with that in mind."

If you are reading this and recognising the markers of an unsafe relationship, coercive control, intimidation, financial abuse, sexual coercion, physical violence, please reach out for specialist support. In Australia, 1800RESPECT (1800 737 732), Lifeline (13 11 14) and your local police are first-line. Domestic violence sits outside the territory this book can responsibly cover, and it always takes priority over family-systems work.

Key Takeaways

The parental subsystem is whatever shape your parenting partnership takes, partnered, single, separated, blended, multi-generational. The principles in this chapter apply to all of them.

What the children read from the adults' relationship, the way conflict is handled, whether it is resolved, whether contempt is present, has measurable effects on their emotional and behavioural development.

Constructive conflict, well-resolved, can strengthen children. Destructive conflict, unresolved, degrades their sense of emotional security in the family.

A chronically difficult child generates strain on the parental partnership. The strained parental partnership becomes less cohesive in its parenting, which intensifies the child's difficulty. The loop is structural and can be changed by changing one part of it.

Sole parents and post-separation co-parents face their own version of these dynamics. Sole parents need a deliberately constructed wider support network. Co-parents need to manage their own conflict at a low temperature, regardless of how they feel about each other.

Useful moves: disagree away from the children when possible, repair publicly, refuse contempt, stay aligned on the child even when you disagree, notice triangulation, protect some maintenance time for the partnership, and get help when the loop is bigger than you can interrupt.

Some partnerships will not recover, and ending a partnership well can be more child-protective than continuing it badly. Domestic violence and coercive control sit outside this book's scope and always take priority over family-systems work.

References

1. Cummings, E. M., & Davies, P. T. (2010). Marital Conflict and Children: An Emotional Security Perspective. New York: Guilford Press.
2. Cummings, E. M., & Miller-Graff, L. E. (2015). Emotional security theory: An emerging theoretical model for youths' psychological and physiological responses across multiple developmental contexts. Current Directions in Psychological Science, 24(3), 208–213. https://doi.org/10.1177/0963721414561510
3. Gottman, J. M. (1994). Why Marriages Succeed or Fail: And How You Can Make Yours Last. New York: Simon & Schuster. (See also Chapter 7.)

CHAPTER 10

When the Parent Becomes the Bad Apple

"And now that you don't have to be perfect,
you can be good."

, John Steinbeck, East of Eden

A Word Before You Read This Chapter

This is the chapter most parents want to skip.

It is also one of the most useful chapters in the book.

Before going any further, one observation. The fact that you have read this far, past the disclaimer, past the Author's Note, past nine chapters about your child, your family system, your sibling subsystem and the wounds underneath, tells me something about you. Parents who do not want to do this work do not arrive at Chapter 10. They put the book down somewhere around the introduction. The defensiveness this chapter sometimes triggers is real, and we will name it as we go. But the willingness is real too, and it has already brought you here. Trust that willingness. It is most of the work.

If you are reading this and feeling pushback already, that pushback is information, not an accusation. Stay with it for a few pages. The point of this chapter is not to add to anyone's shame. It is to name something the rest of the book cannot honestly avoid.

The bad apple effect inside a family does not always come from a child. Sometimes the harmful pattern, the dysregulating influence, the behaviour that is steadily reshaping the household climate, is being carried, partly or fully, by an adult. Sometimes that adult is a partner. Sometimes a step-parent. Sometimes an extended family member who is over a great deal. Sometimes, and this is the version that is hardest to read, the adult is the parent reading this book.

If that sentence triggered a defensive reaction in you, you are doing the human thing. Almost no one likes recognising themselves in a description of the problem they came to a book to solve in someone else.

Three things are true at the same time, and they are worth holding together for the next few pages:

Most parents who become a dysregulating presence in their child's life do not mean to. They are loving people doing their best inside circumstances and histories that have not always given them what they needed.

Recognising the pattern is different from being defined by it. A parent who becomes part of the problem is also the most powerful part of the solution. No one else has the access, the standing or the longevity inside the family system that the parent has.

You will not be able to do this work from a place of self-flagellation. Shame collapses the system, the same way it collapses a child. The corrective stance for this chapter is the same one we have asked of children throughout the book: face it without contempt for yourself, take responsibility for what is yours, and repair what can be repaired.

And, borrowing from Steinbeck, the moment you let go of having to be the perfect parent is also the moment you become free to be a good one. Those are not the same project. They have never been the same project. This whole chapter, in some sense, is built on that distinction.

On those terms, this chapter is for you.

Every Parent Has Hard Days

Before going further, we need to draw a line that this chapter is not about.

Every parent has hard days. Every parent loses their temper sometimes. Every parent says something they regret, lets a screen on for too long, snaps at a child for a reason that has nothing to do with the child, withdraws into their phone when they should be present, raises their voice over a small thing because the small thing is the last small thing in a row of small things.

None of this, on its own, is the bad apple effect. None of this makes a parent harmful.

Children are not damaged by occasional rupture. They are damaged by ruptures that are unrepaired, and by ruptures that become the climate.

Pioneering work by the developmental psychologist Ed Tronick, beginning with what is now known as the "still-face paradigm," established something that should be widely reassuring to parents.[1] Tronick's research found that parents and infants are mismatched, out of attunement with each other, roughly seventy per cent of the time. The mismatches themselves are not what shape secure attachment. What shapes secure attachment is what happens after the mismatch: whether the parent re-attunes, repairs, comes back, and lets the child experience the move from rupture to repair.

Repair, not perfection, is the actual mechanism. The parent who never lost it would be a parent the child could not learn from. The parent who is willing to come back after losing it is the parent the child learns from constantly.

So if you are reading this and thinking, "I yelled at my eight-year-old yesterday," please do not file yourself under bad apple. File yourself under human, and then go and repair.

What this chapter is about is something different. It is about the difference between a hard day and a climate.

Hard Day Versus Climate

A hard day comes and goes. A climate is what your child lives inside.

A hard day is a parent yelling once at the end of a long week. A climate is a parent who yells most days, and the children move through the household waiting for the next time.

A hard day is a parent who collapses into the couch, exhausted, and ignores the children for the evening. A climate is a parent who is consistently emotionally unavailable, and the children have stopped trying to bring things to them.

A hard day is a parent making a sarcastic comment at a partner. A climate is contempt that has settled into the household tone, eye-rolls, mockery, name-calling, and the children are growing up inside that.

A hard day is a parent being controlling about a particular safety issue. A climate is a parent who must control everything, all the time, and the children have learned that initiative is dangerous.

A hard day is a parent feeling anxious and over-reacting once. A climate is a parent whose anxiety is the household's weather, and the children have organised themselves around managing it.

The distinction is not sharp. It is a gradient. The honest question, in any given parental pattern, is whether you have a hard day from time to time, or whether what you started calling hard days has slowly become the texture of the household.

If you are unsure, the most truthful test is to ask the children, when they are old enough, gently, without setting them up to comfort you. "What is it like for you when I am stressed? What do you do when I get angry? What do you wish I would do differently?" The answers will tell you what they have been reading.

Most parents who are willing to ask these questions discover that the children have a much more accurate map of the household's climate than the parents have allowed themselves to see.

The Patterns That Become Climate

When parental behaviour begins to shape the family climate in ways that hurt children, it tends to take one of a small number of recognisable shapes. Most parents who fall into one of these patterns also have many strengths in other parts of their parenting. The shapes are not identities. They are tendencies, and they are correctable.

Chronic anxiety. The parent's nervous system is in a low-grade state of alarm most of the time. Their voice is tight. They scan for threat. They worry aloud. They over-explain risks. The children read this state and either become anxious themselves, or organise their behaviour around protecting the parent from further worry. Anxious-parent households often produce children who present as either deeply anxious or strikingly responsible.

Chronic criticism. The parent finds the thing that is wrong before the thing that is right. They notice what the child has not done. They correct grammar mid-sentence. They critique posture, choices, tone. From the inside, this often feels like high standards. From the child's inside, it often feels like nothing they do is enough, and the wound that builds, slowly, is shame.

Chronic withdrawal. The parent is physically present and emotionally somewhere else. Distracted. On the phone. Lost in their own depression, addiction, work pressure, grief or trauma. Children of withdrawn parents commonly say, in adulthood, that they always knew they were loved, and that they also always felt alone in the house with the parent. Both can be true.

Chronic unpredictability. The parent's mood determines the household, and the children cannot reliably predict which version of the parent they will get. Friendly today, furious tomorrow. Generous now, dismissive later. Children who grow up under unpredictability often develop hypervigilance, they read faces, voices and footsteps for early warnings, and exhaustion that follows them into adulthood.

Chronic contempt. The parent treats family members, often a partner or one specific child, with sneering, mockery, sarcasm or disgust. We have already discussed contempt in Chapters 7 and 9. It is named again here because contempt from a parent toward a child is one of the most enduring wounds in the literature on family harm. Children rarely recover quickly from a parent who looks at them as if they are slightly disgusting.

Chronic explosiveness. The parent operates inside a normal range most of the time and then erupts, verbally, sometimes physically. The eruptions are often followed by remorse, sometimes by apology, sometimes by promises that it will not happen again. Then it happens again. Children of explosive parents tend to live in two states: the calm before the storm, and the storm.

If you recognise yourself in one of these descriptions, the recognition is the first move toward changing it. The recognition is not the failure. The pattern, repeated without recognition, is.

Where the Pattern Often Comes From

Almost no parent designs the patterns described above on purpose. They arrive at them, usually, by carrying them.

A parent who is chronically anxious is rarely a parent without history. They are often a parent who grew up in a household where vigilance was necessary, and the vigilance has continued into a household where it is no longer necessary.

A parent who is chronically critical was, very often, a child who was chronically criticised, and is now passing forward something they did not invent.

A parent who withdraws is often a parent carrying depression, trauma, addiction, grief or burnout that has not been adequately treated. The withdrawal is a symptom, not a choice.

A parent who is unpredictable is sometimes living with untreated mood disorder, with the after-effects of complex trauma, or simply with chronic exhaustion that has been allowed to run for too long.

A parent whose contempt has become a tone is, in many cases, repeating something that was modelled to them in their own childhood, and that they did not have the language or support to name and break.

A parent who explodes is often someone whose nervous system never learned to stay regulated under stress, because the people who were supposed to teach them did not have that skill themselves.

None of this excuses the impact on the child. Children do not get to choose between a wounded parent and a healthy one. They get the parent they have, and they pay for what that parent cannot do, regardless of why.

But knowing where a pattern comes from changes how it can be addressed. Patterns that have a history can be worked with. The work is rarely fast. It is rarely solo. It is also possible.

This is one of the places where this book sits explicitly inside a broader integrative mental-health frame. The trauma and cellular work I described in my earlier book Healing Trauma at the Cellular Level matters here. The lifestyle and metabolic work in The Blood Sugar Solution to Mental Health and Stacking Therapies for Depression Recovery matters here. A regulated parental nervous system is not a personality. It is built. The practical chapters later in this book, particularly Chapter 17, on becoming the safe harbour, return to this practically.

what children pick up when a parent has slipped into one of these patterns, because the picture is more compassionate than parents usually fear.

Children do not, on the whole, conclude that their parent is a monster. They love their parents. They want their parents to be okay. They will defend their parents to other people fiercely, often even to themselves.

What they more commonly conclude is something about themselves.

"Mum is anxious because of me."

"Dad is critical because I am not enough."

"Mum is withdrawn because I am too much."

"Dad is explosive because I cannot do anything right."

Children, especially young children, are wired to take responsibility for what is happening in their environment, because doing so is, paradoxically, easier than living with the helplessness of being a small person inside a state they cannot influence. Self-blame, however painful, returns a small amount of agency to the child. "If I were better, this would not happen."

This is one of the costs that parents most often miss. They believe they are managing their own internal state inside their own head. The child has been picking up the state, attributing it to themselves, and adjusting their behaviour to manage it.

Naming this, out loud, to the child, age-appropriately, is one of the most powerful things a parent can do. "When I get anxious, that is mine, not yours. It is not because of you, and it is not your job to fix it." "When I yell, that is something I am working on. It is not a sign that you are bad." "When I am quiet, it is because I am tired or sad about something that has nothing to do with you." These sentences, said sincerely and repeated over time, take a weight off a child that the parent did not always realise the child was carrying.

Repair, Not Perfection

Almost everything in this chapter resolves into a single principle: the parent does not have to be perfect. The parent has to be willing to repair.

Repair is not a one-time conversation. It is a practice. It includes, at minimum:

Recognising what happened. "I yelled at you this afternoon."

Owning the impact, not just the act. "I can see that scared you."

Taking responsibility without slipping into self-attack. "That was on me. I was already stressed before that conversation, and I took it out on you."

Naming what you are doing about it. "I am working on this. I am going to keep working on this."

Not requiring the child to comfort you. The repair is for the child, not for the parent's shame.

Coming back when it happens again. Because it will. Repair is not a single event. It is the parent showing up, again and again, to do the work in the open.

Children are remarkably forgiving of imperfect parents who repair. They are remarkably scarred by imperfect parents who never do. The decision available to almost every parent reading this chapter, almost every day, is which of those two parents they are going to be.

A parent who learns to repair is not a parent who has stopped being human. They are a parent who has decided that being human in front of their children, and making that humanity available for repair, is a more honest gift than the version of themselves they used to think they had to perform.

When You Need More Than This Chapter Can Offer

Some patterns are bigger than a chapter, a book, or a season of self-reflection. If, reading this, you suspect you are dealing with depression, anxiety, complex trauma, addiction, untreated grief, postnatal mental illness, neurodivergence that has never been formally recognised, or the after-effects of an unsafe childhood, this is one of the situations in which getting your own help is not optional. It is, instead, one of the most child-protective things you can do.

In Australia, the first line for most parents is your GP, who can put together a Mental Health Treatment Plan and refer you under Medicare to a psychologist, psychiatrist or social worker. Beyond Blue (1300 22 4636) and Lifeline (13 11 14) are good places to start if speaking to a stranger feels easier first. Perinatal Anxiety and Depression Australia (PANDA) supports parents with infants and young children. Relationships Australia and Family Relationship Centres support parental and partnership work. Drug and alcohol services in every state and territory will speak to you in confidence.

Outside Australia, the equivalents apply. Many countries have public mental-health pathways through general practice, and most large workplaces have an employee assistance programme that includes a small number of free, confidential counselling sessions.

The honest message of this chapter is that you cannot regulate a household you are not regulating yourself. And you cannot reliably regulate yourself if the things underneath your reactivity have never been treated. Looking after the parent is, in this sense, looking after the child.

A Word for the Reader Who Is Defensive

If you have made it to the end of this chapter and you are still feeling pushback, that is fine.

Defensiveness is not a moral failing. It is usually a sign that something in the chapter has touched a vulnerable place. The vulnerable place is more useful than the defensiveness, but you are entitled to take time getting from one to the other.

The most useful thing you can do, if this chapter has stirred something up, is not to immediately resolve it. Sit with it for a few days. Re-read it once. Notice which sentences hooked. Notice which descriptions you recognised in yourself, even partly. Notice the ones you wanted to deny outright, those are sometimes the ones doing the most work.

If you are partnered, share the chapter with your partner and have a careful conversation about what you each saw. If you are not partnered, share it with a trusted friend, or with a therapist if you have one.

And if you can, and this is the last and most important thing, let your child see you doing this work. Not in detail. Not in a way that asks the child to comfort you. Just enough that the child sees the parent has taken responsibility for being a healthier presence in the household. That visibility itself is repair.

No parent needs to read a chapter like this and feel devastated. Almost every parent reading it can do something useful with it. The bar is not perfection. The bar is willingness.

Key Takeaways

Sometimes the bad apple effect is being carried, partly or fully, by an adult inside the family. Recognising this is not the same as being defined by it.

Every parent has hard days. Children are not damaged by occasional rupture; they are damaged by rupture that becomes the climate. Tronick's research is clear that parent-child mismatch is normal, repair, not perfection, is the actual mechanism of secure attachment.

Chronic patterns that can become climate include anxiety, criticism, withdrawal, unpredictability, contempt and explosiveness. Most parents who fall into these patterns also have real strengths elsewhere; the patterns are tendencies, not identities.

These patterns almost always have a history. They can be addressed. Doing so is rarely fast and rarely solo, and it sits inside the broader integrative mental-health work this book is part of.

Children commonly conclude that a parent's difficult state is their own fault. Naming this clearly to the child, that the state is the parent's, not theirs, removes a weight the child has been quietly carrying.

Repair, not perfection, is the standard. Recognising what happened, owning the impact, taking responsibility without self-attack, naming the ongoing work, and coming back when it happens again, that is the practice.

When the parental pattern is bigger than self-reflection can address, getting your own help is not optional. In Australia, GP, Better Access pathways, Beyond Blue, Lifeline, PANDA and Relationships Australia are first-line.

Defensiveness while reading a chapter like this is not failure. It is information. The bar is willingness, not perfection.

References

1. Tronick, E. Z. (1989). Emotions and emotional communication in infants. American Psychologist, 44(2), 112–119. https://doi.org/10.1037/0003-066X.44.2.112

2. Tronick, E. (2007). The Neurobehavioral and Social-Emotional Development of Infants and Children. New York: W. W. Norton.

3. Mesman, J., van IJzendoorn, M. H., & Bakermans-Kranenburg, M. J. (2009). The many faces of the still-face paradigm: A review and meta-analysis. Developmental Review, 29(2), 120–162. https://doi.org/10.1016/j.dr.2009.02.001

4. Steinbeck, J. (1952). East of Eden. New York: Viking Press.

CHAPTER 11

Peer Groups and the Currency of Belonging

The Adolescent Pivot

Somewhere around the start of adolescence, the centre of gravity of a child's social world begins to move.

Until then, family is the dominant emotional environment. Parents and siblings are the main mirrors. Friendships matter, but they are mostly held inside the wider family frame. As adolescence approaches, this changes. Peers move closer to the centre. Their opinions begin to weigh more than the parents'. Their reactions begin to shape the adolescent's self-image more reliably than the family's. By the middle of secondary school, in most children, the peer group is doing as much identity-shaping work as the home is.

This is not a failure of the family. It is normal development. Human adolescence is, biologically, a period during which the young person is meant to extend their sense of belonging beyond the family unit so that they can eventually function in the wider world. The neurobiology of adolescence, the increased sensitivity of reward circuitry to peer presence and peer evaluation, the slower maturation of the prefrontal regions involved in long-term planning, is built for exactly this transition.

The same biology that makes adolescents capable of forming powerful friendships and intense loyalties also makes them, for a few critical years, more vulnerable to peer influence than at any other time of life. They are wired to listen to the group. The question is what the group is teaching.

This chapter is about that teaching. Specifically, it is about how harmful behaviour gets quietly rewarded inside friendship groups, and how a child learns, often without ever realising it, that the price of belonging in this particular group is to act in ways that go against what they would otherwise believe.

How a Laugh Becomes a Lesson

The most influential body of research on how harmful behaviour spreads through adolescent peer groups comes from the developmental psychologist Thomas Dishion and his colleagues at the Oregon Social Learning Center, working alongside the same coercive-process tradition we met in Chapter 7.

In a 2011 review article in the Annual Review of Psychology, Dishion and Jessica Tipsord summarised three decades of work on what they call peer contagion in child and adolescent development.[1] Their central finding is that adolescent peer relationships do not merely correlate with later problem behaviour, they actively manufacture it, through specific social-reinforcement mechanisms that can be observed and measured in real time.

The mechanism works like this. An adolescent expresses a rule-breaking, hostile or risk-seeking idea, a comment about a teacher, a suggestion about cutting class, a story about something they did or wished they had done, a piece of contemptuous talk about another student. The peer responds with social reinforcement: a laugh, a nod, a "yeah, exactly," a raised eyebrow of approval, sustained eye contact, a follow-up question that invites elaboration.

That reinforcement, repeated, encodes the harmful content as effective. The adolescent has just learned that this kind of talk earns belonging. Their brain, calibrated by evolution to read social signal, will return to the strategy.

The remarkable finding is how small the reinforcement needs to be. A laugh is enough. Sustained attention is enough. The smile of an admired peer at exactly the right moment is enough. None of this requires a peer group to be openly antisocial. It requires only that, at the moment a particular kind of content is offered, the wrong response is given.

Once a friendship dyad or peer group has begun reinforcing harmful content reliably, the slope is established. Studies have followed adolescents whose friendships were organised around shared rule-breaking talk and shown that, all else being equal, those friendships predict significantly elevated rates of antisocial behaviour, substance use and violence in later adolescence.

What is not in those friendships is, just as importantly, what is. There is no equivalent reinforcement of compassion, restraint, kindness, or the idea that another person's feelings matter. Those things may exist between the same children in other moments. They are not the currency of belonging in this particular peer system.

Why Lectures Alone Fail

The reason a parental lecture often does not change a peer-influenced behaviour is not because the adolescent is being defiant. It is because the lecture and the peer reinforcement are operating on different levels.

A lecture is information. The adolescent processes it cognitively. They may even agree with it.

Peer reinforcement is reward. The adolescent processes it, on the whole, sub-cognitively, through reward circuitry that is currently operating on a hair-trigger. The reinforcement comes paired with an immediate, embodied sense of belonging. The lecture comes paired, often, with an immediate sense of being lectured.

Cognition and reward are not equally weighted at this stage of development. Reward usually wins.

This does not mean parents should stop having values conversations. It does mean that parents who pin all their hopes on a particularly well-delivered lecture about the wrong friend group are likely to be disappointed. The deeper work, which we will return to in Chapter 23, is to engineer the social context so that the adolescent is also embedded in groups where prosocial behaviour is the visible currency of belonging.

A child who has only one peer group, and that group reinforces contempt and risk, has very few alternatives. A child who is embedded in two or three different peer environments, sport, music, scouts, faith community, drama, cadets, surf life saving, volunteer work, extended family cousins, has options. Each environment is teaching its own currency. The more diverse the inputs, the less captured the adolescent is by any one of them.

What Peer Groups Reward

explicitly what kinds of behaviour harmful peer groups tend to reinforce. The patterns are remarkably consistent across the research:

Contempt. Mockery of teachers, parents, other students, particular groups. Contempt is a quick, efficient currency. It signals belonging without requiring vulnerability.

Risk. Stories of having taken risks, plans to take more, dares, escalations. Risk is rewarded both because it carries status and because it pulls the group together in shared experience.

Rule-breaking. Skipped classes, lies told to parents, things gotten away with. Each piece of small rule-breaking talk earns its small reinforcement.

Substance use. Casual references, shared first stories, normalisation of frequency. Once a peer group has begun reinforcing this content, the slope to actual substance use is much shorter than parents typically realise.

Sexual content. The earlier-than-actual sexual sophistication of group talk, the pressure to perform a worldly stance, the use of explicit material as a vehicle of belonging. Pornography exposure is now part of this picture in ways the previous generation did not have to consider.

Targeted cruelty. The shared agreement that a particular classmate is the legitimate target of mockery. This is one of the most reinforcing forms of peer talk and one of the most damaging, both to the targeted child and to the group members performing it, who are, with each laugh, slightly hardening their own capacity for cruelty.

If your child has come home recently using language, holding opinions, or describing relationships in ways that surprise you, the question to ask is not, "What is wrong with my child?" It is, "What is the currency of belonging in their current peer system?"

The Paradox of Grouping Struggling Children Together

There is one finding from this body of research that should change how parents, schools and policymakers think about intervention.

The intuitive response to a child whose behaviour is sliding is to put them with other children who are also sliding, on the theory that they will help each other. Group-based behavioural programmes for at-risk youth, residential treatment, alternative classrooms, juvenile-justice cohorts, many of these are built on this logic.

Dishion's research has shown, in multiple controlled studies, that the opposite is more often true. Bringing struggling adolescents together in unstructured or insufficiently supervised settings tends to accelerate, not arrest, harmful behaviour. The mechanism is exactly what we have just described. Place adolescents with shared rule-breaking leanings together for long enough, and they reinforce each other's patterns. The intervention itself ends up doing the same teaching the original peer group was doing.

Researchers call this an iatrogenic effect, treatment-induced harm caused by well-intended grouping. It does not always happen. It happens often enough that it is now considered a serious design constraint on adolescent group programmes.

The corollary for parents is direct. Removing your child from a struggling peer group and placing them with a different struggling peer group is rarely a solution. The right move, where it is possible, is to dilute, to embed your child in environments where prosocial behaviour is the visible norm, and where their existing patterns are no longer the most rewarded thing in the room.

The Quieter Contagion: Co-Rumination, Self-Harm, Disordered Eating

It would be a mistake to treat peer contagion as if it were only about aggression or rule-breaking. Some of the most measurable peer-contagion effects in modern adolescent samples are about distress.

Co-rumination, the pattern in which two or more friends spend extended periods talking together about how bad things are, in detail and repetitively, without moving toward action, is associated with elevated rates of depression and anxiety in both members of the friendship. It looks like emotional intimacy. It functions, increasingly, as a feedback loop that deepens distress.

Self-harm and suicidal ideation also show measurable peer contagion. Once a friendship group includes one member engaging in these behaviours, the risk for the other members rises. This is not a moral failing of the group; it is the same neural machinery of imitation and belonging applied to a particular kind of content.

Disordered-eating thoughts and body-image distress similarly travel through peer networks. Adolescents whose closest friends speak frequently about dieting, calorie restriction, body comparison or specific eating-disorder content are themselves at higher risk of developing the same patterns.

These quieter contagions are easy to miss because they do not look like the bad apple effect parents are usually warned about. There is no broken curfew, no fight, no expelled friend. There is just two friends, on a bedroom floor, in earnest, intimate conversation, slowly making each other's mental health worse.

Parents who can stay close enough to their adolescent's emotional landscape to notice the quality of the friendship, not just its existence, have a better chance of catching these patterns early. We will return to the practical work of monitoring, with care and without surveillance, in Chapter 20.

What Helps

Diversify the peer environments your child belongs to. A child embedded in three or four different groups is much harder to capture by any one of them.

Curate without controlling. Adolescents need to do their own social selection; they will not respond well to direct prohibition of friends. The work, instead, is on the wider context, choosing the activities, the groups, the schools, the camps, the family friends, the extended family they are around, and letting the adolescent select within that context.

Do not try to win the lecture. Information that is delivered without judgement and offered repeatedly, in passing, lands more reliably than the carefully prepared sit-down. The five-minute conversation in the car about something that came up on the radio is doing more work than the half-hour value lecture at the dinner table.

Notice the currency. If your child has come home with a new vocabulary, a new attitude, or a new set of opinions, the question is what kind of content their current peer group is rewarding. The behaviour is downstream of the currency.

Stay relationally available. The single most reliable protective factor against harmful peer influence in the developmental literature is a warm, low-conflict relationship with at least one parent. Not a perfect one. A reachable one.

Get help when the slope is steep. Substance use that has moved beyond experimentation, sustained social aggression, sexualised behaviour, self-harm or eating-disordered content require clinical input. In Australia, headspace centres are designed for exactly this age group and are the usual first stop, alongside a GP and a psychologist.

Key Takeaways

Adolescence is a developmentally normal period during which peer influence rises sharply and parental influence relatively weakens. The biology is built for this.

Peer contagion is the documented process by which peer groups socially reinforce rule-breaking or hostile content through small, immediate rewards, laughter, nods, sustained attention. The behaviour gets encoded as effective.

Lectures alone fail because cognition and reward operate on different levels and reward usually wins at this stage of development.

Peer groups commonly reward contempt, risk, rule-breaking, substance use, sexualised content and targeted cruelty. The behaviour your child brings home is downstream of the currency of their current peer system.

Bringing struggling adolescents together in poorly supervised settings often accelerates rather than arrests harmful behaviour. Diluting into prosocial environments is the more effective move.

Peer contagion also runs through quieter content: co-rumination, self-harm, suicidal ideation, disordered eating. These are easy to miss precisely because they do not look like the standard picture of trouble.

Diversification of environments, relational availability, and early professional input when the slope is steep are the practical core of what works.

References

1. Dishion, T. J., & Tipsord, J. M. (2011). Peer contagion in child and adolescent social and emotional development. Annual Review of Psychology, 62, 189–214. https://doi.org/10.1146/annurev.psych.093008.100412

2. Patterson, G. R., Reid, J. B., & Dishion, T. J. (1992). Antisocial Boys (A Social Learning Approach, Vol. 4). Eugene, OR: Castalia Publishing. (See also Chapter 7.)

CHAPTER 12
School and Classroom Cultures

The Other Half of Childhood

Whatever else a school does, it is the place where your child spends roughly six hours of every weekday for thirteen years. By the time they finish, they will have been in school more often than they have been at home with you while awake.

This makes school the second nervous-system environment of childhood, and in some ways the more demanding one. At home, a child knows the cast. At school, the cast is wider, more varied, and includes adults whose attention is shared across thirty other children. The emotional climate the child enters every morning has been set by people who are not the parents, and is sustained by dynamics the parents largely do not see.

Most parents understand that school matters academically. Fewer have a clear picture of what school is doing to their child as a system, as a place where some of the most important developmental work of belonging, exclusion, modelling, contempt and repair is being learned in real time, every day, regardless of what is being taught in the lesson.

This is the chapter where the bad apple effect leaves the family and meets the institution. Most of what we have already seen, emotional contagion, the social reinforcement of harmful behaviour, the cost of normalised harm, operates equally inside a classroom. The classroom just adds a few extra layers, and a particular kind of authority figure (the teacher) whose ability to hold the system has its own consequences for every child sitting in the room.

What a Single Disruptive Child Does to a Classroom

Chapter 3 introduced the empirical study by economists Kien Le and My Nguyen on Vietnamese fifth graders, which showed that exposure to peers being treated harshly at home produced measurable declines in academic performance for the surrounding children.[1] That study sits inside a larger body of research on what is sometimes called classroom peer effects.

The story it tells is consistent. When a classroom contains a child whose dysregulation is unsupported, repeated disruption, persistent aggression, ongoing crisis behaviour, the cost is paid by every child in the room. Test scores fall. Teacher attention is consumed. Working memory is depressed by the chronic presence of unpredictability. Children begin to organise their attention around the next disruption rather than around the lesson.

These costs are not the dysregulated child's fault. The dysregulated child is, themselves, paying the largest cost. They are also, as we have repeatedly named in this book, often a symptom carrier, for trauma at home, for unmet developmental needs, for an under-resourced classroom or school. The point is not to blame them.

The point is that letting the situation continue without serious support, for the child, for the teacher and for the wider classroom, is not neutrality. It is a decision, and it is being paid for by twenty-eight other children whose education is happening around the disruption.

Australian classroom-management literature, like the broader international evidence base, makes the same point. The single most effective thing a school can do for the surrounding children is to wrap the most dysregulated child in enough support, behavioural, mental-health, family, that they no longer need to dominate the classroom's nervous system to be seen.

The Cost of Hypervigilance

There is a particular finding from research on children in chronically unsafe or unpredictable classrooms that is worth pausing on. When a child has to remain alert to the possibility of disruption, a sudden outburst from a peer, an unpredictable teacher response, a known bully on the perimeter, the cognitive resources that would otherwise be available for learning are diverted into vigilance.

Working memory shrinks. Sustained attention frays. Reading comprehension drops. The child is not failing to try. They are spending their cognitive budget on safety.

This pattern shows up most starkly in children from already strained backgrounds, but it shows up to some degree in any child sitting in a classroom whose climate is unsafe. A child who can mostly relax in their classroom learns. A child who has to keep one eye on the room cannot.

If you are wondering why your child seems to be struggling academically despite being clearly bright, one of the questions worth asking is what the climate of their classroom feels like to them. Not whether they like their teacher in general. Whether they feel safe enough to take their attention off the room.

Classroom Composition Matters

A second strand of research, economic rather than psychological in its methods, has shown that the composition of a classroom shapes what every child learns.

Economists Victor Lavy and Analia Schlosser, working with large Israeli administrative datasets, found that an increase in the proportion of girls in a classroom improves the academic outcomes of both boys and girls.[2] The mechanism is not anything mysterious about gender. It is about classroom climate. Their analyses suggested the gains were mediated by lower levels of disruption and violence, improved relationships between students and between students and teachers, and reduced teacher fatigue.

The wider point is what that finding implies. The composition of a classroom is itself an intervention. If a classroom has a higher density of children whose dysregulation is unsupported, every child in the room pays a cost. If a classroom has been thoughtfully composed, with adequate support for the children most in need of it, every child in the room benefits.

Most parents have very limited control over classroom composition. The ones who do, those choosing between schools, evaluating new placements, advocating during particularly difficult years, should know that this lever exists, and that it matters more than most school marketing material suggests.

School Culture as a System

Above the level of the individual classroom sits the wider school culture. This is the climate set by the leadership, the staff norms, the disciplinary philosophy, the playground supervision, the way bullying complaints are handled, and the unspoken rules about what kinds of behaviour earn social capital among the students.

Some school cultures are deeply protective. Children at these schools, even when they are struggling, are likely to be noticed, supported and held inside a system that can absorb their distress. The children around them are likely to be modelling kindness as the norm, because the institution has made kindness the visible currency of belonging.

Other school cultures are corrosive. The ground rule of the playground is, in practice, that contempt and exclusion are tolerated. Bullying is processed slowly, if at all. Disruptive behaviour is allowed to dominate. The children most in need of help are written off. The children doing well are doing so partly by quietly aligning themselves with the dominant cruel current.

Most schools sit somewhere in between, and the school your child is at may be different from one year to the next, depending on which staff are present, which students are in their cohort, and what is happening at leadership level.

The honest version of this chapter is that you cannot, on your own, change a school culture. You can choose a school where it is possible. You can advocate clearly when the culture begins to slide. You can move your child if the culture has become harmful and the school has shown, over time, that it cannot or will not address it. And you can keep providing your child with what the school cannot, a different set of norms at home, a different model of how human beings can speak to each other, a place where the bad apple effect is not the climate.

What Parents Can Productively Ask of a School

When something is going wrong at school, most parents go in either too soft or too hard. A few questions, asked clearly and without theatre, tend to land better than either.

What is your understanding of what is happening between these children?

What support is being put in place for the child who is dysregulated, and what support is being put in place for my child?

What is the school's plan if this pattern continues?

How will I know whether what is being put in place is working?

What is your timeline?

Is there a wellbeing officer, school counsellor or chaplaincy person who should be involved?

If the school is being defensive, evasive, or making promises without action, you are entitled to escalate, to the head of year, to the principal, to the school board, and ultimately, in Australia, to the relevant state education department or the independent-school regulator. Most schools want to handle these situations well; some are stretched and need the prompt; a few are protecting their reputation more than their children.

Document everything in writing, including the dates of conversations and what was promised. This is not adversarial. It is structural realism. Schools are large institutions, and clarity protects everyone, including the school staff who want to help.

If, after sustained, well-handled advocacy, the school is unable to support your child adequately, changing schools is sometimes the right move. Some children flourish at a different school in a way that surprises everyone, including them. Schools are not interchangeable, and matching your child to the right one matters.

When the School Is Part of the Problem

It is also important to say, plainly, that schools can themselves be part of the bad apple effect.

A teacher whose contempt for a particular child has become a habit. A principal whose authority style runs on humiliation. A coach who blurs sport with personal cruelty. A culture in which staff burnout has spilled over into harshness. A school whose bullying response is to reframe the targeted child as the problem.

Where this is the picture, the chapter on monitoring and gatekeeping (Chapter 20) becomes specifically applicable to school relationships, not just peer relationships. Some adults at school may need to be navigated, escalated, or removed from your child's sphere as the year unfolds. None of this is comfortable. Some of it is necessary.

The honest test is the same one we use for the rest of the book. What is your child being shaped into by their continued exposure to this person or system, and is that shape one you and they can live with?

Key Takeaways

School is the second nervous-system environment of childhood and accounts for an enormous proportion of a child's waking developmental experience.

Empirical research shows that exposure to a single disruptive or harshly-treated child in a classroom measurably depresses the academic performance of surrounding children. The cost of leaving such a child unsupported is paid by everyone in the room.

Children in unsafe classrooms divert cognitive resources into hypervigilance. Working memory and sustained attention shrink. Learning suffers. The child is not failing to try; they are spending their budget on safety.

Classroom composition itself is a measurable intervention. Lavy and Schlosser's research shows that a higher proportion of girls improves outcomes for all children, mediated through reduced disruption and improved relationships.

School cultures range from deeply protective to corrosive. Most parents cannot single-handedly change a school's culture, but they can choose, advocate, document and, where necessary, move.

Productive parental advocacy is structured: clear questions, requested timelines, documented agreements, and willingness to escalate calmly when the school does not deliver.

Where the school is itself part of the harmful pattern, the same monitoring and gatekeeping principles that apply to peers apply to school staff.

References

1. Le, K., & Nguyen, M. (2019). 'Bad Apple' peer effects in elementary classrooms: The case of corporal punishment in the home. Education Economics, 27(6), 557–572. https://doi.org/10.1080/09645292.2019.1667306 (See also Chapter 3.)

2. Lavy, V., & Schlosser, A. (2011). Mechanisms and impacts of gender peer effects at school. American Economic Journal: Applied Economics, 3(2), 1–33. https://doi.org/10.1257/app.3.2.1

CHAPTER 13

Online Spaces and the Wider Adult World

The Two Influences That Walk Past Your Front Door

There are two categories of influence on your child that the family gatekeeping of an earlier era would have caught and that today's family gatekeeping often does not.

The first is online. Your child's phone, tablet or computer is a portable doorway to a parallel set of social environments, peers, communities, public figures, algorithmically promoted strangers, that is shaping them whenever it is in their hands. Most parents under-estimate how much of their child's day is spent inside this doorway, and how much of their child's identity is being formed there.

The second is the wider adult world. Coaches, extended family members, parents of friends, religious leaders, neighbours, family-friends, music teachers, swim instructors, scout leaders, the parent of the child who hosts the most sleepovers. These are the adults around your child whose behaviour your child is reading as data about how grown-ups behave. Most of them are wonderful. Some of them are not. And in many cases, the family has unconsciously continued to expose the child to a person whose behaviour, if it were happening between two children, would have been intervened on long ago.

This chapter takes both in turn. They are different, but they share a common feature: they sit just outside the family's primary regulating circle, and they are doing influence work that the parent does not directly see.

Online Spaces: The Algorithmic Layer

Anyone parenting in the 2020s has watched something happen to children that did not happen to previous generations. Phones came in. Social media came in. Short-form video came in. Group chats moved off the kitchen wall and into the bedroom. Pornography became free and effectively unfiltered. Gambling-mechanic apps colonised play. And the rates of adolescent anxiety, depression and self-harm, particularly among girls, began rising sharply, in country after country, beginning around 2012.

There is now a substantial popular literature attempting to make sense of this. American social psychologist Jonathan Haidt's 2024 book The Anxious Generation argues that the rewiring of childhood by smartphones and social media has been a primary driver of the adolescent mental-health crisis.[1] Sociologist Jean Twenge, in her earlier book iGen, made a similar case from a different angle, that the generation that came of age with smartphones in their pockets is measurably less rebellious, less independent, less mentally healthy, and lonelier than the generation before them.[2]

It is fair to note that the academic debate about the strength of these claims is not settled. Some developmental researchers, including Candice Odgers, have argued that the empirical evidence linking social-media use to mental-health outcomes at the population level is weaker than Haidt's book suggests, and that other explanations (including reverse causation, wider economic and social pressures, and the effects of the pandemic years) deserve more weight. The honest reading, in the middle of an active debate, is that the smartphone story is real but probably not the whole story.

Even allowing for that, three findings from the wider literature are robust enough to act on as a parent.

Adolescents, especially girls, who spend large amounts of unstructured time on social media report worse mental-health outcomes than those who do not. The size of the effect is debated; the direction is consistent.

Pornography exposure has shifted earlier and become more violent in its dominant content over the last fifteen years. Most boys now encounter it well before secondary school, and the content is shaping how they understand sexuality, consent and relationships. Most girls encounter, by adolescence, a sexual culture that reflects this exposure back to them.

Algorithmic feeds are not neutral. They are optimised to maximise time-on-platform, and the content that maximises time-on-platform is, on average, the content that produces the strongest emotional reactions, outrage, comparison, body-shame, fear, contempt. What the algorithm rewards is what the child is repeatedly served.

Whether or not Haidt's book has the precise causal story right, no parent in the 2020s gets to opt out of having a thoughtful position on what their child is doing online and how much of it is healthy. The bad apple effect runs through algorithmic spaces with extraordinary efficiency.

What the Algorithm Selects For

It is worth being specific about what kinds of content the dominant platforms tend to amplify in adolescent feeds, because the picture is more concrete than the abstract worry suggests.

Body-image content. Particularly for girls, feeds rapidly become saturated with curated bodies, comparison content, before-and-after images, fitness and diet content that often slides into eating-disorder territory. Some of this is openly pro-eating-disorder. Most of it is the more insidious version: aspirational, normalising, monetised.

Misogyny and what is sometimes called the "manosphere." For boys, feeds often surface content from a particular constellation of male influencers whose central message is contempt for women, a transactional view of sexuality, status anxiety, and the idea that male emotional vulnerability is weakness. This content is highly effective at recruiting boys who are already lonely, anxious or socially marginalised.

Self-harm, suicide and depression content. Algorithmic surfacing of this content, often misclassified as "relatable" or "mental-health awareness," has been documented in repeated investigative reports. For adolescents already experiencing distress, this content tends to deepen rather than relieve the distress.

Hate content. Racism, transphobia, antisemitism, contempt for particular communities. These are reliably algorithmically promoted to adolescents who engage with adjacent content, and the engagement loop is quick.

Pornography. As mentioned above, mostly free, mostly unrestricted, mostly more violent and more racialised than the previous generation's exposure, and now part of the texture of most adolescents' early sexual development.

Gambling-mechanic content. Loot boxes, in-game economies, prediction markets, sports-betting saturation in advertising. Adolescent brains are particularly susceptible to variable-ratio reward schedules, which is why these mechanics are designed the way they are.

It is not necessary to be a moral panic about all of this. It is necessary to be aware that the bad apple effect, in the algorithmic version, comes home in a child's pocket, and that no child can be expected to navigate it alone.

The Parent's Job, Online

The parental work here is not to remove the internet. The parental work is to delay, structure and accompany.

Delay. The Australian Government has recently legislated a minimum-age requirement for social media platforms. Internationally, similar conversations are underway. Whatever the eventual legal frame, the broader principle is that early adolescent brains and adult-grade algorithmic platforms are not a good match. Holding off on a smartphone, or holding off on social-media accounts within the smartphone, for as long as social pressure makes possible, is one of the most measurably protective decisions parents have available.

Structure. Where devices are present, the architecture matters. Devices that live in shared spaces, not bedrooms. Devices that go to bed before children do. Apps that are present by negotiation, not by default. Notifications turned off. Specific platforms paused at specific points. Australian families have access to the federal eSafety Commissioner's parental-control resources, which are free, well-maintained, and worth using as a baseline.

Accompany. The most reliably protective stance, where structure is in place, is the parent who is present in the digital landscape with the child rather than absent from it. Not as a surveillance officer. As an interested adult who watches the same shows, knows the influencers their child follows, asks about the latest in-game drama, and has a continuing conversation about what is being shown and what their child makes of it. Accompaniment is what stops a child being alone with the algorithm.

Talk early about pornography, before they encounter it. Talk early about misogynistic content, before it becomes their first model of masculinity. Talk early about online predators and grooming, in language a child can hold. Talk in small, regular, low-pressure moments. The five-minute conversation in the car is doing more work than the half-hour talk on the couch.

And take the wider community seriously. Many of the most protective decisions in this space are easier when made together with the parents of your child's friends. The "Wait Until 8th" movement and its Australian equivalents work because individual parents are no longer the only ones holding the line. Coordinate where you can.

The Wider Adult World

Now, the second category. The adults around your child.

Not the algorithm. The actual people. The grandparent whose contempt for a particular family member has begun to leak into family gatherings. The coach who confuses sport with humiliation.

The parent on the sideline whose criticism of his own child is loud enough to be teaching every child in earshot what to expect from a father. The uncle whose drinking is now part of every family event. The friend's parent whose marriage is loudly falling apart in front of the children. The teacher whose entire teaching style runs on shame.

Each of these is, in the language of this book, an exposure. Each is teaching your child something about how adults treat each other, and how adults are allowed to treat children.

Most parents under-recognise how much weight these adults carry in a child's developing model of the world. The child registers everything. The fact that they are silent at the time does not mean they are not learning.

The Sideline-Parent Problem

There is a particular pattern that recurs in Australian community sport, school competitions and weekend activities, and that deserves naming. The sideline parent.

This is the parent, usually a father, sometimes a mother, whose attention to their own child during a game, performance or activity has crossed from supportive to corrosive. They yell at their child. They yell at the coach. They yell at the umpire. They yell at the other team. They mock other children, sometimes in front of those children. They make a small humiliation out of every error.

Most parents around them are uncomfortable. Few say anything. The behaviour continues, week after week.

What every other child on the team is registering is that this is what fathers do. Or that this is what adults do at sport. Or that this is normal, since no one else around is intervening. The sideline parent is, week after week, modelling harmful behaviour in real time on every child within earshot, including the ones who will go home thinking less of their own father, who is quieter, simply because the sideline parent is louder.

If this is happening in a context your child is in, it is reasonable to raise it. Speak to the coach. Speak to the club. Speak to the other parents. Some clubs have explicit codes of conduct that can be invoked. Some need to develop them.

Where the sideline parent is your partner, your sibling, your father, or your friend, and the pattern has been ignored for years, the conversation is harder. It is also one of the more important ones a parent can have, because the alternative is letting the pattern keep teaching your child week after week.

The Toxic Extended-Family Member

Many families contain a relative whose behaviour is widely tolerated for the sake of family peace. The grandparent whose racism is older than the grandchildren. The uncle whose drinking has become part of every Christmas. The aunt whose contempt for a particular cousin is routine.

Loyalty to the family is real, and most parents will not lightly cut a relative out of their child's life. They should not have to. But continued exposure is itself a decision, and it is being paid for in the child's developing model of relationships.

The honest middle path, in most families, is some version of structured limitation. The relative is not severed, but the time spent with them is reduced, the contexts are chosen carefully, and the parent stays in the room rather than letting the child be alone in the relative's orbit. Where the behaviour is more serious, coercion, contempt directed at a child, racialised or homophobic attacks, drunkenness around children, sexualised behaviour, limitation moves toward removal.

Naming the limitation aloud to the child often matters more than the limitation itself. Children are capable of holding complexity. "Uncle X is family, and we love him, and we are not going to spend a long weekend at his house, because the way he treats your mother is not okay," is something a child can hold, and a model of how to hold it.

Coaches, Teachers and Other Authority Figures

A coach can be one of the most formative adults in a child's life. A great one teaches resilience, mastery, teamwork, the value of practice, and what it feels like to be supported by someone who believes in you. A poor one teaches that humiliation is a legitimate teaching tool, that anger is a legitimate response to mistakes, and that adults' moods are children's problems to manage.

If your child has a coach, instructor, teacher or scout leader whose pattern is closer to the second description, you are entitled to act. Speak to them directly if it is safe and appropriate. Speak to the club or school if it is not. Move your child if the pattern is not addressed.

Children are bad at quitting on their own when an adult they have been told to respect is treating them poorly. They need parents to do this work for them, sometimes against the child's own protest. The cost of leaving them inside a humiliating relationship for another season is real.

Key Takeaways

Two categories of influence routinely walk past family gatekeeping today: the algorithmically curated online environment, and the wider adult world your child moves through.

The smartphone-and-social-media story is real, even if the precise causal claims are still debated. The robust findings, that adolescent girls' mental health correlates with social-media exposure, that pornography is now part of early sexual development for most boys, and that algorithmic feeds optimise for emotionally activating content, are enough to act on.

The parental work online is to delay, structure and accompany, not to surveil. The "Wait Until 8th" logic, coordinated parental restraint with other families, is one of the most effective collective moves available.

Adults around your child are continuously teaching them how grown-ups are allowed to behave. Sideline parents, dysregulated extended-family members, humiliating coaches and contemptuous teachers all sit inside the bad apple effect, and all need to be assessed honestly.

Where these adults are inside your family or community circle, the work is some structured limitation, named clearly to the child, rather than silent tolerance.

Children are bad at protecting themselves from humiliating adults. They need their parents to do that work, sometimes over their child's own protest.

References

1. Haidt, J. (2024). The Anxious Generation: How the Great Rewiring of Childhood Is Causing an Epidemic of Mental Illness. New York:

Penguin Press. (Note: while highly influential, some of Haidt's causal claims are contested in the recent academic literature; the broad concerns about algorithmic exposure and adolescent mental health remain credible at the level of correlation and converging evidence.)

2. Twenge, J. M. (2017). iGen: Why Today's Super-Connected Kids Are Growing Up Less Rebellious, More Tolerant, Less Happy — and Completely Unprepared for Adulthood. New York: Atria Books.
3. Odgers, C. L. (2024). The great rewiring: Is social media really behind an epidemic of teenage mental illness? Nature, 628, 29–30. https://doi.org/10.1038/d41586-024-00902-2
4. eSafety Commissioner (Australia). www.esafety.gov.au (accessed 2026).

CHAPTER 14
When the Standard Slowly Slips

The Slow Slip

Most families that arrive at a serious problem did not arrive there in a single step. They arrived through hundreds of small accommodations, each of them, in isolation, reasonable.

A child screams at a sibling. The parents are exhausted. They issue a half-hearted correction and move on. The next time, the same correction. The next time, no correction. By the third month, screaming at a sibling is part of how the household sounds.

A teenager misses curfew by twenty minutes. The parents are tired and choose not to make it the issue tonight. By a year later, the curfew is, in practice, an hour later than it used to be.

A child becomes contemptuous toward one parent. The other parent flinches. The flinch is not followed up on. The contempt continues, mildly. The flinching parent decides not to provoke it further. By the time anyone names it, it is the family's wallpaper.

A device that was a guest in the house has slowly become a roommate, then a tenant, then the central organising feature of every evening. No one decided. It just happened, in fifteen-minute concessions.

This chapter is about how that happens. It is about a phenomenon, well-named in the safety and organisational-behaviour literature, that explains why families and institutions slowly drift past lines they would never have crossed in a single step. Researchers call it the normalisation of deviance, meaning the slow drift away from a standard, not anything about the people inside it.

It is one of the most useful frames in this book, because once you can see it, you can interrupt it. And once you can interrupt it, the family standard begins to recover, often without any of the dramatic interventions parents fear they may have to make.

The Challenger: A Cautionary Story

The most influential study of how this drift happens inside a high-stakes system is the American sociologist Diane Vaughan's 1996 book The Challenger Launch Decision.[1]

Vaughan was trying to explain how engineers and managers at NASA, faced with mounting evidence that the rubber O-rings sealing the joints of the Space Shuttle solid rocket boosters were failing in cold weather, ended up authorising the launch of the Challenger on a near-freezing January morning in 1986. Seventy-three seconds after liftoff, the O-rings on the right booster failed. The shuttle disintegrated. Seven crew members died, including the schoolteacher Christa McAuliffe.

The conventional story, in the immediate aftermath, was one of misconduct. Someone must have known. Someone must have ignored a clear warning. Someone must have been negligent.

Vaughan, after years of archival work, told a different story. There had been no single moment of misconduct. Instead, over the previous decade, the engineers and managers responsible for the O-rings had repeatedly observed evidence of damage that fell outside the original safety specifications. Each time the damage was observed, it was investigated, discussed, classified, and, crucially, deemed an acceptable in-flight risk because the shuttle had returned safely. What had once been treated as a problem became, in the language of the agency, an in-family event. A known concern. Not a crisis.

Over time, what was once a clear breach of the design specifications was incrementally re-categorised as an acceptable feature of normal operation. The engineers were not ignoring the data. The data had simply been re-defined, slowly, into something that no longer demanded action.

On the night before the Challenger launch, when the engineers raised concerns about cold-weather performance, they were operating inside a culture that had spent ten years gradually moving the line. The concern they were warning about was, by 1986, no longer felt as a concern. It was felt as the way things were.

Seventy-three seconds into the flight, the way things were stopped working.

Vaughan's point was not that NASA was uniquely bad. Her point was that any organisation, including a healthy one, can drift past its own standards through a series of locally rational decisions, and that the drift is invisible at the scale of any single decision. The slip only becomes visible from outside, or from later.

Families work the same way.

The Fallacy of Past Success

The cognitive engine of the normalisation of deviance is what Vaughan and others have called the fallacy of past success. The reasoning runs like this:

We crossed this line yesterday. Nothing terrible happened. Therefore the line cannot have been important.

Repeated, this reasoning quietly licenses larger and larger deviations. Each one is justified by the absence of catastrophe in the previous one. The fallacy is that the absence of immediate catastrophe is not evidence of safety. It is evidence that the system has not collapsed yet.

Inside a family, the fallacy of past success usually sounds something like this:

"We have been through this before. He calmed down. It will be fine."

"Nothing has happened yet, even though they have been on the phone all night for months."

"She is teasing him, not really hurting him. They will work it out."

"He has always come back from these things eventually. Last year was worse and he turned a corner."

"They are still going to school. The grades are okay. It cannot be that bad."

Each of these sentences may be locally accurate. None of them are reliable predictors of how the pattern will end. The track record of small concessions, gathered together, becomes the case for one more concession. By the time the household pulls back to recalibrate, the line that used to be obvious is several steps behind.

The honest discipline is to refuse the comfort of the fallacy. The fact that nothing terrible has happened yet is not, by itself, useful information about whether the current trajectory is acceptable.

How Families Drift Past the Line

The drift inside a family typically has the same shape Vaughan documented at NASA, scaled down to a kitchen table.

Step one: a behaviour occurs that, in an earlier version of the household, would have been clearly unacceptable.

Step two: the parents are tired, distracted, or uncertain how to respond. The behaviour is not addressed, or addressed only weakly.

Step three: the same behaviour occurs again, this time in a slightly more developed form. The parents are no fresher than they were last time. The response is again partial.

Step four: the behaviour is recategorised. It is no longer an alarm. It is a feature of this child, this season, this teenager, this household.

Step five: a new behaviour, slightly worse, becomes the new edge. The previously unacceptable behaviour is now the normal background. Energy that would have been spent intervening on the original behaviour is now reserved for the new one.

Step six: a few months later, the household has a new normal. The original line is several steps back. The current line is itself slipping.

The drift is not visible at any single step. It is visible, with painful clarity, in retrospect, usually after a sibling finally complains hard enough to be heard, or a school finally calls a meeting, or an extended family member finally says aloud what they have noticed for months. At that point, the parents often experience genuine shock at how far the household has moved. They were inside the drift.

There is no judgement in this. The drift is a structural property of any system under chronic strain. It is what tired humans inside a feedback loop do. The corrective is not self-flagellation. The corrective is a deliberate, periodic, honest recalibration. The chapter on parental neutralisation that follows looks at the specific cognitive moves that fuel this drift; the rest of this chapter looks at how to interrupt it.

The Markers of a Drifted Household

If you suspect, while reading this chapter, that your household may have been drifting, here are the markers most commonly seen in clinical and family-systems work. None of these is, alone, a verdict. Several of them together are usually a signal worth attending to.

Behaviour that would have alarmed you a year ago no longer alarms you.

You find yourself reassuring outside observers, extended family, a friend, a teacher, that something they have noticed is fine, and you are aware, while doing so, that you are not entirely sure it is.

You catch yourself using phrases like, "That is just how he is," "She has always been dramatic," "It is not as bad as last time," or, "At least it was not like the night when...".

Siblings have begun to behave as if a particular pattern from another sibling is a fact of life that they must work around, not a behaviour that the adults are addressing.

Your partner, your child, or a trusted friend has begun gently raising a concern that you have, repeatedly, dismissed.

Your own emotional reaction inside the home has narrowed. You have stopped reacting strongly to things that, earlier, would have prompted a stronger response.

You have stopped having particular kinds of guests in the house, or stopped going particular places, because of how a particular family member behaves.

Bedtime, mealtime, mornings, transitions, formerly ordinary parts of the day, have become events that require strategy.

You have, in private, stopped imagining the household as a place to bring people. You have begun to keep it more separate from the rest of your life than you used to.

If three or four of these are recognisable, it is worth treating that as a flag. Not as proof that you have failed. As evidence that the system has drifted, and that a recalibration is overdue.

Recalibrating

Recalibration begins, in most family-systems work, with three steps.

First, name the drift, to yourself, before naming it to anyone else. Sit with it for an evening. Write down the behaviours that have become the household's background that you would not have tolerated a year ago. Notice which of them have crept up the most. The point is not to compile evidence. The point is to step out of the drift long enough to see it.

Second, locate the original line. What was the standard you want to hold? What would you have wanted yourself to do, twelve months ago, if you had known where the household would be by now? Write that down too. The original line is rarely as far away as the current state suggests; you have just lost sight of it.

Third, choose a small number of recalibrations. Not every drift needs to be reversed at once. The choice of which to address first is itself an art. The general rule is to pick the slips that are costing the most to the children who are not the source, the siblings, the quieter child, the partner whose patience has run out. Their experience is the most reliable barometer of where the line should sit.

Recalibration also means a conversation, at the right level, with the people in the household. Not a lecture. Not a tribunal. A clear, calm, partnered statement, ideally from both adults where there are two: the household has drifted, here is what we have noticed, here is the standard we are returning to, here is what each of us will do differently. Children, even adolescents, generally respond better to a recalibration that is named than to one that arrives as a series of unexplained new restrictions.

recalibration is rarely a single conversation. The drift took months or years. The recalibration takes weeks of consistent practice. The first time the original line is held, the household will protest. The second time, less. The fourth time, the standard will begin to feel native again.

And recalibrate periodically, not only in crisis. The most protected households are the ones whose adults stop, twice or three times a year, and ask each other an honest question: where have we drifted, and what do we want to bring back?

That deliberate review is the parental version of the safety-management practice that, after Challenger, Vaughan recommended for organisations: build in moments at which the system is asked, formally, whether the slips it has been accepting are still acceptable.

Key Takeaways

Most family problems arrive through gradual drift, not through a single crossed line. Researchers in the safety and organisational-behaviour literature call this the normalisation of deviance, meaning the slow movement of a standard, not anything about the people inside it.

The cognitive engine of this drift is the fallacy of past success: the assumption that because nothing terrible has happened yet, the current trajectory is safe.

Drift typically proceeds through small, locally rational accommodations, each of which licenses the next, until the household has a new normal that an outside observer would not recognise as healthy.

Markers of a drifted household include: behaviour that would have alarmed you a year ago no longer doing so; reassuring outside observers about something you are unsure of; using phrases like 'that is just how he is'; siblings behaving as though a pattern is a fact of life; declining to invite people in.

Recalibration is a three-step practice: name the drift to yourself, locate the original line, and choose a small set of recalibrations that begin to restore the standard.

Recalibration is best done periodically, not only in crisis. Households that build in regular review are far less likely to find themselves several steps past the line they meant to hold.

References

1. Vaughan, D. (1996). The Challenger Launch Decision: Risky Technology, Culture, and Deviance at NASA. Chicago: University of Chicago Press.

2. Vaughan, D. (1999). The dark side of organizations: Mistake, misconduct, and disaster. Annual Review of Sociology, 25, 271–305. https://doi.org/10.1146/annurev.soc.25.1.271

CHAPTER 15

How Parents Talk Themselves Out of Acting

An Honest Mirror, Not an Accusation

Most of the drift described in the last chapter is enabled by something that happens silently inside the parent. Before a household can normalise harmful behaviour, the parents have to find a way to live with not addressing it. The mind needs a story. The story needs to be at least partly believable, at least to the person telling it.

These stories have been studied, and they have a name.

In 1957, two American sociologists named Gresham Sykes and David Matza published a short article in the American Sociological Review.[1] Their argument was startling and humane. People who act against their own stated values, they wrote, do not, on the whole, hold a different value system from anyone else. They mostly hold conventional values. What they have learned, instead, is a small set of cognitive moves that allow them to suspend those values long enough to act in ways that violate them.

Sykes and Matza identified five recurring moves. They called them denial of responsibility, denial of injury, denial of the victim, condemnation of the condemners, and appeal to higher loyalties.

Their theory was originally developed in a particular context, early sociological research on adolescents in trouble with the law, and the academic name they gave it, neutralisation, is the term still used in the literature today. Over the seventy years since, the framework has been extended far beyond its original context. It has been recognised at work, in sport, in marriages, in politics, in environmental decision-making, and almost anywhere people's actions have come into conflict with their stated values. The same five moves keep appearing.

Including, with quiet regularity, in parenting.

This chapter takes the five moves and looks at how each one shows up in parental thinking when a household has begun to drift. The point is not to accuse anyone. Most of us use all of these at various points; they are normal cognitive shortcuts under stress, and they have served real protective purposes in our own lives. The question is not whether you have ever used them. The question is whether one or more of them has become, in your household, a chronic substitute for action.

An honest mirror, not an accusation, is the right way to read what follows.

Denial of Responsibility

The first technique says, in effect, that the situation is happening to the parent rather than being shaped by them.

"He cannot help it. It is the ADHD."

"She is a teenager. This is what teenagers do."

"He is going through a phase."

"She gets it from her father. There is nothing I can do."

"It is the school. It is the phone. It is the friends. It is the year we have all had."

Each of these sentences may have a real grain of truth in it. Children do go through phases. ADHD is real. Teenagers do go through difficult patches. Phones and peer groups and pandemic years do shape behaviour.

The neutralisation is not in the diagnosis. It is in the conclusion that follows it. The conclusion that follows it, in a household that has drifted, is: therefore there is nothing for me to do. The recognition of an external cause has been used to license parental withdrawal from the response.

The corrective sentence is the one that holds the diagnosis and the responsibility together. "He cannot help his initial reactivity, and we still have to teach him not to hit his sister." "She is a teenager, and these patterns will still shape who she is, and we still have a job here." "The phone is a real factor, and so is whether the phone lives in her bedroom at night."

Denial of responsibility tends to feel true. That is why it is effective. The corrective is not to pretend you are responsible for everything. It is to notice when the partial truth has been doing the work of relieving you of the part that is yours.

Denial of Injury

The second technique says that nothing real is being damaged.

"They are just brothers. They will sort it out."

"It is just teasing. She does not really mean it."

"He is just venting. It does not affect them."

"This is what kids do. We did the same things at their age."

"No one is bleeding. It is fine."

Denial of injury is one of the easiest neutralisations to slip into because so much of family conflict is invisible from the outside. There are no hospital bills. There are no broken bones. The cost is in atmosphere, in confidence, in a sibling's nervous-system baseline, in a child's sense that home is a safe place to be. None of these are easy to point to. All of them are real.

If you find yourself saying, repeatedly, that no real damage is being done, the test is what the receiving children look like over time. Not what they say in the moment, when they are loyal to the family and accustomed to the climate. What they look like quietly, away from the household, when the pressure has dropped. Are they more anxious than they used to be? More withdrawn? More vigilant? Less themselves?

If the answer is yes, the injury is real. The neutralisation is no longer affordable.

Denial of the Victim

The third technique reassigns the cost. The harm did happen, but the person on the receiving end somehow deserved or invited it.

"She knows exactly how to push his buttons."

"He was asking for it."

"She set him off. She always does."

"He needs to toughen up. He cannot expect the world to handle him gently."

"Everyone is being too sensitive. It is just words."

This neutralisation often shows up in sibling work, particularly when one sibling is a chronic harmer and the other has, over years, developed survival strategies that look like provocation from the outside. The younger sibling is fed up. The younger sibling has learned to swing first because they get hit anyway. The younger sibling has begun to taunt because the older sibling will explode regardless and it is at least under their control if they trigger it.

From the outside, with the wrong frame, this can look like the younger sibling being the actual problem. The neutralisation lets the parent step back from the harder work of recognising that the younger sibling has adapted to a system that is making them less, not more, of themselves.

The corrective question is, "Is this person actually inviting harm, or are they responding, with the strategies available to them, to harm that has already been happening?" Answering that question honestly often shifts where the parental energy needs to go.

Condemnation of the Condemners

The fourth technique points the camera at whoever has raised the concern.

"The school is just being precious. You should see what they tolerate from other kids."

"My mother is overreacting. She always thinks something is wrong."

"You do not understand what we live with. You are not in this house."

"The therapist is biased toward the other parent."

"The family doctor is judgemental. We are not going back."

There are two truths in tension here. Sometimes the school really is being precious. Sometimes the relative really is overreacting. Sometimes a particular professional really is the wrong fit. Defensiveness is not always wrong.

But when condemnation of the condemners has become a chronic move, when every outside party who has raised a concern has, over time, been categorised as biased, ignorant, judgemental, vindictive or out of line, the most likely explanation is not a coordinated external misjudgement. It is that the household has drifted far enough that the people outside the drift are calling it from where they sit, and the people inside the drift are reorganising their assessment of the people outside rather than the other way round.

If you find yourself repeatedly dismissing the people who care about your family as being the ones who do not get it, take a careful breath. Sometimes that is true. Often, when it has become a pattern, what has happened is that the household has moved further from its own values than the parents inside it have recognised.

Appeal to Higher Loyalties

The fifth technique says that some larger value must be honoured, and the harm in question is the necessary cost.

"He is family. We do not abandon family."

"We have to be loyal. He has been through so much."

"We promised we would always have the door open."

"She is my child too. I cannot just take sides against her with the other children."

"We are not the kind of people who do that."

Appeals to higher loyalties are often beautiful. The values they invoke, family, loyalty, unconditional love, refusal to abandon, are real values, and worth holding.

The neutralisation is in using one value to suspend another, without acknowledgement. The appeal to higher loyalty for one child often comes at the cost of a duty owed to a different child. The promise of unconditional family belonging often becomes a license for the behaviour of one member to be unconditionally tolerated. The refusal to take sides often becomes the refusal to protect the child being harmed.

It is possible to honour the higher loyalty and the duty to other children at the same time. "We do not give up on family, and we are also not going to let you treat your sister this way," is not a contradiction. It is what loving leadership inside a complex family actually sounds like.

When you notice yourself reaching for a high-value sentence to relieve yourself of a specific intervention, the question to ask is which other value you have just suspended in order to honour it.

The Self-Compassion Move

If reading the last six pages has made you uncomfortable, that is exactly what the chapter is meant to do.

It is also why the chapter ends here, before it does any further damage.

There is a real risk, with material like this, that a parent reads it and falls off the other side of the cliff. They go from drift, to recognition, to a kind of total self-condemnation. Every sentence they have ever said now feels like a neutralisation. Every accommodation they have ever made now looks like complicity. The shame is enormous.

Please do not do that.

These are normal cognitive moves under stress. We have all used all five of them at various points, including in places that have nothing to do with parenting. They are not signs of moral failure. They become a problem only when they have become chronic, when one or two of them have begun running the household, and when they are no longer being noticed.

Once you can see them, they lose most of their power. The ability to catch yourself mid-sentence, to think, that is a denial of responsibility, what is mine here?, is the entire corrective. It is also a skill that strengthens with practice, the same way any other regulatory practice does.

The point is not to become a parent who never neutralises. That parent does not exist. The point is to become a parent who notices the move quickly enough that it cannot organise the household.

And to be willing, and this is the hardest part, to invite the people closest to you to point out the moves you have stopped seeing. A partner who can say, gently, "I think we are denying the injury again," is doing some of the most important work a parent can ever be asked to do. So is the friend who is willing to say, kindly, that something is bigger than the household has been treating it as.

Steinbeck's line from Chapter 10 is worth holding here too. You do not have to be perfect. You can be good. Catching the neutralisation, naming it without contempt for yourself, and stepping back into the room is exactly what good looks like.

Key Takeaways

Households drift past their own standards because the people inside them tell themselves stories that license inaction. Sykes and Matza named five of these stories: denial of responsibility, denial of injury, denial of the victim, condemnation of the condemners, and appeal to higher loyalties.

Each move usually contains a partial truth. The trouble is not in the truth; it is in the conclusion that follows it.

Denial of responsibility uses external causes to license parental withdrawal from the response.

Denial of injury underestimates the cost being paid in atmosphere, confidence and nervous-system baseline.

Denial of the victim mistakes the receiving child's adaptive strategies for provocation.

Condemnation of the condemners categorises the people raising concerns as the problem.

Appeal to higher loyalties uses one value to suspend another without acknowledgement.

All of us use these moves sometimes. They become a problem when they have become chronic and are no longer being noticed.

The corrective is not self-condemnation. It is the practice of catching the move quickly enough that it cannot organise the household, and the willingness to invite trusted people to point out the moves you have stopped seeing.

References

1. Sykes, G. M., & Matza, D. (1957). Techniques of neutralization: A theory of delinquency. American Sociological Review, 22(6), 664–670. https://doi.org/10.2307/2089195
2. Maruna, S., & Copes, H. (2005). What have we learned from five decades of neutralization research? Crime and Justice, 32, 221–320. https://doi.org/10.1086/655355

CHAPTER 16

The Biological Floor: The Body Beneath the Behaviour

If we want better behaviour, we must build better conditions.

The Body Underneath the Behaviour

Most of this book has been about what families and the world around them do to children, patterns, contagion, sibling subsystems, peer groups, school cultures, online environments, the slow drift of standards, the moves we make under stress to talk ourselves out of acting.

All of that matters. But all of it is happening on top of something more fundamental: a child's body.

A child's nervous system is not a passive recipient of the household climate. It is the primary instrument the child has for being in the world. It registers tone before it registers words. It tightens or softens depending on whether the people around it are tightened or softened. It absorbs sleep, food, light, rhythm, movement, screens, pollution and stress, and it gives back, in the form of behaviour, exactly what it has been taking in.

If a child's biology is in decent shape, the parenting strategies in this book have something to land on. The child has the regulatory bandwidth to receive a boundary, repair a rupture, work with the parent on a problem.

If a child's biology is in poor shape, if their sleep has collapsed, their blood sugar is on a roller-coaster, they are not moving, they are saturated with screens, they are running on chronic stress and have not been outside in days, the same parenting strategies will, much of the time, fail. Not because the strategies are wrong. Because the body underneath them cannot do what the strategy is asking of it.

This chapter is the chapter that holds the rest of the book accountable. It is also,, a single chapter rather than the four it could have been, because the deeper biological work has already been written down at length elsewhere, in my three earlier books, which the closing section of this chapter points to for parents who want to go further.

The aim here is the bridge. To put the body underneath the behaviour, in language that does not require any prior reading, and to give parents enough of a frame to act on it.

When Biology Goes On Watch

The most useful single concept here is one developed by an American physician-scientist named Robert Naviaux. He calls it the Cell Danger Response.[1]

Naviaux's idea is biologically detailed and worth several books on its own. The version a parent needs is simpler.

Inside every cell in your child's body sits a small population of structures called mitochondria. They are best known as the energy-producing engines of the cell, but they are also something else, they are the cell's alarm system. When a mitochondrion senses danger, whether from physical injury, infection, toxin exposure, malnutrition, or psychological stress, it shifts the cell out of normal operation and into defensive mode. Energy production changes. Membrane chemistry changes. The cell pulls back from its ordinary work and prepares to defend itself.

This is the Cell Danger Response, or CDR. It is not a flaw in the system. It is one of the most ancient, conserved, intelligent mechanisms in living biology. It is what allows a body to survive a cut, fight off a virus, recover from a fall, get through a crisis. It is meant to come on, do its work, and turn off again so that healing can begin.

The healing process that follows the CDR is what Naviaux calls salugenesis, from the Latin salus, meaning health. Salugenesis is the body's active, organised, multi-stage rebuilding programme. It is what actually repairs a wound, resolves an infection, restores a depleted nervous system, returns a stressed mind to baseline. Naviaux's 2023 paper in the journal Mitochondrion is the most thorough scientific account of how this rebuilding actually unfolds at the cellular level.[2]

The trouble begins when the CDR cannot turn off.

Modern children, in modern environments, are routinely exposed to a constellation of stressors their biology was not built to manage in chronic form. Family stress that does not resolve. Sibling dysregulation that does not let up. Peer-group conflict that follows them home through the phone. Algorithmic feeds that rev up arousal and perpetuate it. Diets dominated by ultra-processed foods that destabilise blood sugar and disturb the gut. Sleep that is too short and too late, on every school night for years. Sunlight they barely meet. Movement they barely get. Connection that is filtered through devices.

When these inputs run long enough, the CDR does not switch off. The biology stays on watch. Cells stay in defensive mode. Salugenesis stalls.

What this looks like in a child, on the outside, is exactly what most parents read in this book have been describing throughout. Reactivity. Anxiety. Anger that explodes faster than it used to. A sleep-cycle that has gone off the rails. Eating that is dysregulated. Mood that is heavier. Concentration that is patchy. Behaviour that does not respond to discipline because the child is not, in the moment, capable of regulating well enough to receive it.

The behaviour is the visible top of the iceberg. The biology is most of what is underneath.

What Holds a Child's Biology in Defence

Almost every theme this book has covered, when traced down far enough, is a way the CDR can be kept switched on in a child's body.

Chronic family stress keeps it on. A child raised inside the kind of climate Chapters 9 and 10 described, sustained marital tension, parental dysregulation, contempt running through the household tone, has a nervous system that almost never gets to come down to baseline.

Sibling-system contagion keeps it on. A child living next to a chronically dysregulated sibling, the matching response, the inertia, the endless escalation we mapped in Chapter 7, is doing low-grade alarm work most of the day.

Peer conflict keeps it on. A child whose friendships have become organised around contempt, exclusion or unreliable belonging is biologically vigilant whenever the phone buzzes.

Online environments keep it on. Algorithmic feeds optimised for emotional arousal, the steady drip of comparison and outrage, late-night scrolling that pushes against the child's sleep, every one of these is, biologically, the equivalent of a small alarm bell ringing every few seconds.

Bad sleep keeps it on. Unstable blood sugar keeps it on. Lack of daylight keeps it on. Lack of movement keeps it on.

And, uncomfortably, even some of the harder work this book has asked parents to do can, in the short term, keep it on. Recalibration is stressful. Repair is uncomfortable. Holding a boundary the family has been ignoring for months produces, in the first few weeks, more activation, not less.

All of this is normal. The point is not to remove every stressor. That would be neither possible nor developmentally healthy. Children need to meet stress and recover from it. That is how their nervous systems get built.

The point is to make sure that, alongside the stress, the conditions for recovery are reliably available. The CDR is meant to switch off. Salugenesis is meant to follow. The body, given the conditions, will do this work on its own.

Those conditions are what the rest of this chapter is about.

The Biological Floor

What I will call the biological floor is the set of basic conditions a child's nervous system needs in order to keep coming back to regulation. They are not optional. Every child has them. Most children, in modern households, are not getting them in adequate measure, and the behavioural cost of the deficit is large.

The floor has six planks.

Sleep

Sleep is the single most important plank, and the one most easily lost. Children and adolescents are chronically under-slept in the era of screens, and the cost is paid in regulation, in mood, in immune function, in concentration, and in behaviour.

The numbers are not subtle. School-age children need around nine to eleven hours per night. Adolescents need eight to ten. Most Australian children, by mid-primary school, are getting at least an hour less than they need. Most Australian adolescents, by Year Nine, are running on a deficit of two hours a night, every night, for years.

Practical floor: a consistent bedtime, a consistent wake time, no devices in the bedroom overnight, the last hour before sleep low-stimulation, screens out of the room at least an hour before lights-out, and a cool, dark, quiet sleep environment.

Of all the things this chapter recommends, sleep returns the largest behavioural change for the smallest investment of effort. If you do nothing else, look honestly at sleep first.

Blood Sugar and What Children Eat

Stable blood sugar is the second plank. A child whose glucose is on a roller-coaster, sugary breakfast, mid-morning crash, sweet lunch, afternoon collapse, is a child whose nervous system is being asked to regulate inside a body that cannot.

Modern Australian children eat a diet that, on average, is dominated by ultra-processed foods, refined carbohydrates, vegetable seed oils and added sugar. The metabolic and mental-health implications of this pattern are now extensively documented and were the subject of my third book, The Blood Sugar Solution to Mental Health.[3]

Practical floor: protein and healthy fats at breakfast, not just refined carbohydrate. Vegetables and protein at lunch and dinner. Fewer between-meal sugary snacks. Water as the default drink. Whole foods over packaged. Steady meals at predictable times. Limits on the most addictive ultra-processed lines.

None of this needs to be perfect, and the point is not to police every birthday cake. The point is the steady-state diet, six or seven days a week. That is what the child's biology runs on.

Movement, Sunlight and Time in Nature

The third, fourth and fifth planks belong together because they are recovered together. Children need to move, every day, for at least an hour, ideally outdoors, ideally in daylight, ideally in some kind of contact with the natural world.

Movement returns the body to its evolutionary baseline. Daylight, especially morning daylight, sets the circadian system that drives sleep, mood, hormones and alertness. Time in nature reduces sympathetic arousal in ways that have been measured repeatedly across cultures and ages.

Practical floor: walking or cycling to school where possible. After-school sport, scouts, surf life saving, dance, parkour, anything that gets the body moving. Weekends that include time outside rather than time on screens. Family rituals built around being outdoors, bushwalks, beaches, gardens, river swims, backyard cricket.

Children whose week includes plenty of movement, daylight and natural environments are markedly more regulated than children whose week does not. This is not a luxury. It is part of the floor.

Screens and Stimulation

The sixth plank is the inverse of the others. The child's nervous system needs not just inputs, but the absence of certain inputs. It needs unstructured boredom, downtime, slow attention, time without the next dopamine hit.

Modern devices are very good at preventing this. Phones, tablets and televisions deliver continuous, finely-tuned stimulation at a rate the child's nervous system was never designed to metabolise. Some children show this damage as anxiety. Some show it as dysregulation. Some show it as the slow narrowing of attention. Some show it as the simple inability to be alone for ten minutes without reaching for a screen.

Practical floor: screens have boundaries. They are not the default activity. They are not in the bedroom. They are not at meals. They are not the first thing in the morning. The child has device-free hours every day. The household models the same restraint the children are being asked to practice.

Chapter 13 covered the algorithmic and content concerns in detail. The point here is biological. Even if the content were entirely benign, the volume and tempo of screen stimulation would still be doing damage to a developing nervous system. The content layer matters. The exposure layer matters too.

Connection and Co-Regulation

The biological floor is not only about what enters the body and what does not. It is also about who the child is regulating with.

The American neuroscientist Stephen Porges, in his work on what he calls polyvagal theory, has spent decades documenting that the human nervous system is not, on the whole, a solo regulator.[4] It is a relational regulator. A child's vagal tone, the readiness of their body to return to calm after stress, is built, over years, through repeated experiences of being co-regulated by an adult who is themselves regulated.

This is the biology underneath every chapter on parenting in this book. When a parent stays steady in the face of a child's storm, they are not just modelling self-control. They are giving the child's body a regulating other to attune to. When a parent repairs after rupture, they are not just teaching apology. They are demonstrating that connection is recoverable, which the child's nervous system records.

Practical floor: presence over performance. Time together that is unhurried, undistracted and frequent. Conversations that are not transactional. Moments of physical co-regulation, hugs, sitting together, walking side by side, that the child can bank against the next storm. Adults around the child who model regulation rather than reactivity. A household whose tempo lets the child breathe.

All the rest of this book's parenting work, calm authority, repair, accountability without shame, builds on this floor.

A Note for Parents Who Want to Go Deeper

If this chapter has felt like the tip of an iceberg, that is because it is.

The trauma and Cell Danger Response material is treated at length in my first book, Healing Trauma at the Cellular Level: The Role of the Cell Danger Response in PTSD and Trauma Recovery, which Robert Naviaux generously wrote the foreword for.[5] That book is the place to go if you want to understand the biology of stuck healing in detail, and the somatic, integrative and trauma-specific therapies that help it move again.

The lifestyle, layered-healing approach to depression is treated in my second book, Stacking Therapies for Depression Recovery: A Layered Healing Approach.[6] It is a more practical book, organised around the small, evidence-supported steps that, stacked together, produce real change in mood and resilience over time. It is also written with parents in mind in several places.

The metabolic, blood-sugar and nutritional-psychiatry territory is treated in my third book, The Blood Sugar Solution to Mental Health.[7] That book covers continuous glucose monitoring, ketogenic metabolic therapy, fructose, seed oils, sleep, screen time, EMFs, sunlight, grounding, gut health, hormones across life stages, and the wider field of metabolic psychiatry now emerging in clinical practice.

None of those books is required reading for the rest of this one. This chapter is meant to stand on its own as the bridge. But for any parent who recognises, reading these last few pages, that the biology underneath their child is asking for more than a chapter of attention, the deeper work is there.

Build the Conditions, the Behaviour Follows

There is a way of reading parenting books that ends in a kind of exhaustion. Each new chapter recommends a new strategy, the parent agrees the strategy is reasonable, the strategy fails to take hold in the actual household, and the parent concludes, wrongly, that the failure is theirs.

Often the failure is not in the strategy. The strategy was being asked to work on top of a child whose biology was not in any condition to receive it.

The most freeing recognition this chapter can offer is also the simplest. If your household is not getting the biological floor, if sleep is broken, blood sugar is wild, movement is rare, daylight is scarce, screens are saturating, connection is thin, most of the parenting strategies in this book will not work as well as they could.

The corrective is not heroic. It is structural. Build the floor, gently and over time, in ways the household can sustain. Do not try to do all six planks at once. Pick the one most clearly broken and work on that for a month. Then the next.

Families who put the biological floor back in, who fix the sleep, steady the eating, get the kids moving and outside, dial back the screens, restore daily connection, and who stay with it consistently often see the behaviour they were worrying about begin to soften within weeks, sometimes within the first month. The foundational work does not replace the parenting work that follows in the rest of this book. It stabilises the child. And once the child is stabilised, every parenting strategy that comes after, calm authority, repair, accountability without shame, collaborative problem-solving, the rest, lands more reliably than it would have on a body that could not yet regulate.

If we want better behaviour, we have to build better conditions.

That is the chapter, and it is the bridge. From here, the rest of the book turns to what parents do, the ten chapters of practical work that follow.

Key Takeaways

Behaviour does not happen in a vacuum. It happens on top of a body. A child whose biology is in poor shape cannot reliably receive the parenting strategies the rest of this book recommends.

The Cell Danger Response, described in Robert Naviaux's work, is the body's ancient and intelligent shift into defensive mode under threat. It is meant to switch off. Salugenesis, the body's healing programme, is meant to follow.

Modern children are routinely exposed to chronic stressors that keep the CDR switched on: family tension, sibling dysregulation, peer conflict, algorithmic feeds, broken sleep, unstable blood sugar, scarce movement, scarce daylight, thin connection.

The biological floor, sleep, blood sugar, movement, sunlight, screens, and co-regulating connection, is not a luxury. It is what makes the rest of parenting possible.

The deeper biological story is treated at length in my three earlier books. This chapter is the bridge, not the substitute.

If we want better behaviour, we must build better conditions. Most of the parenting work in the rest of the book sits on top of this floor.

References

1. Naviaux, R. K. (2014). Metabolic features of the cell danger response. Mitochondrion, 16, 7–17. https://doi.org/10.1016/j.mito.2013.08.006
2. Naviaux, R. K. (2023). Mitochondrial and metabolic features of salugenesis and the healing cycle. Mitochondrion, 70, 131–163. https://doi.org/10.1016/j.mito.2023.04.003
3. Porges, S. W. (2011). The Polyvagal Theory: Neurophysiological Foundations of Emotions, Attachment, Communication, and Self-Regulation. New York: W. W. Norton.
4. Doney, G. (2024). Healing Trauma at the Cellular Level: The Role of the Cell Danger Response in PTSD and Trauma Recovery.
5. Doney, G. (2026). Stacking Therapies for Depression Recovery: A Layered Healing Approach.
6. Doney, G. (2026). The Blood Sugar Solution to Mental Health: Unlocking the Link Between Blood Sugar and Mental Health Recovery.

CHAPTER 17

Becoming the Safe Harbour: The Regulated Parent

The State, Not the Script

Most parenting advice arrives as a script. Say this. Do not say that. Use these words in this situation. Avoid those words in that situation.

Scripts have their place, and a few of them, like the one we will return to in Chapter 25 on repair, are useful. But the deeper truth is one most experienced parents already half-know.

What lands with a child is not, in the end, the script. It is the state of the parent saying it.

The same words can be said two different ways and produce two different households. "I can see you are angry. It is not okay to hit your sister," said by a parent who is themselves activated, sounds like criticism. Said by a parent whose nervous system is steady, the same sentence sounds like leadership. The child responds to the second very differently from the first. Their body has registered which one they are dealing with before their ears have finished processing the words.

This chapter is the first of ten on what parents can do. It comes first because everything that follows depends on it. Calm authority does not mean knowing the right line. It means being the kind of presence in the room that the right line can come out of. The script needs the state.

The good news is that this is something parents can learn, even mid-life, even mid-storm, even after years of parenting in a different mode. The state of your nervous system is not a personality. It is a practice.

What "Safe Harbour" Actually Means

The phrase a safe harbour gets used a lot in parenting writing, sometimes loosely. What it does and does not mean.

A safe harbour is not a parent who is calm all the time, never raises their voice, or has done so much of their own work that nothing their child does can ruffle them. That parent does not exist.

A safe harbour is a parent who, on most occasions, can be steadier than the storm. Whose nervous system, in the moments that matter, is more regulated than the child's. Who can be approached when something has gone wrong without the child first having to scan for whether today is a safe day or a dangerous one. Who, when they do lose it, comes back. Who is, on average and over time, predictable.

Predictable is the word that does most of the work here. Children do not need a parent who has climinated reactivity from their lives. They need a parent whose general operating temperature is reliable enough that the child can plan around it.

A child who can plan around their parent's emotional weather can take risks. They can fail. They can come back from school with a hard day. They can admit to a mistake. They can ask a question they are uncertain about. They can be seen falling apart and trust that they will be helped back together rather than punished for the falling.

A child who cannot plan around the parent's weather does the opposite. They become careful. They hide things. They manage the parent before they manage themselves. They stop bringing the truth home.

A safe harbour is, in this sense, less about the parent's peak moments and more about their average. The peaks pass. The average is what the child lives inside.

The Biology of a Regulated Parent

Chapter 16 introduced Stephen Porges's polyvagal work and the basic finding that human nervous systems are relational regulators rather than solo ones. That work matters specifically here.[1]

When a parent is regulated, heart rate steady, breathing slow, voice unhurried, face relaxed, their nervous system is sending a continuous, low-volume signal of safety to anyone in the room. The signal is sent through tone, through breath, through the pace of speech, through micro-expressions on the face. A child's nervous system reads that signal automatically and, where the parent is sufficiently steady, downshifts its own arousal toward the parent's.

When a parent is dysregulated, heart rate climbing, breath shallow, voice tight, face tense, their nervous system is sending the opposite signal. The child reads the threat and matches it. Their own arousal climbs. Whatever conflict the room was originally about now has two people activated, and the work of resolving it has become considerably harder.

This is what Ed Tronick's work on rupture and repair, introduced in Chapter 10, was showing in slow motion in the still-face paradigm.[2] Children are not just listening to parents. They are reading them, second by second, and adjusting.

one of the most useful things a parent can ever learn is how to read their own nervous system before their child reads it for them. Most of the disasters in any given household happen in the small window between the parent becoming dysregulated and the parent recognising they are dysregulated. By the time recognition arrives, words have already been said. The child is responding. The escalation has begun.

Closing that recognition gap is most of the work of this chapter.

Reading Your Own State Before You Speak

Bodies tend to give honest signals about what state they are in, if the person inside the body is paying attention. Most parents, mid-storm, are not. They are too busy reading the child.

It is worth, in calmer moments, learning to recognise your own activation early. The signals are not subtle. They are usually some combination of:

A tightening across the shoulders or jaw.

A small change in breath. Faster. Higher in the chest. Sometimes briefly held.

A heat in the chest, a flush in the face, or a cool tightness in the gut.

A particular tone in the inner voice, sharp, sarcastic, certain. The voice that wants to land a line.

A narrowing of attention. The room shrinks. The only thing in your field of view is the child or partner you are about to react to.

A pull toward decisive action right now. The sense that something must be said or done immediately.

These signals are useful information. They are the body telling you, before you have spoken, that the next thing out of your mouth is unlikely to come from your most regulated self.

If you can learn to notice them in time, even five seconds before the line you were about to deliver, you will, over months and years, have changed your household.

The Pause

The single most useful regulatory skill any parent can practise is also the simplest. It is the pause.

A pause does not need to be long. Three seconds is enough. Twenty seconds is plenty. The point is not to become reflective in the middle of a meltdown. The point is to interrupt the chain that runs from activation, to reactive thought, to spoken word, to escalation.

Inside the pause, several useful things can happen.

Breath can lengthen. A slower, longer out-breath in particular is one of the most reliable activators of the calming branch of the autonomic nervous system. Two long out-breaths, in the middle of a hard moment, can be enough to drop you a notch.

A hand can move to the chest, the belly, or the back of the neck. Touch on those areas is calming for most people. Children, watching, also register that you are using a self-soothing gesture rather than a reactive one. They learn from this without being taught.

The eyes can move. Looking briefly away from the child, around the room, or at the floor, breaks the locked stare that activates threat circuitry on both sides. This is not avoidance; it is a very small reset.

A sentence can be said internally before any sentence is said externally. The sentence does not have to be wise. "Slow down," works. "Not now," works. "I can wait," works. "What is the actual problem here?" works.

Children, especially older ones, are not unsettled by a parent pausing. They are unsettled by a parent reacting. A parent who can say, "Give me a second," and use it to find their feet again, is modelling something the child needs to learn for themselves anyway.

If you do nothing else from this chapter, practise the pause. It is small. It is portable. It is doing more than almost any single piece of advice in this book.

When You Cannot Be Regulated in That Moment

Some moments are too much for a pause. The child has done something that has hit one of your own old wounds. You are exhausted in a way no breathing technique is going to fix in twenty seconds. Your partner has just walked out of the room mid-conflict. You have been holding it together all day for the children and the day has finally caught you.

On these days, the corrective is not to perform regulation you do not have. It is to step out.

"I need a minute. I will come back when I am calmer."

"This is not a good moment for me to talk about this. I will come back to you in twenty minutes."

"I can feel I am about to say something I will regret. I am going to step into the kitchen for a moment."

These sentences are not weakness. They are leadership in a different form. A parent who can name their own state and step out is showing the child that adults, too, get dysregulated, and that the way to handle it is to recognise it and pull back rather than to take it out on whoever is closest.

The non-negotiable is the return. A parent who steps out and does not come back has not regulated. They have abandoned the room. The child reads that as withdrawal. The repair has not happened.

A parent who steps out and comes back twenty minutes later, calmer, willing to engage, has done the actual work. They have shown that activation passes, that the child is not so dangerous to be near that they have to be cut off, and that the relationship resumes once the storm has settled. That sequence is the one that builds a child's long-term capacity to manage their own dysregulation.

Repair Is the Other Half of Regulation

No parent, however much practice they have had, will be regulated all the time. Tronick's research, again, is the bedrock here. Parent and child are out of attunement most of the time. What matters is that the rupture is repaired.

We will give repair its own full chapter in Chapter 25. The point worth making here is that repair is not a separate skill from regulation. It is regulation's other half.

When you have lost your temper, the work is not to pretend it did not happen and not to spiral into self-attack. The work is to come back, when you are calmer, and name it. "I yelled before. That was not okay. I was already stressed about something else, and I took it out on you. I am sorry."

That sentence does several things at once. It accurately models what an adult does after a regulatory failure. It protects the child from concluding that the parent's state was their fault. It re-establishes the safe harbour. And it models, in plain view, the very practice you are trying to teach the child.

Children are not damaged by parents who get it wrong. They are damaged by parents who get it wrong and do not come back. The practice of coming back is more powerful, in long-term terms, than the practice of getting it right the first time.

The Long Practice

Daniel Siegel and Mary Hartzell, in their book Parenting from the Inside Out, argue that one of the strongest predictors of how a person parents is whether they have done the work of understanding their own childhood, not in a navel-gazing sense, but in the specific sense of knowing where their own reactivity comes from, and whose voice it actually is when they are most activated.[3]

Most parents, in their most reactive moments, are not really arguing with the child in front of them. They are arguing with someone older. A parent of their own, perhaps. A teacher. A sibling. A first partner. Someone whose treatment of them, decades ago, taught their nervous system to react in the very particular shape it now reacts in.

Recognising that the trigger has a longer history than the current moment is not an excuse. It is a doorway. It is the start of the practice that, over years, allows a parent to be regulated in situations that previously hijacked them.

This is the long-arc work that this chapter cannot do on its own and that no single chapter can do. It is the work of paying attention to your own reactions, noticing patterns, finding the older sources, and, where needed, getting some help with the parts that have been carried for too long. For Australian parents, that help can come from a GP-referred psychologist, a family therapist, an integrative health practitioner, or, for trauma-specific work, a clinician trained in modalities like EMDR, somatic experiencing, brainspotting or family-systems therapy.

The work is slow. It is also possible. A parent who, at fifty, is more regulated than they were at thirty has done the most useful kind of family work there is. The household will be reading the difference for years.

Regulation is a practice, not a personality. You do not need to start at the top of it. You need to start.

What Helps

Look after the floor. Chapter 16's biological floor applies just as much to the parent as to the child. A parent who is sleeping six hours a night, eating poorly, never moving, never outside, never connecting with their partner or friends, and always on a screen will not, on average, be a regulated parent. The architecture matters.

Practise the pause when there is no crisis. Most people cannot reliably reach a regulatory move under stress that they have not practised in calm. Use ordinary, low-stakes moments, a bit of traffic, a slow queue, a small frustration, to practise lengthening the breath and recognising activation. The pause then becomes available when you need it.

Name your weather to the people in your home. "I am tired today." "I am stressed about work, and it is not about you." "I have a short fuse this afternoon. I am going to try not to use it on anyone." This is not over-sharing. It is calibration. The household reads weather more accurately when the weather is named.

Notice the triggers that recur. If the same kind of moment is reliably setting you off, that is data. Write it down. Look at it when you are calm. Where is this coming from? Whose voice is it? Some triggers will reduce just by being recognised. Others will need more focused work.

Get help with the patterns that are bigger than self-management can reach. A short course of psychotherapy or trauma-informed clinical work, by a registered clinician, often does more for parental regulation than years of solo trying.

Be patient with yourself. Parental regulation is not a state you arrive at. It is a practice you keep returning to, every day, for as long as you are parenting. The progress shows up over years. The household will show you it is showing up.

Key Takeaways

What lands with a child is not the script but the state of the parent saying it. Calm authority is a state before it is a sentence.

A safe harbour is not a parent who is calm all the time. It is a parent whose general operating temperature is predictable enough that the child can plan around it.

Parents' nervous systems regulate children's nervous systems through tone, breath, pace and face. This is the polyvagal mechanism behind the parenting strategy.

Most reactive moments are preceded by recognisable body signals. Closing the gap between activation and recognition is most of the practical work of this chapter.

The pause is the simplest, most portable regulatory tool a parent has. Practise it in calm before you need it in storm.

When you cannot be regulated in the moment, naming it and stepping out is leadership, not weakness, provided you come back.

Repair is the other half of regulation. Children are not damaged by parents who get it wrong. They are damaged by parents who get it wrong and do not come back.

Most parental triggers have a longer history than the moment they appear in. Recognising that history is the doorway to the long-arc practice. Help, where needed, makes that work faster and gentler.

Regulation is a practice, not a personality. Start where you are.

References

1. Porges, S. W. (2011). The Polyvagal Theory: Neurophysiological Foundations of Emotions, Attachment, Communication, and Self-Regulation. New York: W. W. Norton. (See also Chapter 16.)
2. Tronick, E. Z. (1989). Emotions and emotional communication in infants. American Psychologist, 44(2), 112–119. (See also Chapter 10.)
3. Siegel, D. J., & Hartzell, M. (2003). Parenting from the Inside Out: How a Deeper Self-Understanding Can Help You Raise Children Who Thrive. New York: Tarcher / Penguin.

CHAPTER 18

Calm Authority: Bigger, Stronger, Wiser and Kinder

Three Doors a Parent Can Walk Through

Most of the time, when a household reaches the moment where something has to be said or done, the parent has three available stances to walk into.

The first is the permissive stance. The parent feels the moment, registers the child's distress, and lets the boundary go. The child is upset, and the parent does not want to make it worse, so the rule does not get held. The screen stays on. The dessert is given. The bedtime is renegotiated. The harm to a sibling is excused because the harming child was, after all, having a hard day. The household is, briefly, peaceful. The cost is paid in the next round, when the child has correctly read the lesson: enough escalation will move the parent.

The second is the punitive stance. The parent registers the same moment, but this time the activation in their own body wins. The voice rises. The threat lands. The consequence is bigger than the offence. The child is shamed in the process of being corrected. The household is, briefly, quiet. The cost is paid in the relationship, in the child's nervous system, and in what the child has just learned about how adults handle the moments that frighten them.

The third is the authoritative stance, and it is the one this chapter is about. The parent stays present. The boundary is held.

The child's feelings are welcomed but their behaviour is not. The correction lands without humiliation. The relationship survives the moment. Over weeks and months, this stance is, by a wide margin, the one most strongly associated with healthy child outcomes in the developmental literature.

The American developmental psychologist Diana Baumrind, in a series of landmark studies in the 1960s and 1970s, named these three stances and produced the empirical evidence that has organised the field since.[1] [2] Her finding was simple and stable. Children raised by parents whose dominant style was authoritative, warm, clear, firm, responsive, fared better, on almost every measure, than children raised by parents whose dominant style was permissive or authoritarian.

The hard part is that no parent stays in one door all the time. Every parent walks through all three, in different moments. The work is to make sure the third door is the one being walked through most often, and the one being walked back to after the others have happened.

This chapter is about how to keep finding the third door.

The Phrase

The most useful single shorthand for the authoritative stance comes from a body of clinical work in attachment-based parenting called the Circle of Security.

Developed by the American clinicians Bert Powell, Glen Cooper, Kent Hoffman and Bob Marvin, working from John Bowlby's attachment theory, Circle of Security has been used in thousands of clinical settings around the world to help parents find the role their child's nervous system most needs them to play.[3] Its central image is a circle on which a child moves, sometimes outward toward exploration, sometimes inward toward comfort. The parent's job is to be the secure base the child leaves from and the safe haven the child returns to.

And the parent's steady stance, in both directions, is captured in a phrase that has become one of the most widely repeated formulas in modern attachment-informed parenting:

Bigger. Stronger. Wiser. Kind.

I have, throughout this book, used a small variant, Kinder, in the comparative, because that is the form the phrase has come to take in my own clinical use, and because what the moment usually asks of a parent is not generic kindness but a kindness that is greater than the storm in the room. The original phrase, however, is Powell, Cooper, Hoffman and Marvin's, and the credit belongs to them.

Whichever form, the four words name something a parent can do in any difficult moment. They are simple enough to remember inside a hard moment. They are deep enough to take a lifetime to live inside.

The next four sections take each in turn.

Bigger

Bigger does not mean physically bigger. It means taking up the leadership space in the moment, rather than handing it to the child.

Most household conflicts that escalate do so because the parent has, without quite meaning to, become the same size as the child. The child is upset; the parent meets the upset with their own. The child is angry; the parent matches the anger. The child is testing a limit; the parent feels small in the face of the test and either gives way or strikes back.

Being bigger is not being domineering. It is being the larger emotional container in the room. Big enough to hold the child's feelings without being knocked over by them. Big enough that the child can throw the full weight of their distress at the parent and still find a steady person on the other side.

Practically, bigger sounds like, "I can hold this. We are okay," being communicated through tone and posture before any words are spoken. Big enough to be the adult, even when the child is doing their best to recruit you into being something else.

Stronger

Stronger is the part that holds the line.

It is the parent who can say, "No," and mean it, without flinching, without escalating, without explaining for ten minutes. It is the parent who, when the child is hitting their sister, gets between them. It is the parent who, when the bedtime arrives, walks the child to bed even when there is protest. It is the parent who, when the screen needs to go off, takes it.

Strength here is not force. It is reliability. The child can lean on the parent's strength to find their own boundaries. They learn what the limits actually are because the parent holds them consistently. They learn that protest does not move the limit, which is, paradoxically, what allows them to stop spending their energy on protest and start spending it on the actual task of growing up.

A parent who is too strong has crossed into authoritarianism. A parent who is not strong enough has crossed into permissiveness.

Stronger, in the Circle of Security sense, is the calm, unflustered firmness that says, in effect, the line is here, I am not arguing about it, and I love you all the way through.

Wiser

Wiser is the part that looks beneath the behaviour.

A reactive parent sees the behaviour and responds to it. A wiser parent sees the behaviour and asks what it is signalling. The hitting may be a missing skill in frustration tolerance. The lying may be a child whose truth has previously been used against them. The defiance may be a child trying to recover a sense of agency in a system where they feel controlled. The withdrawal may be a child whose nervous system is overwhelmed.

Wiser does not mean clever. It does not mean having the right diagnostic label. It means refusing to take the surface of the moment as the whole story, and being willing to ask what is happening underneath before responding.

Crucially, wiser does not require the parent to delay action. The boundary still gets held in the moment. The wisdom is in what comes after, in the slower work of figuring out what the behaviour was pointing at, and in adjusting the household over time to address the underlying need.

A parent who is wiser is, in practice, the parent who has read the chapters of this book on the wounds, the family system, the biological floor and the peer environment. The wisdom is what those chapters become inside a real moment.

Kinder

Kinder is the part that almost everyone misses.

It is what makes the difference between authority that builds a child up and authority that wears them down. The line being held with warmth is a different experience for the child than the line being held with contempt, even when the line is the same line. Children read the parent's underlying disposition while the line is being held, and what they record is not just what the parent said but how the parent felt about them while saying it.

Kinder does not mean softer. It does not mean dropping the boundary, lowering the standard, or apologising for being the adult. It means doing the hard part, saying the no, holding the limit, refusing the harmful behaviour, with affection still visible in the parent's face and voice. The child should be able to feel, even mid-correction, that they are loved.

The deeper version of kinder is being kinder than the moment is asking you to be. The child has just done something difficult. Most of you wants to be sharp. Kinder is the bit of you that overrides that impulse, holds the line anyway, and somehow communicates, with a tone of voice or a hand on the shoulder, that the relationship is still intact.

Children who are corrected with kindness can metabolise the correction. They can take it in, sit with it, and integrate it. Children who are corrected with contempt cannot. The shame the contempt creates blocks the learning the correction was meant to deliver.

Kinder is also, very often, kinder to yourself. A parent who is harsh with themselves over their own perceived failures will be harder to live with than a parent who has decided to take themselves on with the same warmth they are trying to extend to the child.

The Trap of Permissiveness Disguised as Kindness

There are two recognisable ways the authoritative stance can collapse, and both deserve naming clearly because both are common.

The first is permissiveness disguised as kindness.

This is the parent who has read enough modern parenting literature to know that they want to be warm, attuned, and respectful of their child's feelings, and who, in their effort to be those things, has stopped holding the line. The child gets bigger. The behaviour gets harder. The household gets less safe. The parent, sensing this, doubles down on warmth and connection, on the theory that the child must just need more love.

More love is rarely the missing piece in this version. The missing piece is the limit.

Validation is not a substitute for a boundary. "I can see you are angry, and you cannot hit your sister," is the move. "I can see you are angry, here is some chocolate, please stop," is not. The first sentence holds both halves of the work. The second has surrendered the second half in the hope of buying peace, and the child has just learned that peace is buyable through escalation.

If your household is currently characterised more by feelings management than by limits, this is the trap to watch for. The corrective is not less warmth. It is more spine, alongside the warmth that is already there.

The Trap of Authority That Has Slipped Into Authoritarianism

The opposite trap is authority that has slipped into authoritarianism, often through exhaustion or under stress.

This is the parent who, two months ago, was warm, clear and firm, and who, after enough sleep deprivation, work pressure, financial strain or repeated child dysregulation, has become harsh. The voice is louder than it used to be. The consequences land faster and bigger than they used to. The patience that was previously available has narrowed. The home has begun to feel, even to the parent, less warm than it should.

This trap is, often, the more painful one to recognise, because the parents most likely to be in it are also parents who care a great deal about not being in it. They were raised, perhaps, in households that ran on harshness, and they have spent years deliberately not parenting that way. The drift back into harshness, when it happens, feels like a betrayal of who they wanted to be.

If you recognise yourself here, the corrective is not self-condemnation. It is the work this book has been pointing toward all along. Look at the floor, sleep, blood sugar, movement, connection. Look at your own nervous system and what is currently overloading it. Look at whether your own old wounds are being activated by particular behaviours of your child. Get help if the load is bigger than self-management can address. Repair, where you have crossed lines, with the children who are the receiving end of it.

The authoritative stance is recoverable. It is recoverable from either trap. The work is to know which trap you tend toward, and to set your corrective in that direction.

Loving Leadership When No One Is Watching

There is a final test of the authoritative stance that is worth saying clearly. It is the test of how the parent behaves when no one outside the household is watching.

It is not difficult, on a good day, to be calm and warm and firm in front of other parents at a school pick-up, in front of in-laws at Christmas, in front of friends at a barbecue. The performance is supported by the audience.

What the child registers is what happens at home, on the wet Tuesday evening, when the dinner has burned, the homework has not been done, the younger sibling has just spilled milk for the third time, and the parent is two days behind on sleep. That is the parent the child is forming their model of the world around.

Loving leadership when no one is watching is not the same skill as loving leadership when someone is. It runs on what is already in the parent, after the social motivation has been removed. The parent who, on the wet Tuesday, can still pause, take a breath, get bigger than the storm, hold the line, look beneath the behaviour and stay kinder than the moment is asking them to be, that is the parent the household is built around.

If that parent is not yet you, on every Tuesday, you are still in the long practice. The practice does not require you to arrive there to be worth doing. It only requires you to keep going.

What Helps

Pick the door before the moment. Most authoritative responses are pre-decided, not improvised. If you have already thought, on a calm afternoon, about what you will do when bedtime is refused or the screen has to come off, you will be much steadier when the moment arrives. Improvisation is what produces both permissiveness and harshness.

Use the four words. In the middle of a hard moment, the prompt Bigger, Stronger, Wiser, Kinder is short enough to actually use. Run through it as a mental checklist. Am I bigger than this storm right now? Am I being strong enough to hold the line? Am I looking beneath what I am seeing? Am I being kinder than this moment is pulling me toward?

Mind the kinder. The first three Bs are easier for most parents than the fourth. Kindness is the one that gets eroded first under stress. Watch for it.

Repair the slips. If you have walked through the wrong door, repair afterwards. The chapter on repair (Chapter 25) shows the practical script.

Watch the trap you tend toward. Most parents lean toward one trap more than the other. Knowing which one is yours, and which conditions push you into it, is half the work of staying out of it.

Audit how the household feels when no one is watching. Do this with care, not contempt for yourself. The wet Tuesday version of you is the one the children are learning from. Improvements there matter most.

Key Takeaways

There are three doors a parent can walk through in any difficult moment: permissive, punitive (authoritarian), or authoritative. The third has the strongest empirical support, dating back to Diana Baumrind's landmark research.

The most useful shorthand for the authoritative stance is the Circle of Security phrase Bigger, Stronger, Wiser and Kind. I use Kinder for emphasis. The credit for the original belongs to Powell, Cooper, Hoffman and Marvin.

Bigger is taking up the leadership space rather than becoming the same size as the child.

Stronger is calm, reliable firmness. Not force. Not harshness.

Wiser is looking beneath the behaviour at the wound, the missing skill, or the unmet need underneath it.

Kinder is correcting without contempt, being kinder than the moment is asking you to be. This is the part most easily eroded under stress.

Two common traps: permissiveness disguised as kindness (where validation has replaced limits) and authority that has slipped into authoritarianism (where exhaustion has narrowed warmth). Both are recoverable. Both have their own corrective.

The truest test of the authoritative stance is how the parent behaves when no one outside the household is watching. The wet Tuesday version of you is what the children are forming their model of the world around.

References

1. Baumrind, D. (1966). Effects of authoritative parental control on child behavior. Child Development, 37(4), 887–907. https://doi.org/10.2307/1126611
2. Baumrind, D. (1971). Current patterns of parental authority. Developmental Psychology, 4(1, Pt. 2), 1–103. https://doi.org/10.1037/h0030372

3. Powell, B., Cooper, G., Hoffman, K., & Marvin, B. (2014). The Circle of Security Intervention: Enhancing Attachment in Early Parent–Child Relationships. New York: Guilford Press.
4. Hoffman, K., Cooper, G., & Powell, B. (2017). Raising a Secure Child: How Circle of Security Parenting Can Help You Nurture Your Child's Attachment, Emotional Resilience, and Freedom to Explore. New York: Guilford Press.

CHAPTER 19

All Feelings Are Welcome. All Behaviours Are Not.

The Two Halves

This chapter is built around a principle that has come into wide use in current attachment-informed parenting writing. Its phrasing in this form is most commonly attributed to Dr Aliza Pressman, a developmental psychologist and host of the podcast Raising Good Humans, whose 2024 book The 5 Principles of Parenting brought it into broad circulation.[1] The underlying idea, of welcoming the inner experience while still holding limits on the outer behaviour, runs further back through the attachment-informed parenting tradition, including the RIE work of Magda Gerber, Daniel Hughes's PACE model in therapeutic parenting, and the writing of clinicians such as Janet Lansbury, Daniel Siegel and Becky Kennedy.

The principle, in Pressman's form, is simple.

All feelings are welcome. All behaviours are not.

It is a useful single line because it does two things at once. It tells the child that whatever they feel, they are still safe with the parent. It tells the child, at the same time, that the family will not be rearranged around feelings that have turned into harm.

The principle is simple to say. It is much harder to live, because most parents, in any given moment, can manage one half well or the other half well, but rarely both at once. Some of us are good with feelings. Our children come to us with their tears and their fears and we sit with them. We struggle, however, when those feelings turn into hitting, lying, or screaming at a sibling. The boundary feels mean to us. We hesitate. The behaviour continues.

Others of us are good with behaviour. We hold the line. The hitting stops. The screen goes off when it is meant to. The bedtime is bedtime. We struggle, however, when the child is in the middle of a feeling we do not know what to do with. We move past it. We tell them to calm down. We get on with the day. The child learns that their inner world is something to manage privately.

The work of this chapter is to show what it looks like to do both halves at once.

Why Both Halves Matter

If you only welcome feelings, you have a household that runs on emotion. The child whose mood is loudest sets the temperature. Limits become negotiable, because every limit produces a feeling, and feelings are sacred. Siblings who are not the loudest learn to take up less space. The child causing the most disruption is rarely the one who is unhappiest with the arrangement.

If you only enforce behaviour, you have a household that runs on compliance. The child does what they are told. The behaviour, on the surface, is good. Underneath, the child is learning that their inner experience does not register, and that being a child is something to perform rather than something to live. Some of these children grow into anxious, perfectionistic adults. Others grow into adults who, the moment compliance is no longer enforced, swing the other way and do not know what to do with the freedom.

Both half-versions produce children who carry a wound. The child whose feelings ran the household carries the wound of never having felt firm ground under them. The child whose behaviour was managed without their feelings being seen carries the wound of having been treated as a problem rather than a person.

Both halves matter because each one protects something different. The first half protects the child from shame. The second half protects everyone from harm. A household that does both is a household where the child can feel safely, fully, and without having to earn their parents' attention through good behaviour, and where the people inside the household are also safe from each other.

Two Things Can Be True

The American clinical psychologist Becky Kennedy has built much of her widely-read parenting work on a closely related principle, which she calls two things can be true.[1] Her version goes like this. Your child can be deeply upset about a decision. You can also have made the right decision. Both are real at the same time. The parent does not have to choose between holding the line and loving the child through their reaction to it.

It is a useful frame because it reflects how children actually experience the moment. When a child is told no, several things are happening inside them at once. They are angry. They are disappointed. They may feel rejected. They may feel ashamed. They may also, somewhere deeper, feel a small relief at the firmness, because firmness is reassuring even when it is unwelcome.

A parent who can hold all of that at once gives the child permission to feel it all. They do not need the child to stop being upset before they can be loved. They do not need to soften the line to make the upset go away. The child gets to be both upset and held. The parent gets to be both firm and warm.

If you can take only one thing from this chapter into a hard moment, take that. Two things can be true. Your child can be furious with you. You can also be doing the right thing. The fury does not have to change your decision, and your decision does not have to deny their fury.

What This Sounds Like

The principle becomes practical at the level of sentences. What does a parent actually say in the middle of a hard moment to do both halves at once?

A child has just hit their sibling.

Half-feelings: "I can see you are angry." Half-behaviour: "It is not okay to hit." Together: "I can see you are angry. It is not okay to hit your brother. I am going to help you calm down, and then we are going to work out what happened."

A teenager is refusing to come off the screen.

Half-feelings: "I know you are in the middle of something and you do not want to stop." Half-behaviour: "The screen is going off in five minutes." Together: "I know you are in the middle of something and it is annoying to be interrupted. The screen is going off in five minutes. We can talk about how to make this work better another time, but it is not a tonight conversation."

A child is crying because a friend has been unkind at school.

Half-feelings: "That sounds really hard. I am so sorry." Half-behaviour: not strictly needed here, because nothing has gone wrong with the child's behaviour. Together: presence, listening, sitting with them, and offering the next step only when they are ready.

A teenager has lied about where they were last night.

Half-feelings: "I understand telling me the truth felt scary, especially given how I have reacted in the past." Half-behaviour: "Lying about where you are is not something we can keep doing. We need to come up with a plan, and there are going to be some changes." Together: a conversation that begins with curiosity about what made the lie feel necessary, before moving to consequences and a path forward.

Notice what these examples have in common. The feeling is named first, briefly, without overworking it. The boundary is named clearly, without softening it. The child's relationship with the parent is not in question while the boundary is being held. The next step is described without becoming a lecture.

Notice also what is not in the examples. There is no negotiation of the boundary. There is no shaming of the feeling. There is no demand that the child stop feeling what they are feeling before the conversation can happen. The parent is doing both halves at once, and trusting the child to grow into the size of what they are being asked to hold.

Naming the Feeling Is Half the Regulation

There is a useful piece of neurobiology behind why the feeling-naming half of this principle works as well as it does. Daniel Siegel and Tina Payne Bryson, in The Whole-Brain Child, summarised it under the phrase name it to tame it.[2]

When a child is in the middle of a strong feeling, the parts of their brain most involved in language and reflection are largely offline. The parts most involved in fight, flight or shutdown are running the show. The body is activated. Words are not coming.

When a parent calmly names the feeling, several things happen. The child hears their internal experience put into language they can process. The act of putting words on the experience engages the more reflective parts of the brain. The activation, in many cases, drops a notch. The child becomes more able to receive whatever else is going to happen next.

This does not always work in the heat of the moment. Some children, when they are deep into a meltdown, cannot receive any words at all. The naming has to wait. The first task is presence and physical safety, with words coming later, once the child has begun to come back online.

But for most children, in most moments, the simple act of having a parent accurately describe what they are feeling does real regulatory work. "You are really frustrated about this," lands differently from "Calm down." The first sentence joins the child where they are. The second tells them to be somewhere else.

The Hard Cases

There are some moments where the principle is harder to apply. They deserve naming honestly.

Public meltdowns. The supermarket aisle, the school pick-up, the family gathering. The temptation, in these moments, is to skip the feelings half because of the audience. Other adults are watching. Some are judging. The pressure is to make the child stop, fast, by any means available. If you can hold the principle even partially in public, you will model something the watching adults rarely see, and you will protect your child from the experience of being shamed in front of strangers. Sometimes the right move is to remove the moment from the audience by leaving, doing the regulation work elsewhere, and coming back later. There is no rule that says the work has to happen in front of everyone.

Behaviours you find personally repellent. A child who is being deliberately cruel to a younger sibling, a teenager who is sneering, a child who is doing something that hits a particular nerve in the parent. The half-feelings part can feel almost impossible to do here. The honest move, when you are activated, is the regulation work from Chapter 17. Take the pause. Step out if you need to. Come back when you can hold both halves. If you cannot do both at once, hold the boundary first and do the feelings half later, in repair. That sequence is imperfect but workable.

Behaviours that have become patterns. The same hitting, the same lying, the same eye-roll, again and again. By the seventh time, the parent is exhausted and the warmth has gone. The principle still applies, but the parent is going to need to address the pattern, not just the moment. That is the territory of Chapters 21 and 27, where collaborative problem-solving and longer-term work come in.

Children whose feelings have stopped landing. Some children, especially adolescents who have been hurt before, will reject any attempt to name what they are feeling. "You don't know what I'm feeling." "Stop trying to therapise me." In these cases, the work is patient. Stop naming. Just stay close. Be available. Wait. The naming will become possible again when the relationship has been rebuilt.

What Children Take From This Over Time

If a child grows up inside this principle, several things tend to happen.

They learn that their inner world is welcome. The full range of human feeling is allowed in the house, including the difficult, the dark, and the inconvenient. They do not have to perform a particular emotional state to belong.

They learn that feelings and behaviour are different. What you feel is not the same as what you do. Both matter, but they are answered with different responses. The first gets curiosity and care. The second gets a clear, fair, predictable response.

They learn that limits are an act of love, not the absence of it. The parent who holds the line while still being warm is doing something the child can feel, even if they cannot articulate it. Over the years, the child internalises the same combination, and begins to apply it to themselves and to others.

They learn that two things can be true. They can be upset and still loved. They can be wrong and still worthy. They can be in trouble and still cared for. They can be having a hard time and still be a good person. This is one of the most useful frames a child can take into adulthood, and it almost always begins inside the household where it was modelled by a parent.

What Helps

Practise the formula, then forget it. "I can see you are X. It is not okay to Y. We are going to Z." Run that template in your head until it is available without thinking. Once it is, the words will come naturally in your own voice, and the formula will recede.

Name only what you can see. Do not project. "You look really frustrated" is better than "I know exactly how you feel right now." If you guess wrong about what they are feeling, they will tell you, and the conversation will be richer for it.

Watch for the half you tend to drop. Most parents lean toward one half more than the other. Knowing which one is yours, and watching for it under stress, is half the work of staying balanced.

Repair the half you missed. If you held the line but skipped the feeling, you can come back later and say so. If you sat with the feeling but did not hold the line, you can come back later and name the limit. Repair is not failure. It is the second chance the principle was always going to need.

Slow the moment down. Most household conflicts are running faster than they need to. A few seconds of pause before the response usually allows both halves to be present. The pause from Chapter 17 is doing the work here too.

Use the principle on yourself. "I am exhausted. I am also going to make dinner anyway." "I am angry with my partner. I am also not going to take it out on the kids." "I feel guilty about losing it earlier. I am also going to repair it without spiralling into self-attack." The principle works for parents too.

Key Takeaways

All feelings are welcome. All behaviours are not. The two halves protect different things, and a household that does both protects both.

If you only welcome feelings, you get a household that runs on emotion. If you only enforce behaviour, you get a household that runs on compliance. Both produce wounded adults.

Becky Kennedy's two things can be true is the same principle in another form. Your child can be deeply upset and you can still be doing the right thing. The fury does not have to change the decision, and the decision does not have to deny the fury.

Naming a child's feeling, when they can hear it, does real regulatory work. Siegel and Bryson called this name it to tame it.

Hard cases include public meltdowns, behaviours you find personally repellent, behaviours that have become patterns, and children whose feelings have stopped landing. Each has its own modification of the principle.

Children raised inside this principle learn that their inner world is welcome, that feelings and behaviour are different, that limits are an act of love, and that two things can be true.

Watch for the half you tend to drop, and repair the half you missed. The principle works for parents too.

References

1. Pressman, A. (2024). The 5 Principles of Parenting: Your Essential Guide to Raising Good Humans. New York: Simon Element / Simon & Schuster.

2. Kennedy, B. A. (2022). Good Inside: A Practical Guide to Resilient Parenting Prioritizing Connection Over Correction. New York: Harper Wave / HarperCollins.

3. Siegel, D. J., & Bryson, T. P. (2011). The Whole-Brain Child: 12 Revolutionary Strategies to Nurture Your Child's Developing Mind. New York: Bantam.

CHAPTER 20

Parental Monitoring, Gatekeeping and Protective Supervision

Why Monitoring Matters

There is a long-running tension in parenting writing between two ideas. The first is that children need autonomy, privacy, and the room to make their own decisions. The second is that children need adults who know what is going on in their lives, who hold the perimeter of the household, and who can step in when something is going wrong.

Both ideas are right. The work is not to choose one over the other.

The construct that holds the two together, in the developmental and prevention literature, is parental monitoring. It is not surveillance. It is not control. It is the steady, age-appropriate awareness a parent has of what their child is doing, who they are with, what kinds of pressures and influences they are facing, and what kinds of help they may need.

The most cited single paper on parental monitoring is Thomas Dishion and Robert McMahon's 1998 review, which formalised the construct and broke it down into a small number of recognisable practices a parent can do.[1] The reason their framework matters here is straightforward. The bad apple effect, as we have traced it through the last several chapters, runs through influences that often sit just outside the parents' direct view. Peer groups. Online spaces. Coaches. Extended family. Sibling dynamics that intensify when no adult is in the room. Monitoring is the work of keeping enough eyes on those influences that the family system can intervene before a slow slide becomes a crisis.

It is also, on the harder end of the continuum, the work of protecting children from harm coming from inside the family itself. We will get there in this chapter, slowly and carefully. The starting point is the ordinary, everyday version, which most parents are already doing in some form.

The Five Pieces

Dishion and McMahon's framework, simplified for parents, breaks monitoring into five practices. They are not separate skills so much as different angles on the same overall posture of awareness. A parent who is doing all five well is doing parental monitoring as the literature describes it.

The first is tracking. Knowing where your child is, who they are with, what they are doing, and how those things are going. For a primary school child, tracking is easy. For a teenager, tracking is a continuing negotiation that has to balance their growing autonomy against your continued responsibility. The work is not to know everything. The work is to know enough that, if something is going wrong, you would not be the last person in the household to find out.

The second is communication, sometimes called elicitation. Creating the conditions in which the child will tell you what is going on. This is more about your reactions than your questions. A child who has learned that telling their parent about a hard moment leads to a calm conversation will tell their parent again. A child who has learned that telling leads to overreaction, lectures, or punishment will not. Communication is not interrogation. It is a long, low-key practice of being a person your child finds it useful to talk to.

The third is gatekeeping. Deciding who and what is allowed into your child's life. The friend who can come over. The friend's house your child can stay at. The phone they have or do not have. The platforms that are on the phone. The coach you keep them with or move them away from. The extended family event you protect them from. Gatekeeping is parenting that is willing to absorb the temporary anger of a child in exchange for the longer-term protection of their development.

The fourth is environmental structuring. Building the day, the week, the home and the schedule so that the right kinds of things happen by default. After-school activities that anchor the week. Family meals at predictable times. Devices that live in shared spaces. Bedtime routines that hold. Environmental structuring reduces the number of moments in which a child has to make a difficult decision alone.

The fifth is rule-setting and enforcement. Clear, fair, predictable expectations, applied consistently, with consequences that are proportionate and reliable. Rule-setting is not the loudest part of parenting, and the parents who are best at it tend not to be the parents who are constantly arguing about rules. They are the parents whose rules are simply the way things are in the family, and whose children, even when grumbling, know the rules will hold.

Most parents are already doing some version of all five. The work of this chapter is to look at each of them, ask which ones have slipped, and to think carefully about the harder end of the continuum, where the gatekeeping and structuring move into a posture called Protective Supervision.

The Continuum

Monitoring is not one thing applied at one intensity. It is a continuum that adjusts to the child, the moment and the situation.

At one end of the continuum is ordinary supervision. The kind that runs through most households on most days. You know roughly where your children are. You know who their friends are. You ask about their day. You drive them to and from places. You notice if something seems off. You do not control every minute of their lives, and you do not need to.

Further along the continuum is heightened monitoring. The phase a parent moves into when something has shifted. A new peer group that worries you. A grade that has dropped. A child who has gone quiet. A pattern of behaviour that has begun to feel unsafe. Heightened monitoring tightens the lens. More questions. More involvement. More environmental structure. Less unsupervised time. It is not punishment. It is the family system paying attention to what is happening, and increasing its responsiveness for a season.

Further along still is what this chapter calls Protective Supervision. This is a specific posture used when one child in a family has caused, or is at risk of causing, sustained harm to another child or to a particular adult in the household. It is not a permanent state. It is not exile. It is a structured, time-limited arrangement of supervision that prioritises the safety of the child being harmed while help is put in place for the child who has been harming.

Most families never need to reach the third end of this continuum. The chapter is going to spend more pages there than the everyday parts because the third end is where families most often get it wrong, and where the cost of getting it wrong is highest.

When Protective Supervision Is Needed

Protective Supervision is not the response to ordinary sibling conflict. Children fight. Children push each other. Children, in the rough and tumble of growing up, sometimes hurt each other in ways that need to be addressed but do not require a structural change to how the household runs.

The threshold is sustained, repeated, serious harm from one child toward another, where the harm has continued despite earlier interventions and where the receiving child no longer feels safe in their own home.

Specific patterns that warrant the conversation include:

Repeated physical aggression that has injured a younger or smaller sibling, especially when it has happened in moments where adults were not present.

Sustained intimidation, threats, or coercive behaviour from one sibling toward another that has produced a measurable change in the receiving child, such as withdrawal, anxiety, fearfulness around the harming sibling, or unwillingness to be alone with them.

Any pattern of sexualised behaviour from one sibling toward another that goes beyond age-appropriate exploration, including behaviour that involves coercion, secrecy, or a significant developmental gap between the children. A 2024 systematic review out of the Australian Catholic University's Institute of Child Protection Studies and Brave Hearts provides one of the clearest contemporary summaries of what this pattern looks like and what protects children inside it.[2]

Repeated cruelty involving the deliberate weaponisation of a younger sibling's vulnerabilities (their body, their fears, their friends, their possessions) in a way that has continued after parents have intervened.

Behaviour from a child or adolescent who has begun, under the influence of an external peer group, an online community, or a substance, to bring harmful behaviour into the home in a way that is not safe for siblings.

Where one or more of these patterns is present and has not responded to earlier interventions, Protective Supervision is the next step. Not as a punishment. As a way of keeping the receiving child safe while the harming child gets the help they need.

What Protective Supervision Looks Like in Practice

Most parents who first hear the idea of Protective Supervision imagine something dramatic. It is rarely dramatic. It is structural.

In a household that has moved into Protective Supervision, the practical changes are usually some combination of the following.

The two children are not left alone in a room together. An adult is present, or in clear earshot, when they are in the same space.

Bath time, getting changed, and other vulnerable moments are restructured so that there is no opportunity for the harming child to be alone with the receiving child.

If the children share a bedroom, they are separated for sleeping for as long as the pattern is active, even if this requires creative use of household space.

Transitions that have historically been unsafe (after-school for an hour or two before adults are home, weekends, school holidays, car trips) are explicitly covered. An adult is present, or another arrangement is in place.

The receiving child has reliable access to a parent at any time without having to navigate the harming child to get there.

The harming child knows the rules of the supervision, has them explained calmly, and is told both why the rules are in place and that they are not permanent.

Both children are receiving help. The receiving child for the impact on them. The harming child for whatever is driving the behaviour.

The supervision is reviewed regularly, by the parents, ideally with input from a clinician working with the family, and adjusted as the situation improves.

not a punishment regime. It is the same kind of structural arrangement a child-protection professional would recommend, applied at home, and held until it is no longer needed.

Why It Is Protection, Not Exile

clearly, because parents often get this wrong, that Protective Supervision is not exile. The harming child stays inside the family. They are not cut off from love. They are not told they are bad. They are told that some things are not safe right now, that the family is going to make sure those things do not happen again, and that the people who care about them are going to help them work out why this has been happening.

What Protective Supervision is, in attachment terms, is the parent finally functioning as both halves of the safe harbour at once. The harming child needs containment. The receiving child needs protection. The parent's job is to provide both.

There are two failure modes parents commonly fall into instead.

The first is to treat the harming child as the only problem. To exile them, in practice if not in word. To stop trusting them, stop including them, stop protecting their dignity. This intensifies their shame, hardens their identity around the harm they have done, and often escalates the pattern. It also teaches the receiving child that the family handles harm by ostracising rather than addressing, which is its own quiet wound.

The second is to under-respond. To minimise. To tell the receiving child that their sibling did not really mean it, that they need to toughen up, that brothers and sisters fight. This abandons the receiving child to a household that has demonstrated it will not protect them. It also tells the harming child that what they are doing is, in some sense, allowed. The pattern continues.

Protective Supervision is the path between those two failures. It contains the harm without rejecting the harming child. It protects the receiving child without making them an object the family avoids talking about. It is harder to do well than either of the two failure modes, which is partly why the failure modes are so common.

The Hardest Conversations

Putting Protective Supervision in place requires conversations that most parents have never had to have, and that most parents are not prepared for. Three of them are worth naming.

The conversation with the harming child. This needs to be calm, clear, low on shame, and high on continuity of love. "We have noticed that what is happening between you and your sister is not okay, and we are going to be making some changes to how things work for a while. We are not punishing you. We are making sure no one else gets hurt while we work out what is going on. We love you, and we are going to keep loving you all the way through this." Adapt the words to the age. Hold the underlying message constant.

The conversation with the receiving child. This is the easier conversation in one way and the more important in another. The receiving child needs to hear, clearly, that the parent has seen what has been happening, that it was not okay, that it is not their fault, and that the family is putting arrangements in place to keep them safe. They also need to be told what those arrangements are, in concrete detail, so they can stop spending their energy worrying about whether the parent will follow through.

The conversation with each other, as parents (or co-parents, or extended-family carers, or whoever is doing the parental work). Protective Supervision is hard to maintain when only one adult in the household is committed to it. Both adults need to be aligned. If you are co-parenting across two households, and the second household is not maintaining the supervision, that is a serious issue that often requires outside input. If your partner is undermining the arrangement, that needs addressing as the underlying problem before the supervision can hold.

These conversations are not one-off events. They are revisited. The supervision is reviewed. The children are checked in with. The arrangement adjusts as the situation moves.

When You Need Outside Help

Almost every situation that calls for Protective Supervision also calls for outside clinical help. Parents acting alone, on goodwill and best intentions, rarely have the bandwidth, the training, or the perspective to manage this work without support.

In Australia, the first line for most families is a GP, who can refer to a psychologist, a paediatric mental-health service, or a family therapist under Medicare. Headspace centres are the usual entry point for adolescents. State and territory child and adolescent mental health services (CAMHS) cover the more complex cases. The Royal Children's Hospital Mental Health programmes in Melbourne, Sydney Children's Hospitals Network, and equivalents in other states all run specialist programmes for sibling and family conflict involving sustained harm.

Where the harm is sexualised in nature, specialist services are essential. The 2024 Australian systematic review on sibling sexual abuse identified a recurring pattern in which families, faced with a disclosure, responded with disbelief, minimisation, or attempted in-house management.[2] The pattern is understandable and almost always makes the situation worse. Specialist help is required. Brave Hearts, Bravehearts, the eSafety Commissioner's resources, and state-based child-protection helplines can provide initial guidance.

If you are reading this chapter and recognising that your family is in or near the Protective Supervision territory, please do not try to manage it alone. The chapter has tried to give you a frame that is honest and usable. The implementation, in any real family, deserves a professional in the room with you.

What Helps

Audit the five pieces of monitoring once a year. Tracking, communication, gatekeeping, structuring, rule-setting. Ask yourself which of the five has slipped. The slipped one is usually the one to work on next.

Notice the early signals. The receiving child going quiet around a particular sibling. A drop in their willingness to be in shared spaces. A change in their sleep, appetite, or school engagement. These signals show up before the harm is loud. They are worth attending to.

Believe the children. When a child tells you that something has been happening with a sibling, take it seriously. The minimisation reflex is automatic in most parents. Override it.

Move along the continuum without shame. Heightened monitoring is not a failure of parenting. Protective Supervision is not a failure of parenting. They are correct responses to specific situations. Treating them as last-resort options the family must avoid usually means the family delays them past the point at which they would have helped most.

Pair every supervision arrangement with help for both children. The receiving child needs to be seen and supported. The harming child needs to be assessed and helped. Without both, the supervision is just containment, and containment alone rarely produces lasting change.

Get help. This chapter cannot replace a professional in the room. If you are in this territory, find one.

Key Takeaways

Parental monitoring, formalised in Dishion and McMahon's 1998 framework, is the steady, age-appropriate awareness a parent has of what their child is doing and what kinds of influences they are facing. It is not surveillance.

Monitoring breaks into five recognisable practices: tracking, communication, gatekeeping, environmental structuring, and rule-setting. Most parents are already doing some version of all five.

Monitoring sits on a continuum, from ordinary everyday supervision to heightened monitoring during a difficult phase to Protective Supervision when one child is causing sustained, serious harm to another.

Protective Supervision is not exile. It is a structured, time-limited arrangement that keeps the receiving child safe while the harming child gets the help they need. It contains harm without rejecting the harming child.

The threshold for Protective Supervision is sustained repeated serious harm despite earlier intervention, including patterns such as physical aggression, intimidation, coercive sexualised behaviour, and the deliberate weaponisation of a sibling's vulnerabilities.

Two failure modes are common. Treating the harming child as the only problem (effectively exiling them) intensifies shame and often worsens the pattern. Under-responding abandons the receiving child and tells the harming child that the behaviour is allowed.

Putting Protective Supervision in place requires conversations with the harming child, the receiving child, and the parents themselves, and almost always requires outside clinical help.

If your family is in or near this territory, do not try to manage it alone. In Australia, the first line is a GP referral, with headspace, CAMHS, Brave Hearts, the eSafety Commissioner, and state child-protection helplines available depending on the situation.

References

1. Dishion, T. J., & McMahon, R. J. (1998). Parental monitoring and the prevention of child and adolescent problem behavior: A conceptual and empirical formulation. Clinical Child and Family Psychology Review, 1(1), 61–75. https://doi.org/10.1023/A:1021800432380
2. Falkiner, E., Tener, D., Tucci, J., et al. (2024). The risk and protective factors, response to disclosure, and interventions for sibling sexual abuse: A systematic review. Child Abuse & Neglect, 158, 107107. https://doi.org/10.1016/j.chiabu.2024.107107

CHAPTER 21

Collaborative and Proactive Solutions

Why Punishment Stops Working

Most parents arrive at this chapter having tried punishment first.

They have grounded the child. Taken the phone. Put them in time-out. Removed the screens. Cancelled the weekend. Gone through the standard repertoire of consequences that the parenting culture treats as the default response to a child who is not behaving the way the parent needs them to behave.

For some children, in some situations, punishment works well enough. The behaviour stops. Life carries on. Nothing more is needed.

For other children, in many other situations, punishment does not work. The behaviour comes back. The consequences get larger. The child becomes either more defiant or more shut down. The household tightens around the conflict. The parent reaches for something bigger to make the point land. The child meets that with more of the original behaviour. Both of them are exhausted, and neither of them can remember exactly when the cycle started.

If you are reading this chapter and recognising your household, the most useful thing the chapter has to offer is the recognition that the cycle is not a failure of your parenting. It is a failure of the model. Punishment, applied to certain kinds of behaviour, was never going to work. The behaviour was not, in those situations, a motivational problem. It was a skill problem. And punishing a child for a missing skill does not produce the skill. It produces a tired child and a tired parent.

The framework this chapter is built around is the response to that recognition. It is called Collaborative and Proactive Solutions, or CPS. It was developed by an American clinical psychologist named Ross Greene, building on his earlier book The Explosive Child and elaborated, with his colleague J. Stuart Ablon, in the more clinical Treating Explosive Kids and the school-focused Lost at School.[1] [2] [3]

CPS is not a soft alternative to discipline. It is a different way of thinking about what the behaviour was telling you in the first place.

Kids Do Well If They Can

The CPS framework runs on a single starting premise that, once a parent has sat with it for a while, changes how almost every difficult moment looks.

Kids do well if they can.

Most adults, faced with a child who is not behaving well, default to the assumption that the child is choosing not to. The behaviour is read as defiant, manipulative, attention-seeking, or motivated by some hidden gain. The corrective, on this reading, is to make the alternative more painful or the desired behaviour more rewarding. Either way, the child has to be motivated into the right choice.

Greene's argument, drawn from decades of clinical work with children whose behaviour had not responded to conventional approaches, was that this assumption is, in most cases, simply wrong. Kids who could behave well, in his experience, were already behaving well. Kids who were not behaving well were not, on the whole, choosing the behaviour. They were running into something they could not yet do.

The behaviour was the visible evidence of a missing skill.

Once you can see this, the parenting work changes. The question stops being how do I make my child do this. The question becomes which skill is missing, and how do I help my child build it.

The skills that tend to be missing in children whose behaviour is challenging are not the skills most adults expect. They are not honesty, respect, kindness, or any of the moral categories the surface behaviour seems to violate. They are more fundamental: flexibility, frustration tolerance, problem-solving, emotion regulation, language processing, the capacity to manage transitions, the capacity to handle unexpected change. When one or more of these is lagging, the child runs into demands they cannot meet, and the meltdown, refusal, aggression or shutdown follows.

The behaviour, on this reading, is not the misbehaviour. It is the symptom.

Lagging Skills, Not Lazy Children

Pause on how this reframes some of the language parents commonly use.

A child who refuses to start their homework is often described as lazy. Through the CPS lens, the more accurate description is usually a child whose executive function (the capacity to initiate, sequence, and sustain effortful tasks) is not yet equal to what the homework is asking of them. The lazy framing leads to a punishment. The skill-gap framing leads to scaffolding the start of the task.

A child who explodes at small frustrations is often described as having a bad temper. The more accurate description is usually a child whose frustration tolerance is lagging behind their age. The bad-temper framing leads to consequences for the explosion. The skill-gap framing leads to building tolerance, in small increments, over time.

A child who lies repeatedly, even when caught, is often described as dishonest. The more accurate description, in many cases, is a child for whom the cost of telling the truth has, for one reason or another, become higher than they can manage. The dishonest framing leads to harsher punishments for lying. The skill-gap framing leads to working out why the truth has become unsafe.

A teenager who blows up over screen limits is often described as addicted, defiant, or entitled. The more accurate description is often a teenager whose flexibility and capacity to handle transitions have not yet caught up to the abrupt demands the rules are placing on them. The addicted framing leads to escalating restrictions. The skill-gap framing leads to a different kind of conversation about how the transition could be made bearable.

None of this means the behaviour is acceptable. It is not. The skill-gap framing does not remove accountability. It just reframes what the work needs to be. Accountability without the skill-building does not produce change. Skill-building without accountability is permissiveness. The CPS framework, when applied properly, holds both.

Plan A, Plan B, Plan C

Greene names three options a parent has when an unsolved problem is in front of them.

Plan A is imposing the parent's will. "This is how it is going to be." The parent decides, the rule is enforced, the child complies or there is a consequence. Plan A is the default mode in most households. It is also the mode most likely to produce the meltdown, the dig-in, the shutdown, when applied to a problem that is sitting on top of a lagging skill.

Plan B is collaborative problem-solving. The parent and the child sit down together, work out what is making the situation difficult, and reach a solution that addresses both the parent's concerns and the child's. Plan B is the heart of the CPS approach.

Plan C is setting the problem aside for now. Not every issue can be solved at once. A parent can decide that this particular problem, this particular week, is not the one to focus on. The parent does not pretend the issue is fine. They simply choose not to make it the front of the queue.

The intuition most parents bring is that Plan A is the responsible adult option, Plan B is for when things have gone wrong, and Plan C is giving up. Greene's argument is the opposite. Plan B should be the default for any recurring problem that is sitting on top of a skill gap. Plan A is for safety emergencies and a small number of non-negotiables. Plan C is a deliberate triage tool that prevents a household from trying to solve everything at once and burning everyone out.

Most households improve significantly when they make two shifts. They use Plan A less. They use Plan B more.

The Plan B Conversation

Plan B has three steps. They have to happen in order. Skipping or reversing them is the most common reason CPS conversations go wrong.

Step one is the empathy step. The parent's only job is to find out, in the child's own words, what is making the unsolved problem hard for them. The parent does not negotiate, defend, lecture, or offer solutions. They listen. They ask follow-up questions. They reflect back what they have heard. They keep going until they have a real understanding of the child's perspective.

What this sounds like, in a real moment, is something like, "I have noticed that getting started on homework is really hard for you most days. What is up with that?" And then a long, patient willingness to sit with the answer, even if the first answer is, "I don't know." "I don't know" is rarely the final answer. It is usually the start of one. Wait. Ask follow-ups. "Is it the maths in particular, or is it any homework? Is it the time of day? Is it being told to start? Is it that you cannot find a place to do it? Is it that your sister is annoying you while you are trying to work?" Keep going gently until you have something concrete.

Step two is the define step. Now the parent gets to share their concerns. Not their solutions. Their concerns. Why does this problem matter to the parent. What worries them about it. What they are seeing or hearing. "My concern is that when the homework does not get started, you are still up at ten trying to finish it, and you are getting four hours of sleep, and the next day is even harder."

Step three is the invitation step. The parent invites the child to think together about a solution that addresses both sets of concerns. "I wonder if we can come up with a way that the homework starts earlier, that does not feel as hard for you and that means you are not still up at ten. What do you think might work?"

The solution, when it comes, is meant to do three things. It addresses the child's concern. It addresses the parent's concern. It is realistic for both of them to do.

Notice what is not in this conversation. The parent has not asserted authority. The parent has not lectured. The parent has not threatened. The parent has not bargained. The parent has, instead, treated the child as a person whose perspective on a real problem is useful information.

Most children, when they are met this way, respond. Not always immediately. Not always in the first conversation. But over time, with practice, the child learns that this kind of conversation is what their parent reaches for, and that the parent is interested in solutions that work for both of them. Once that has been established, the child becomes, increasingly, a participant in the solving rather than the problem to be solved.

A Worked Example

It is worth running a real example, in something like real time, to show what this looks like.

The unsolved problem: an eleven-year-old who blows up most evenings when asked to come off his game and start dinner.

Plan A version: "Off the game now. I told you twenty minutes ago. If you cannot do this you are losing the game for a week."

Outcome: meltdown, slammed door, dinner ruined, parent angry, child resentful, problem reappears tomorrow.

Plan B version, evening one, in a calm moment well before dinner:

Parent: "I have noticed that coming off the game when it is time for dinner has been really hard for you. What is up with that?"

Child, after a long pause: "I don't know."

Parent: "Is it that you have been in the middle of a round?"

Child: "Yeah, kind of. If I leave a round my team loses and they get angry at me."

Parent: "Right, so it is not just the game, it is what happens with the other players if you leave mid-round. That is useful for me to know. How long does a round take?"

Child: "About fifteen minutes. Sometimes longer."

Parent: "Got it. So when I call you for dinner, you might be ten minutes into a round you cannot leave. That makes sense. My concern is that dinner ends up being twenty minutes late, the food gets cold, and we are all stressed by the time we sit down. I wonder if we can come up with a way that you do not get stuck mid-round when dinner is ready, and dinner can still happen on time. What do you think might work?"

Child: "What if you give me a fifteen-minute warning before dinner, so I can finish the round I am in or not start a new one?"

Parent: "That sounds workable. Let us try that for a week. If it works, we keep doing it. If it does not, we come back and try something else."

What just happened. The parent learned something they did not know (that the child's reaction was not about the game, it was about the team dynamic). The child was treated as a person whose situation made sense. A solution emerged that addressed both sides. The household has one fewer recurring conflict to manage. None of this required a punishment, a power struggle, or a lecture.

It also took five minutes.

Why CPS Sits Beside Boundaries, Not Against Them

Some parents worry that CPS is permissiveness in a more polite costume. It is not. The boundaries are still there. The household standards are still held. What CPS changes is how those boundaries are arrived at when the issue is recurring and the previous approach has not worked.

There are still moments where Plan A is the right answer. Safety. Non-negotiables. Things that simply cannot be open to discussion. CPS does not abolish those moments. It just stops them being the default response to every difficulty.

A household running on CPS as its default for recurring problems, with Plan A reserved for the things that require it, tends to have fewer overall conflicts than a household running on Plan A for everything. The collaboratively-arrived-at solutions hold better. The child has buy-in. The relationship is not constantly being strained by power struggles. The boundaries that do require Plan A get clearer attention because they are not lost in the noise of constant smaller battles.

When CPS Does Not Work the First Time

It is also worth being honest that the first attempt at CPS often does not produce a clean result.

The child may not engage. They may say "I don't know" and refuse to go further. They may suggest a solution that is wildly unrealistic. They may agree to a plan and not follow through. They may say all the right things in the conversation and do none of them later.

None of this is a sign that the framework is broken. It is a sign that, like any other practice, CPS takes time to land in a household that has not used it before.

Some practical adjustments help. Choose your moment. Plan B works best in calm conditions, well away from the actual problem situation. Trying to run a Plan B conversation in the middle of a meltdown is a setup for failure. Save the conversation for a quiet evening, a car ride, a walk. Choose your battle. Pick one unsolved problem to start with. Ideally not the biggest one. A win on a smaller issue builds the practice for harder issues later. Be patient with the empathy step. This is the step where most parents rush. Slow down. Get the child's perspective fully, even if it takes three sittings. Be honest in the define step. Your concerns matter too. The conversation is not just about validating the child. It is about both of you understanding the situation. Be willing to revisit. The first solution may not work. That is expected. Plan B is a recurring practice, not a single conversation.

If, after several genuine attempts, CPS is still not landing in your household, that is a signal that there is something else going on. The child may have a developmental or mental-health need that is bigger than the framework can address alone. The parent may be carrying patterns that are interfering with the conversation. The marriage or co-parenting relationship may need to be addressed first. None of these mean CPS is wrong. They mean the situation needs more than CPS by itself, and outside professional input is the next step.

What Helps

Read the Greene books. The Explosive Child is the accessible introduction. Lost at School covers the school-based applications, which are useful even for parents who are not directly involved in school problems. Treating Explosive Kids is the more clinical text, useful for therapists or for parents who want the deeper version.

Identify your top three unsolved problems. Write them down. Notice which of them are recurring, which are small enough to start with, and which are tied to particular times of day or particular triggers.

Choose one to start with. Run a Plan B conversation in calm conditions. Notice what comes up. Notice your own urge to skip the empathy step or to rush to a solution. Resist both.

Use Plan C honestly. Not every problem can be tackled at once. Setting some aside for now is not failure. It is triage.

Reduce Plan A to where it actually belongs. Safety. Non-negotiables. Genuine emergencies. Most of what currently runs on Plan A in a typical household does not need to.

Get help when CPS is not landing despite genuine effort. A clinician trained in CPS, or a family therapist, can usually help identify what is interfering. The CPS Institute (Lives in the Balance, Greene's organisation) has a directory of trained practitioners.

Key Takeaways

Punishment works, sometimes. For many recurring behaviour problems it does not, because the behaviour is sitting on top of a missing skill rather than a motivational deficit.

Collaborative and Proactive Solutions, developed by Ross Greene, runs on the premise that kids do well if they can. Children whose behaviour is challenging are not, on the whole, choosing the behaviour. They are running into demands that exceed their current skills.

The skills most often lagging are flexibility, frustration tolerance, problem-solving, emotion regulation, and the capacity to handle transitions. The behaviour is the visible top of those skill gaps.

Greene names three options for any unsolved problem: Plan A (impose the parent's will), Plan B (collaborate to solve it), and Plan C (set it aside for now). Most households improve when they use Plan A less and Plan B more.

Plan B has three steps: empathy (understand the child's perspective), define (share the parent's concerns), invitation (work out a solution together). The order matters. The empathy step is where most parents rush.

CPS is not a replacement for boundaries. Plan A still exists for safety and genuine non-negotiables. CPS just stops Plan A being the default for every recurring difficulty.

First attempts at CPS often produce imperfect results. The framework, like any practice, takes time to land. Where genuine attempts are not working, outside professional help is the next step.

References

1. Greene, R. W. (2014). The Explosive Child: A New Approach for Understanding and Parenting Easily Frustrated, Chronically Inflexible Children (5th ed.). New York: Harper. (See also Chapter 2.)
2. Greene, R. W., & Ablon, J. S. (2006). Treating Explosive Kids: The Collaborative Problem-Solving Approach. New York: Guilford Press.
3. Greene, R. W. (2008). Lost at School: Why Our Kids with Behavioral Challenges Are Falling Through the Cracks and How We Can Help Them. New York: Scribner.

CHAPTER 22

Parenting a Neurodivergent Child

Why This Chapter Belongs Here

Many of the parents who pick up this book are reading it because of a particular child. Not children in general. One specific child whose behaviour is harder to understand, whose distress lands harder, whose patterns do not respond to the strategies that worked with their siblings or the ones recommended by friends.

For a meaningful proportion of those parents, the underlying picture is neurodivergence. The child has ADHD, or autism, or sensory processing differences, or a learning difference, or a combination. Some of these children have a formal diagnosis. Many do not, often because the assessment process is slow and expensive and most parents do not start it until things get hard enough that they have to.

The framework this book has built holds for neurodivergent children. The Cell Danger Response is the same. The wounds underneath behaviour are the same. The need for repair after rupture is the same. The same calm authority works.

What changes is the application. The decode step looks for different things. The discipline step has to fit a different developmental capacity. The repair step often takes longer and is sometimes nonverbal. The biological floor matters more, not less. The peer environment is harder to navigate, and the cost of getting it wrong is steeper.

This chapter exists because a parent of a neurodivergent child reading the rest of this book deserves a place where their reality is named directly, where the adjustments they need are described concretely, and where the resources they can turn to are listed plainly. The shorter version of this chapter could be inserted into Chapter 21. Greene's collaborative problem-solving framework, which Chapter 21 builds on, is particularly well suited to neurodivergent children, and one of his most-cited lines, kids do well if they can, is the central claim this chapter rests on.

But neurodivergent children deserve a chapter, not a footnote. A parent flipping through the contents page should be able to find this chapter at a glance.

What "Neurodivergent" Means in This Book

The term neurodivergent is broad, deliberately so. It covers a range of brain-and-body differences from what the dominant culture treats as typical. The most commonly named are ADHD, autism, dyslexia, dyscalculia, dyspraxia, sensory processing differences, language-based learning differences, Tourette's and tic disorders, and giftedness (particularly twice-exceptional, where a child is both gifted and has a learning difference or other neurodivergence).

The term has its critics, and the boundaries between categories have been redrawn many times. For the practical purposes of this chapter, those debates do not need resolving. What matters is that an estimated one in five children meets criteria for at least one form of neurodivergence under the broad umbrella, and the proportion is higher in any clinical or therapy population. If you are reading a book like this one, the odds your child or someone close to them is neurodivergent are real.

Some parents reading this will know which categories apply to their child because the child has been formally assessed. Many will not. Many parents recognise patterns that fit but have not yet pursued diagnosis, often because of cost, time, family disagreement, or the worry that a label will close more doors than it opens. None of those reasons is unreasonable.

What this chapter argues is that you do not have to wait for a diagnosis to start adapting your parenting to the child you actually have. The work of recognising what your child needs and adjusting accordingly is available right now, regardless of where you are in the assessment process.

The Same Framework, With Adjustments

The framework this book is built on does not need to be replaced for neurodivergent children. It needs to be applied with a different sense of what your child is actually capable of in any given moment, and a different timeline for how change happens.

Decode first becomes more important, not less. Neurodivergent children's behaviour is more often misread than typical children's behaviour. What looks like defiance is usually a transition the child cannot yet manage. What looks like rudeness is usually language processing or social communication that has not landed the way the parent assumed it would. What looks like attention-seeking is usually genuine sensory or emotional dysregulation that the child does not have other tools to manage. The clinical psychologist Mona Delahooke, in her book Beyond Behaviors, frames this as a body-up rather than a top-down view of behaviour. The behaviour is the visible top of an underlying biological state, and the work of the parent is to read what the body is telling you before responding to what the behaviour appears to be saying.[1]

Discipline becomes about scaffolding more than consequences. A neurotypical seven-year-old who hits a sibling can usually take in a calm correction, sit with the consequence, and adjust over weeks. A neurodivergent seven-year-old, depending on their profile, may not be able to take in any correction in the moment because their nervous system is still flooded, may hold the consequence with shame that lasts much longer than was intended, and may need months rather than weeks to begin adjusting because the underlying skills are still being built. None of this means consequences do not apply. It means the consequences have to fit the child's actual capacity rather than their chronological age, and the timeframe for change has to be longer.

Repair becomes longer, and sometimes nonverbal. A neurotypical child can usually do a verbal repair conversation within hours. A neurodivergent child may need more time before they can engage with words at all. Some children who would not be able to do a repair conversation can do a repair through a shared activity (a walk, a game, drawing together). Some can repair through a written note. Some can only repair through your reliable presence over the next few days. All of these are legitimate forms of repair. The four-part script in Appendix A still applies; the medium and the timing change.

The biological floor matters more. A neurotypical child operating on poor sleep, unstable blood sugar and saturated screen time will be more reactive than they need to be. A neurodivergent child in the same conditions can be barely functional. Sleep, food, movement, sunlight and downtime are not lifestyle suggestions for these children. They are the conditions that determine whether anything else you try will work.

ADHD: Executive Function as the Hidden Issue

ADHD, in current understanding, is most usefully thought of as a developmental delay in executive function rather than as a deficit of attention. Children with ADHD are not failing to attend. They are struggling to direct attention, sustain effort over time, regulate emotional intensity, and bridge the gap between intention and action. The underlying brain systems involved (prefrontal cortex, dopamine signalling, working memory networks) are usually functioning, just on a slower developmental timeline.

What this means for parenting is that strategies which assume executive function is in place will fail. Telling an eight-year-old with ADHD to go and pack their school bag is not unreasonable to an adult. To the child, the instruction triggers a multi-step task (decide what to pack, find each item, sequence the packing, hold the goal across distractions, complete it without abandoning halfway) that their brain genuinely cannot run yet. The child is not refusing. They are running into a capacity gap.

The parenting adjustments are practical. External scaffolding replaces internal executive function. Visual lists, checklists on the fridge, photographs of what a packed bag looks like, the parent staying nearby while the task happens (body doubling), tasks broken into single steps with a check-in between each. The point is not to do the task for the child. The point is to make the structure visible and external until the child's own internal structure has caught up.

The role of medication is one of the harder conversations in this territory and is outside this book's scope. The honest position is that for many children with ADHD, well-managed medication, in combination with the right scaffolding and a good educational fit, makes the difference between a child who is constantly failing and a child who can function. For other children, medication is not the right answer. Either way, this is a conversation between you, your child, your GP, and a paediatrician or psychiatrist with ADHD expertise, not a conversation a book can settle.

Autism: Meltdowns Are Not Tantrums

The single most important distinction for parents of autistic children to understand is the difference between a tantrum and a meltdown.

A tantrum is goal-directed. The child is upset because they want something. The behaviour is, in some sense, a strategy. When the goal is achieved or the situation changes, the behaviour usually subsides. Tantrums respond to limit-setting and consistent consequences over time.

A meltdown is not goal-directed. The child's nervous system has been pushed past what it can manage and has lost the regulatory capacity that would normally keep behaviour in check. The child is not choosing the behaviour. They are caught in it. Meltdowns do not respond to consequences in the moment, because the part of the brain that would receive the consequence is offline. Meltdowns subside when the nervous system has recovered, which sometimes takes hours and sometimes the rest of the day.

Treating a meltdown like a tantrum makes everything worse. The child is punished for behaviour they could not control, the relationship is damaged, and the next meltdown arrives faster because the child's baseline arousal is now higher. Treating a tantrum like a meltdown produces its own problems, but in autistic children the more common error by far is the first one.

What helps during a meltdown is not correction. It is reduction of demand. Lower the lights. Lower the noise. Lower the language. Stay close enough to be safe but not close enough to add stimulation. Wait. Most autistic children, when met this way, come down faster than parents expect.

The Australian psychologist Tony Attwood, whose long-running clinical work on autism remains one of the standard references for parents and practitioners, has been making this distinction for decades, alongside the broader point that autistic children read social and emotional cues differently rather than not at all.[2] More recently, the writer and psychologist Devon Price, in Unmasking Autism, has put forward a related argument about the cost autistic children pay when they are forced to perform neurotypical behaviour they do not actually have, and about the long-term mental-health damage that masking produces.[3]

Both of these strands of work converge on the same parenting implication. Your autistic child is not a broken neurotypical child. They are a different kind of child. The framework still applies. The application has to fit who they actually are.

PDA: When Standard Approaches Make Things Worse

There is a particular profile within autism, and increasingly recognised in some children outside the autism category, that warrants its own brief treatment. It has historically been called Pathological Demand Avoidance and is more recently being renamed by autistic adults as Persistent Drive for Autonomy. The clinical label is in flux. The pattern is recognisable.

A child with a PDA profile reacts to demand in ways that go well beyond ordinary pushback. Even small demands (please put your shoes on, time for dinner, can you brush your teeth) can produce intense distress, refusal, sometimes meltdown, sometimes bargaining, sometimes elaborate avoidance. The child is not, in any usual sense, being defiant. Their nervous system experiences demand itself as a threat to autonomy that they have to neutralise to feel safe.

The standard parenting strategies designed for typical or even most neurodivergent children make this picture worse. Firm limits, clear consequences and the calm-authority stance described in Chapter 18, applied to a PDA child, often increase the distress and intensify the avoidance. The child experiences the firmness as more demand, and the system escalates.

What works with PDA children is sometimes called declarative or low-demand parenting. Demands are framed as observations or invitations rather than directives. Choices are given. The child's autonomy is respected at every available point. Routines are flexible. Negotiation is constant. To a parent expecting standard authority to work, this looks like permissiveness. It is not. It is the only stance that allows the PDA child to do anything at all without spiralling.

If you are reading this section and recognising your child, please take that recognition seriously. PDA is poorly understood by most clinicians and is often misdiagnosed as oppositional defiant disorder, with consequences that can be damaging. The PDA Society in the UK and a growing Australian community of practitioners and parents (including writers like Eliza Fricker) have built up considerable practical literature on how to parent these children well. You are not alone in finding this hard. The standard playbook does not work, and that is not your fault.

Sensory Processing and the Body Underneath the Behaviour

Many neurodivergent children have sensory profiles that look very different from the average. Some are over-responsive to certain inputs (loud noises, particular textures, bright lights, strong smells, certain food textures) and will go into distress around them. Others are under-responsive and seek out intense input (deep pressure, spinning, jumping, crashing into things, eating non-food items, mouthing objects long after the typical age). Many children have a mixed profile, over-responsive in some channels and under-responsive in others.

What this means in practice is that a meaningful portion of behaviour parents read as defiance, attention-seeking or fussiness is actually a sensory-driven attempt to get to a tolerable state. The child refusing to put on the school uniform is not being precious. The seam at the neckline is genuinely intolerable to their nervous system in the way an inch of sandpaper down your collar would be to yours. The child climbing on the back of the couch repeatedly is not being naughty. Their proprioceptive system is asking for input the rest of the day has not provided.

The clinical specialty that addresses this directly is occupational therapy with a paediatric sensory focus. A good OT can map your child's sensory profile, identify the inputs they are seeking or avoiding, and put together a sensory diet that meets the child's needs proactively rather than reactively. For many neurodivergent children, this kind of OT input is one of the most useful interventions available, and Australian families can access it through Medicare, NDIS, or private practice depending on circumstances.

Stuart Shanker's self-regulation work, particularly in his 2016 book Self-Reg, makes a compatible point at a more general level: behaviour that looks like misbehaviour is often a stress response, and the most useful intervention is not consequence but reduction of stressors and increase of regulating inputs.[4]

The Particular Vulnerability to the Bad Apple Effect

Neurodivergent children are particularly exposed to the bad apple effect, in two related ways.

First, they are more often misread by the people around them. Family members, teachers, coaches, peers, and other adults frequently read their behaviour as wilful when it is not, and respond with the harshness, exclusion or contempt that this book has spent twenty-five chapters describing the cost of. The result is that neurodivergent children pile up rejection, shame, and the wounds described in Chapter 6 at a rate that neurotypical children do not. By adolescence, many neurodivergent children carry a long tail of misreading by adults who should have known better, and they are particularly vulnerable to peer environments that finally seem to accept them, even when those environments are themselves harmful.

Second, the constant low-grade demand to mask, to perform a neurotypical version of themselves to fit in, exacts a cost the rest of this book has only glanced at. Devon Price's work on masking is particularly clear on this. A child who has spent the school day suppressing their actual nervous-system needs, hiding stim behaviours, performing eye contact and small talk and the social routines they do not have native access to, comes home depleted in a way their parents often misread as ordinary tiredness. The depletion is real and accumulates. Mental-health outcomes for autistic adults who masked through their childhood are substantially worse than for those who did not, and the differential is now well-documented.[3]

The implication for parents is straightforward. Home has to be the place your neurodivergent child is allowed to unmask. The stim behaviours, the routines, the food preferences, the silence, the lack of eye contact when they are tired, the long hours alone in their room with the special interest, the refusal of social demands they have already met all day at school. All of this is recovery work. A child who is allowed to do it at home, without judgement, comes back online. A child who has to mask at home as well does not.

What Helps

Read your child's actual profile, not the diagnosis label. Two children with the same diagnosis can have wildly different presentations. Spend the time noticing what your child specifically struggles with, what they are drawn to, what reliably helps and what reliably does not. Your accumulated observations are usually more useful than any general framework.

Lower the demand load. Most neurodivergent children are under significantly more demand than their parents realise. School is demand. Social interaction is demand. Sensory environments are demand. Family expectations are demand. If your child is constantly meltdowning by the end of the day, the realistic answer is rarely to add more strategies; it is to remove demand from the parts of the day where you can.

Build the biological floor first. Sleep, food, movement, sunlight, screens, downtime. Chapter 16 applies with extra weight here. A neurodivergent child running on poor sleep and unstable blood sugar is not going to benefit from any of the practical work in the rest of this book.

Find the right professionals. A paediatrician with neurodivergence expertise. A psychologist who specialises in your child's particular profile. An occupational therapist for sensory work. A speech pathologist for autism or language differences. A school that gets it. None of these are easy to find in Australia, and the wait times can be long. Start the search early.

Find your community. Other parents of neurodivergent children are one of the most useful resources you have. They can tell you which paediatricians actually listen, which schools are worth the commute, which OTs are good with PDA, which strategies they have tried and which were a waste of money. Australian organisations including Reframing Autism, the ADHD Foundation Australia, Yellow Ladybugs (for autistic girls and gender-diverse children), and a number of state-based parent support networks are good places to start.

Resist the pressure to fix your child. The framing in older parenting and clinical literature is sometimes that neurodivergence is a problem to be solved. The framing this book takes, in line with most contemporary evidence-informed practice, is that neurodivergence is a way of being that comes with real strengths and real costs, and the parenting work is to support the child to grow into themselves, not into a neurotypical version of themselves. The work is hard enough without adding the goal of normalisation on top of it.

Forgive yourself the days when you do not get it right. Parents of neurodivergent children are often exhausted, often blamed by family members and school staff who do not understand what is happening, and often carrying their own undiagnosed neurodivergence which makes the work harder. Repair is available here too. Most of what this book has said about repair applies. Apply it.

Getting Help in Australia

Diagnosis pathways. A GP referral to a paediatrician is the typical first step for school-age children. For older adolescents and adults, a GP can refer to a psychiatrist or to a psychologist who does formal assessment. The NDIS (National Disability Insurance Scheme) covers some neurodivergent children and adolescents, depending on diagnosis and functional impact, and can fund occupational therapy, speech pathology, psychology, and other supports.

Medicare-funded supports. The Better Access initiative provides rebates for psychological care under a Mental Health Treatment Plan from a GP. Some neurodivergent children also qualify for paediatric items under Medicare with sufficient diagnosis.

School-based supports. Australian state education departments operate funded support programmes for children with diagnosed disabilities, including some neurodivergence categories. Independent and Catholic schools have their own support programmes, of varying quality. School psychologists, learning support staff, and inclusion coordinators are the people to ask for.

Specific organisations worth knowing. The Australian Autism Alliance, Reframing Autism, the ADHD Foundation, ADHD Australia, Yellow Ladybugs, the Australian Dyslexia Association, the Auscap (Australian Association for Cognitive and Behaviour Therapy) directory of clinicians, headspace for adolescents.

And the lived-experience material. Increasingly, the most useful guidance for parents of neurodivergent children comes from neurodivergent adults writing about their own experience. Devon Price, Hannah Gadsby (whose autism diagnosis came in adulthood), Eliza Fricker on PDA parenting, Kristy Forbes's Australian work on autistic identity, and the broader autistic and ADHD social-media communities. Read across these sources rather than relying on any single one.

Key Takeaways

Neurodivergence is common, and the framework this book has built holds for neurodivergent children. What changes is the application: decode looks for different things, discipline has to fit a different developmental capacity, repair takes longer.

ADHD is most usefully understood as a delay in executive function. External scaffolding replaces internal executive function until the child's own structure catches up.

Meltdowns are not tantrums. The child cannot receive correction during a meltdown, because the part of the brain that would receive it is offline. Lower the demand, wait, and address the situation later.

PDA (Pathological Demand Avoidance / Persistent Drive for Autonomy) is a profile in which standard authority-based parenting makes things worse. Low-demand, declarative, autonomy-respecting approaches work where firm limits do not.

Sensory processing differences underlie a meaningful portion of the behaviour parents misread as defiance or fussiness. Occupational therapy with paediatric sensory expertise is one of the most useful interventions available.

Neurodivergent children are particularly vulnerable to the bad apple effect: they are more often misread by adults, accumulate more rejection and shame, and pay a high cost for masking. Home has to be the place they are allowed to unmask.

Australian pathways include GP referrals to paediatricians or psychiatrists, the NDIS where applicable, Medicare's Better Access initiative, school-based supports, and a growing list of organisations and clinicians with neurodivergence expertise.

The work is to support your child to grow into themselves, not into a neurotypical version of themselves.

References

1. Delahooke, M. (2019). Beyond Behaviors: Using Brain Science and Compassion to Understand and Solve Children's Behavioral Challenges. Eau Claire, WI: PESI Publishing.

2. Attwood, T. (2007). The Complete Guide to Asperger's Syndrome. London: Jessica Kingsley Publishers.

3. Price, D. (2022). Unmasking Autism: Discovering the New Faces of Neurodiversity. New York: Harmony Books.

4. Shanker, S. (2016). Self-Reg: How to Help Your Child (and You) Break the Stress Cycle and Successfully Engage with Life. New York: Penguin Press.

5. Greene, R. W. (2014). The Explosive Child (5th ed.). New York: Harper. (See also Chapter 21.)

CHAPTER 23

Engineering a Positive Peer Culture

The Other Direction

Most parental anxiety about peer influence runs in the same direction. Worry about the friend who is a bad influence. Worry about the group at school. Worry about the online community. Worry about who your child is going to come home talking like.

All of those worries are reasonable, and the chapters on peer groups, online spaces and the wider adult world have already taken them seriously.

What this chapter is about is the reverse problem, which gets less attention but does at least as much work. The same biological and social mechanisms that allow harmful behaviour to spread through a peer group also allow prosocial behaviour to spread. Belonging is contagious. Kindness is contagious. Discipline, in the better sense, is contagious. The currency of the room is what shapes the children inside it. The question for parents is not just how to keep harmful currencies out. It is how to deliberately put their child inside rooms where the currency is something worth catching.

This is the work I will call, borrowing a phrase from the clinical literature, engineering a positive peer culture. The phrase is older than the current parenting moment, and it carries a useful seriousness. Parents are not merely supervising friendships. They are shaping the social environments in which their child is going to be formed.

Why Diluting Beats Forbidding

The temptation, when a friendship or peer group is going wrong, is to forbid. "You cannot see that boy any more." "That group is not allowed to come over." "You are not on that platform."

Sometimes the forbidding is exactly the right move, especially with younger children, with safety-relevant situations, or where a particular individual has crossed a clear line. Most of Chapter 13 was about when parents should be willing to do exactly that.

But forbidding alone, applied to most peer-group concerns, does less than parents hope. Older children push back. Adolescents resent the directive and often go around it. The forbidden friendship can take on the gloss of forbidden fruit. A child who is told not to spend time with a particular peer often spends more attention on them, not less.

The deeper move, in most situations, is to dilute rather than to forbid. Place your child in three or four other peer environments, each with its own currency of belonging, each prosocial in its own way. The original difficult friendship may continue, but it is now one of several peer worlds your child belongs to, and its hold on their identity weakens. The child has somewhere else to be. Somewhere else they are known, valued, included. The harmful peer group is no longer the only social oxygen available.

This is the principle the developmental psychologist Thomas Dishion has been pointing at across his life's work, applied in reverse. If concentrating struggling young people together accelerates the spread of harmful behaviour, embedding a young person inside multiple prosocial environments correspondingly slows it.

Positive Peer Culture as a Clinical Concept

The phrase positive peer culture, capitalised, refers to a specific clinical model originally developed by Harry Vorrath and Larry Brendtro in the United States in the 1970s and 1980s.[1] It was used in residential treatment settings, schools and youth programmes to deliberately reorient peer dynamics so that the peer group itself, rather than only the adults, supported prosocial behaviour, accountability and growth.

The model rested on a simple observation. In any group of young people, peers exert enormous influence over one another's behaviour. In the wrong settings, that influence runs toward harm, in exactly the way the chapter on peer contagion described. In the right settings, structured by the adults, the same mechanism of peer influence can be turned around. Young people can hold each other to higher standards than the adults could enforce alone. The peer group becomes a force for growth rather than a force for erosion.

Most parents will not be running a residential programme. The relevance of Positive Peer Culture for ordinary families is more modest but no less real. The clinical model demonstrates, with decades of evidence behind it, that the social environment is not a fixed input. It is something adults can shape. The currency of belonging in a young person's life is largely the result of which environments they have been placed inside, and the parents who think carefully about that placement are doing some of the most consequential parenting work available to them.

What Makes a Peer Environment Prosocial

Not every well-intentioned activity produces a prosocial peer culture. Some sports clubs, music ensembles, religious communities and youth groups, despite the worthy frame, run on bullying, exclusion or contempt as much as the wider culture does. The label of the activity is not the same as the quality of the peer environment inside it.

Some of the markers of a prosocial peer environment are worth naming, because they help parents tell the difference between the version that does the work and the version that does not.

Adult presence and competence. A few attentive, regulated adults are visible at all times. They notice what is happening between the young people. They intervene early when the tone is going wrong. They model the behaviour they expect.

A clear, fair, well-held standard. Children can articulate what is expected and what is not. The standard is the same for all of them. When someone breaks it, the response is consistent and proportionate.

An emphasis on contribution, mastery, or service. The currency of belonging is not status, looks, social rank, or ironic distance. It is whether the young person turns up, tries, contributes, develops. Children who are clumsy, awkward, new, or different have a path into belonging through effort.

Repair when things go wrong. Conflicts happen. They are addressed openly. Apologies are made. Relationships are rebuilt. This is the most reliable single test of whether a peer environment is healthy. Healthy environments repair. Unhealthy ones absorb harm into a code of silence.

A sense of purpose larger than the group itself. The young people are doing something. Building, performing, learning a skill, helping someone, training for an event, working toward an outcome. The shared purpose pulls the social dynamic forward.

If a peer environment your child belongs to does not show these markers, it is worth noticing. The brand on the door does not guarantee the quality of the room.

The Australian Options

Australia is, despite the more recent narrowing of childhood, still relatively rich in good peer environments for children and adolescents. The list of options most worth knowing about, by age and inclination, includes the following.

Sport. Junior football, netball, soccer, hockey, basketball, cricket, rugby, AFL, Auskick, Little Athletics, swimming clubs, rowing, skating, martial arts, surfing, tennis. Most local clubs run on goodwill from volunteer parents and coaches, and the quality varies, but the broad model of regular training, weekly competition, mixed-age relationships and physical effort is one of the strongest peer-culture engines available. A well-run team is a peer environment that does enormous developmental work without the children being aware it is happening.

Surf life saving. The nipper programmes that run along the Australian coastline are some of the strongest examples of structured peer environment with adult supervision, physical challenge, and explicit service ethic the country produces. For families near a coastline, this is worth taking seriously even if the child is not particularly drawn to swimming.

Scouts, Guides, JOEYs, Cubs, Venturers, Cadets. The scouting and equivalent traditions, run by long-standing volunteer organisations, are explicitly designed to do exactly the work this chapter is describing. They produce mixed-age peer groups, structured outdoor and skill-based activity, ethical framing, and genuine adult mentoring.

Music ensembles, choirs, bands and orchestras. Group music-making is one of the most cognitively demanding forms of peer cooperation a young person can participate in. Local choirs, school bands, community orchestras, rock bands and jazz ensembles all do the work. The skill demanded by playing or singing together produces a peer environment that runs on contribution and mastery rather than social rank.

Drama and dance. Theatre groups, dance companies and performing arts programmes provide a very different kind of structured peer culture, often well suited to children who are not drawn to traditional sport but who flourish in expressive group work.

Volunteer organisations. Conservation Volunteers, Rotary's youth programmes, RFS or SES cadet schemes, environmental clean-up groups, animal-shelter volunteering. Service-oriented activities embed young people inside groups whose purpose is explicitly outside the group itself.

Religious and faith-based youth communities. For families connected to a faith tradition, well-run youth groups can be powerful prosocial environments. The same caution applies as for any other activity: the brand does not guarantee the room. A well-led youth group is gold; a poorly-led one can be the opposite.

Outdoor education programmes. School camps, residential outdoor programmes, the Duke of Edinburgh's International Award scheme, Outward Bound Australia. Time in the outdoors, in mixed-ability groups, doing physically demanding, real-world tasks, is one of the most reliably formative peer experiences available to a young person.

None of these will work for every child. The point is not to enrol every child in everything. The point is to keep two or three of them running through your child's life at any given time, so that the social oxygen of their week is not coming from one source alone.

Service and Contribution

Worth singling out, because it does specific work that the other options do not always do, is service. Activities in which a young person is contributing to someone else, in a real way, with a real cost in time and effort.

Volunteering at a shelter, a food bank, an aged-care home, an animal rescue, an environmental project. Helping with a community event. Tutoring a younger child. Caring for an elderly neighbour's garden. Working a shift at a community kitchen.

What service does, in a young person's life, that no amount of consumption can do, is shift the centre of gravity from self to other. The young person becomes someone whose contribution is visible, valued, and consequential. They register, in their body, that they have something to give. Over time, this translates into a kind of self-respect that is much harder to dislodge than the version that comes from being told they are wonderful.

Service environments also tend to attract a particular kind of peer. Young people who choose to spend a Saturday morning helping rather than scrolling tend to be young people whose currency is closer to the one you want your child to be inside.

If your child does not currently have any service activity in their week, this is one of the most useful additions a parent can prompt. Start small. A monthly commitment is enough.

The Family as the First Peer Culture

Before any of the external environments, there is the household itself.

The family is the first peer culture a child belongs to. The siblings are the first peers. The parents are the first models of how adults talk to each other and to children. The currency of belonging in the family is the currency the child will calibrate every later peer environment against.

If the family runs on contempt, the child will be drawn to peer environments that run on contempt. Those will feel familiar. The respectful environment will feel slightly off, slightly boring, slightly hard to relax into.

If the family runs on warmth, repair, contribution and the basic dignity of every member, the child will calibrate accordingly. They will be drawn, more often than not, to peer environments that work the same way, and they will feel the wrongness of environments that do not.

This is one of the deeper reasons all the earlier chapters in this book matter. The work of becoming the safe harbour, of holding calm authority, of doing repair, of refusing contempt at the family level, is also the work of giving your child a set of internal standards that will guide their future peer choices long after you are not in the room.

Engineering a positive peer culture, in the largest sense, begins inside the front door.

Curate, Do Not Control

There is one final tension worth naming. Most adolescents will resist a parent's attempt to control their friendships directly. Tell them you do not like a particular friend, and the friendship often becomes more central. Insist on a particular activity, and the resistance to that activity will frequently be larger than the activity itself.

What works better, especially with older children and adolescents, is to curate the wider environment without controlling the specific choices.

You decide which neighbourhood you live in. You decide which school they go to (or which school they go to within reach). You decide which activities they are exposed to early enough that the activity becomes part of their life. You decide which community you are part of, which family friends are in regular contact, which kinds of holidays they have, which kinds of conversations are normal at your dinner table.

Inside that curated context, the child makes their own choices. The peer group they end up in is, formally, theirs. The fact that they ended up in it, rather than another, is in part the result of the context their parents put them inside.

Most of the parental power in this work is upstream of the choice your child appears to be making. Use that power early. By the time you are arguing with a fifteen-year-old about a particular friend, the work that would have most changed the picture was done years before.

What Helps

Pick two or three prosocial environments and keep them running through the year. Sport plus music plus a service commitment is a strong default. Adjust to your child's interests and your family's circumstances.

Vet the environments. Watch a training session. Stay around for the first few weeks. Notice the adults. Notice what is laughed at and what is not. The brand on the door is not the room.

Coordinate with other parents. Some of the most effective peer-environment work happens when several families decide together that a particular sport, club or activity is going to be a fixture of their kids' weeks. The combined effort is greater than any single family's.

Make the time. Prosocial environments compete with screens. They will lose the competition unless they are written into the week as fixtures. Treat the training, the rehearsal, the volunteer shift as non-negotiable in the way only family priorities can be.

Do not over-program. A child does not need to be in five activities to belong inside two or three good peer environments. Over-programmed children burn out and drop everything, which leaves them with no peer environment at all. Two or three deep is better than five shallow.

Watch transitions. The shift from primary to secondary school, the move to a new neighbourhood, the loss of an activity, the end of a season. These are the moments peer environments collapse without anyone noticing, and they are the moments to deliberately rebuild.

Audit the household culture. The first peer culture is the family one. The work of the rest of this book applies here too.

Key Takeaways

The same biological and social mechanisms that let harmful behaviour spread through peer groups also let prosocial behaviour spread. Parents can use the second direction deliberately.

Diluting harmful peer influence by embedding a child in two or three prosocial environments works better, in most situations, than forbidding the harmful one outright.

Positive Peer Culture is a clinical model with decades of evidence in residential and school settings. The principle for ordinary families is the same. Adults can shape the social environments their children are formed inside.

A prosocial peer environment shows certain markers: attentive adult presence, a fair well-held standard, contribution and mastery as the currency of belonging, repair after rupture, and a sense of purpose larger than the group itself.

Australian options worth knowing about include sport, surf life saving, scouting and equivalent youth movements, music and performing arts ensembles, volunteer organisations, faith-based youth communities and outdoor education programmes.

Service activities do specific developmental work no amount of consumption can replace: they shift the child's centre of gravity from self to other, and they attract a particular kind of peer.

The family is the first peer culture. The currency of belonging at home calibrates the child's later choices about which external peer environments to seek out.

The most effective parental work in this area is upstream: curating the environments your child is exposed to, rather than trying to control individual friendships once a difficult one is already in place.

References

1. Vorrath, H. H., & Brendtro, L. K. (1985). Positive Peer Culture (2nd ed.). New York: Aldine de Gruyter.
2. Brendtro, L. K., Brokenleg, M., & Van Bockern, S. (2002). Reclaiming Youth at Risk: Our Hope for the Future (Rev. ed.). Bloomington, IN: Solution Tree Press.
3. Modecki, K. L., Blomfield Neira, C., & Barber, B. L. (2018). Finding what fits: Breadth of participation at the transition to high school mitigates declines in self-concept. Developmental Psychology, 54(10), 1954–1970.

CHAPTER 24
Holding the Line With Family and Visitors

The People Who Come Through Your Door

Most of this book has been about who is inside the household and what is going on between them. This chapter is about who comes in.

Extended family who visit, sometimes for hours, sometimes for weekends, sometimes for months. Friends of the parents who pass through. Friends of the children who do the same. The other parent at a sleepover. The coach who has Wednesday afternoon. The neighbour who comes for dinner. The former partner picking up a child. The new partner of a former partner. Any of these adults can become, briefly or extendedly, part of the household's emotional weather.

Most of them are wonderful. A grandparent whose presence steadies the children. An old friend whose laugh changes the room. A coach whose attention is one of the better influences in your child's life.

Some of them are not. A relative whose drinking has shifted from holiday tradition to weekly distress. A coach whose contempt for the children has been ignored too long. A friend's parent whose home turns out to run on rules and tones that you would never permit. A new partner whose presence makes one of your children visibly tense.

The principle of the bad apple effect, once you can see it, applies just as fully to these visiting adults as it does to children.

The chapter on online environments and the wider adult world (Chapter 13) introduced this. This chapter takes it further into the practical work of holding the line at the front door.

Sutton's Standard, Translated

In 2007, the Stanford organisational psychologist Robert Sutton published a now-famous book on what happens to teams that tolerate one persistently nasty person. He titled it bluntly, in his own deliberately abrasive language, and his argument was simple. Systems that allow chronic interpersonal cruelty from any one member, regardless of that person's other contributions, end up paying a much higher price than the cruelty is worth. The most useful thing leaders can do for their teams, Sutton argued, is to hold an absolute, unyielding standard against this kind of behaviour.[1]

The same principle applies, with a careful translation, to the family and visiting adults who shape your children's environment.

You are the leader of your household in a way no other adult in your child's life will be. The standard for how the people inside your home, and the people who come into it, treat your children and treat each other is yours to set. If you tolerate behaviour that contradicts that standard, your children read the toleration as the actual standard, regardless of what you say.

The translation is not about being harsh. It is about being clear. Some adults in your child's life will, through their own circumstances, history or character, be unable to behave in ways that fit your household. The work is to recognise that, name it without contempt, and adjust the access those adults have to your child accordingly.

Why Family Is the Hardest Place

The harder version of this work is rarely with strangers. It is with family.

Most people will, given a chance, hold a clear line with a stranger whose behaviour is harming their child. They will not invite that stranger into the home a second time. They will speak to the school, the coach, the club. They will protect their child.

The same people will tolerate behaviour from an extended family member that they would never accept from a stranger, often for years, often at real cost to the children inside their household.

The reasons are familiar. Loyalty. Family obligation. Cultural expectation. Not wanting to fracture relationships that have lasted decades. Fear of how a sibling, parent or in-law will react if a line is drawn. Fear of becoming the relative who is talked about. Memories of the same relative being warmer or kinder in earlier years. The hope that this Christmas will be different.

All of these reasons are real, and many of them are decent. The cost of letting them override your protective work, however, is paid by the children who are inside the household when the relative arrives.

Lindsay Gibson, in her widely-read book Adult Children of Emotionally Immature Parents, has documented the long shape of that cost as it plays out in adulthood.[2] The relatives whose behaviour was tolerated when their grandchildren or nieces and nephews were young become the relatives those grown children are now in therapy about. The pattern was visible at the time. It was simply not addressed.

If you are in this territory now, you are in the position to do the addressing your own parents, perhaps, did not do.

Specific Patterns

It helps to be clear about what kinds of behaviour, in visiting adults, are worth taking seriously enough to act on. The list overlaps with what Chapter 13 sketched and is worth restating with a sharper edge here.

An adult who routinely speaks to a child or about a child with contempt. Mockery of the child's body, fears, interests, achievements or vulnerabilities. Sneering at choices the parents have made about the child's care. Comments framed as jokes that, when looked at honestly, are not jokes.

An adult who is drunk or substance-affected around the children, repeatedly, in ways that change the household's emotional weather and that the children clearly register.

An adult who undermines the parents' authority directly in front of the children. The relative who tells your child the rule you just enforced is silly. The grandparent who slips the child the thing the parent has just said no to. The former partner who tells the child the rules at this house do not apply.

An adult whose discipline of children, when given any access to them, runs on shame, threats, hitting, public humiliation, or sustained anger. Your house is not an environment in which other adults are entitled to discipline your children. Even if those adults disagree with how you discipline them.

An adult whose attention to a particular child has become inappropriate. Excessive private time alone with one child. Comments about the child's body. Gifts or attention that make a parent's gut tighten. The sex of the adult and child are not the only thing that matters here. The pattern is what matters. Trust your gut on these.

An adult whose hostility toward your partner, the other parent, or another family member has begun spilling into the children's experience. The grandfather who cannot get through a Sunday lunch without disparaging your wife. The mother-in-law who makes a small comment about your husband every time she visits. Children read these patterns. They take notes about how adults are allowed to treat each other.

An adult who is in active, untreated mental-health crisis or addiction, where the unpredictability of their state is itself the harm. This is the most painful version of this conversation, because the harm is often not the adult's fault. The cost to the children is still real.

Each of these warrants different responses, but each warrants a response.

What Children Are Reading

When parents do not respond to a pattern in a visiting adult, the children take notes. The notes are rarely about the adult. The notes are about the parent.

If your child is watching you tolerate, year after year, a relative whose behaviour is clearly not okay, your child is concluding several things in their developing model of the world.

First, that this kind of behaviour is, in some sense, allowed. It happens. It does not produce a response. Therefore it is part of the range of how adults can behave.

Second, that you, the parent, do not have the standing or the willingness to stop it. Your authority, in the rest of the household, is now read against this gap.

Third, that they, the child, are not quite as protected as they have otherwise been told they are. The same parent who reassures them in other contexts is not, in this context, intervening.

These conclusions are rarely articulated. The child will not, at age nine, sit you down and explain them. They become part of the deep background of the child's expectations, and they show up in adult life decades later, often as a quiet difficulty trusting one's own perception of what is acceptable.

Acting on a visiting adult's behaviour, even imperfectly, even slowly, even in small ways, sends a different note. The note says that the parent has noticed, that the standard exists, and that the child is going to be defended. That note becomes part of the background too.

Setting the Standard at Your Door

There are several layers of response available to a parent dealing with a visiting adult whose behaviour is concerning. Most situations call for the lighter layers first, with the stronger ones reserved for cases where the lighter ones have not worked.

The first layer is private feedback. Quietly, without an audience, you say to the relative what you have noticed and what you would like to be different. "Mum, when you mock his interests in front of him, it lands harder than I think you realise. I would like you to stop doing it." Most people, given that feedback once, in private, with respect, will adjust. Not all. Some will adjust briefly and slip back. Some will be insulted that you raised it at all. The first layer tells you which kind of relative you are dealing with.

The second layer is in-the-moment intervention. When the behaviour happens, you respond at the time. Not aggressively. Not with a scene. With a clear short sentence. "That is not how we speak in this house." "I would like that to stop now, please." "He is leaving the room. We are going to give him some space." The intervention is for two audiences at once. The visiting adult, who learns where the line sits in your home. And the children, who watch you draw it.

The third layer is structural limitation of access. If the behaviour continues despite the first two layers, the relative's access to your home and to the children begins to change. They are not the babysitter any more. They are not invited for the weekend. They are seen at neutral venues, for shorter periods, with a parent visibly in the room. They do not have unsupervised access to a particular child. None of this requires a public announcement. Most of it is simply how things now happen.

The fourth layer is removal. In rare cases, the pattern is severe enough, or the relative's response to feedback is hostile enough, that they no longer come into your home and the children no longer go into theirs. This is hard, and it is usually done slowly, and it sometimes ends with a relationship that does not recover. But it is sometimes necessary. The children's safety inside their own home is not a negotiable item.

Most parents reading this chapter will not need the fourth layer. Many will need the second and third. All will, at some point in raising children, need at least the first.

The Other Parent Across Households

A particular version of this work, deserving its own brief mention, is the situation in which the visiting adult is the other parent or someone else from the post-separation household.

If you are co-parenting across two households, you do not control what happens in the other household. You do control what happens in yours, and you control the boundary at your front door.

If the children are returning from the other household having been around an adult whose behaviour is concerning, the same layers of response apply, with the difference that you may need legal advice, family-dispute-resolution support, or formal child-protection involvement to address the pattern.

In Australia, Family Relationship Centres, family lawyers, and (in serious cases) state child-protection services are the practical avenues. Headspace, GP referrals to a child psychologist, and family therapy can support the children themselves, regardless of what happens with the other household.

What does not work is asking the children to manage the situation themselves. Children should not be the ones reporting on what happens at the other house, mediating between adults, or carrying messages. Their job is to be children. Yours is to do the harder adult work.

The Conversation You Are Avoiding

Most parents who read a chapter like this can name, within thirty seconds, the relative or visiting adult whose behaviour they have been quietly tolerating for too long.

The conversation with that person, when it eventually happens, almost never goes as badly as the imagined version. It is also almost never as conclusive as parents hope. The relative often hears it, half-takes it on, slips back, hears it again, takes it on slightly more, slips back less. The household climate begins to recalibrate. The children read the recalibration.

The cost of not having the conversation, in most cases, is greater than the cost of having it. The first few weeks after a difficult conversation with a relative are uncomfortable. The years that follow, when the household is no longer organised around tolerating the pattern, tend to be quietly relieved.

If you cannot bring yourself to have the conversation, that is also useful information. Not having the conversation may be a sign that the relative's hold on you, individually, is itself an unresolved issue worth your own attention, perhaps with a clinician you trust. Many of us inherit the patterns we then struggle to address in our parents and siblings. Recognising that, and getting your own help with it, is part of how the family system finally changes.

What Helps

Be clear, in your own head, about your standard. What kinds of behaviour from a visiting adult are not okay in your home. Write it down if it helps. The clarity makes the rest much easier.

Notice the patterns, not the events. A single bad afternoon from a relative is not a campaign. A pattern repeated over months is. Most of the work in this chapter is about patterns.

Use the lightest layer that works. Private feedback first. In-the-moment intervention next. Structural limitation if the first two have not worked. Removal only if necessary.

Do not require a perfect script. The relative who hears your feedback once is doing some of the work. The relative who needs the same conversation three times is still adjusting more than they would have if you had said nothing.

Coordinate with your partner, where you have one. The most successful versions of this work happen when both adults in the household are aligned about the standard and willing to back each other in the conversations. Where you are not aligned, that disagreement is itself worth addressing first.

Get help where the pattern is bigger than the household. A family therapist, a clinician familiar with intergenerational patterns, a colleague who has been through similar work. You do not have to figure this out alone.

Let your children see some of it. Not all of it. They do not need to be in the difficult conversations. They do need to see, over time, that you are noticing things, drawing lines, and behaving differently from how the previous generation may have behaved. That visibility is itself part of how they internalise a different standard for their own future relationships.

Key Takeaways

The bad apple effect runs as readily through visiting adults as through children. The people who come into your home are part of your household's emotional weather while they are there.

Sutton's principle from organisational psychology applies, with translation: a household that tolerates chronic interpersonal cruelty from any one adult, regardless of their other contributions, ends up paying a higher price than the toleration is worth.

Family is the hardest place to hold this standard. Loyalty, obligation, cultural expectation and fear of fracture all push parents toward toleration. The cost of toleration, however, is paid by the children inside the household.

Patterns to take seriously include sustained contempt, repeated drunkenness around children, undermining of parental authority, shame-based discipline by relatives, inappropriate attention to a particular child, hostility spilling into the children's experience, and active untreated mental-health or addiction crisis.

Children take notes about what their parents tolerate. The notes shape their long-term model of how adults are allowed to behave and how protected they are.

There are layered responses available: private feedback, in-the-moment intervention, structural limitation of access, and (rarely) removal. Most parents will need the first three at various points in raising children.

Co-parenting across households introduces a particular version of this work, where the structural levers are different and outside professional help is often necessary.

The conversation you have been avoiding usually goes better than the imagined version, and the long-term cost of not having it is greater than the cost of having it.

References

1. Sutton, R. I. (2007). The No Asshole Rule: Building a Civilized Workplace and Surviving One That Isn't. New York: Business Plus / Warner Books. (See also Chapter 1.)

2. Gibson, L. C. (2015). Adult Children of Emotionally Immature Parents: How to Heal from Distant, Rejecting, or Self-Involved Parents. Oakland, CA: New Harbinger Publications.

3. Cavaiola, A. A., & Lavender, N. J. (2000). Toxic Coworkers: How to Deal with Dysfunctional People on the Job. Oakland, CA: New Harbinger Publications. (See also Chapter 1.)

CHAPTER 25
Repair After Rupture

Why Repair Is the Engine

Of all the practical work this book is asking parents to do, repair is the single most important.

It is the move that lets every other piece of the parenting work be imperfect. Calm authority does not have to be perfect, because there is repair. Holding the line does not have to be perfect, because there is repair. Welcoming feelings does not have to be perfect, because there is repair. Even the parents who arrive at this book having got many things wrong for years can become safer parents to their children, in months, by becoming reliable repairers.

Repair is also where most parents have the least training. The previous generation, on the whole, did not repair. Their parents did not repair. Most of us were raised inside households where rupture was followed by silence, distance, or eventually a return to normal without anyone naming what had happened. We carry that pattern into our own parenting without thinking, until something interrupts it.

The premise of this chapter is that the something can be us. We can become parents who repair. The skill is not innate. It is learnable. And when it lands inside a household, the household begins to feel different in ways that are easy to feel and hard to articulate.

Children raised by parents who repair are not children whose parents never get it wrong. They are children who have learned that getting it wrong is recoverable. That is one of the most useful things a child can learn, and it stays with them.

What Repair Actually Means

Repair is the name attachment researchers give to the deliberate process of returning to connection after something has ruptured it.

The American developmental psychologist Edward Tronick, whose still-face research was introduced in Chapter 10, gave the field one of its most reassuring findings in this area.[1] Parents and infants, in his observational studies, were out of sync with each other most of the time. Roughly seventy per cent of the time, by his measurements. The infants whose attachment outcomes were best, however, were not the ones whose parents stayed in sync the most. They were the ones whose parents reliably moved back into sync after the disconnections. The ruptures themselves were not the problem. The repairs after them were doing the work.

What this means in practical terms is that repair is not a sign of failure. It is the visible part of the parenting that actually builds secure attachment.

It also means that repair is not optional. A household in which ruptures happen and are not repaired is not a household where everyone has decided to move on. It is a household where the unspoken cost of each rupture accumulates, and the children quietly learn that disconnection is something they have to manage on their own.

Repair is also not the same as apology, although apology is often part of it. An apology is a single sentence. A repair is the relational move underneath the sentence. You can apologise without repairing. You can also repair, in some situations, without using the word sorry, although in most cases the word is part of how repair gets done.

The Four-Part Repair

A repair, properly done, has four pieces. They do not have to happen in the order listed, but all four usually need to be present for the repair to land.

The first piece is naming what happened. "I yelled at you when you came in from school today." "I lost my temper in the kitchen." "I said something unkind about your friend." The naming is concrete. It does not generalise ("I have been a bit stressed lately"). It does not minimise ("I got a bit cross"). It says, accurately, what occurred.

The second piece is taking responsibility. "That was on me. I was already stressed before that conversation, and I took it out on you. It was not okay." The taking of responsibility does not include explanations that function as excuses. It is allowed to include some context, briefly, but the context is not the load-bearing part.

The third piece is validating the impact. "I can see that hurt you. I can see you got really small for the rest of the afternoon." "I think it scared you." "I think it made you feel like I do not love you, which is not what is true." This is the part most parents skip, and it is the part the child most needs.

The fourth piece is naming what you are doing about it. "I am working on this. When I notice myself getting like that, I am going to step out of the room before I say anything." "I am going to keep working on it. I will get it wrong again. I am sorry." This is the part that turns the repair from a one-time event into a practice the child can rely on.

The whole conversation, in many cases, takes about two minutes. The cumulative impact of doing it consistently, over years, is enormous. The rare-but-perfect repair is far less powerful than the regular, imperfect, slightly clumsy repair done two hundred times across a childhood.

Repair After You Lost It With Your Child

The most common situation calling for repair is also the one most parents most often avoid.

You yelled at your child. Or said something sharp. Or threw the device across the room. Or used a tone that, replayed in your head an hour later, makes you wince. The child, depending on age, has either gone quiet, withdrawn to their room, or escalated their own behaviour in response.

Most parents, in the hours afterward, feel a familiar combination of guilt and reluctance to bring it up. The reluctance has several common voices. The child seems okay now, why stir it up. They will be embarrassed if you make a thing of it. You do not want them to think you are weak for apologising. You will sound performative if you say sorry too formally. You are not sure you did anything that wrong, given the circumstances. They started it.

Each of these voices has a small piece of plausibility, and each of them, taken together, is the reason the rupture goes unrepaired. The default position in most households is that ruptures simply pass without explicit acknowledgement. The household reverts. Everyone gets through the next meal. The thing is, in some sense, over.

It is not over for the child. The child has filed the moment somewhere, and what they have learned about it depends on whether you come back to it.

The repair, in practice, can be very short. "I want to talk to you about earlier. I yelled at you. That was not okay. I was already stressed about other things, and I took it out on you. I am sorry. It was not your fault. I am working on this and I will keep working on it." That is the entire conversation. It does not require you to explain the other things, defend yourself, or get the child to forgive you on the spot. It just needs to be said.

Some children will say it is fine. Some will need a longer conversation. Some will use the moment to tell you something else they had been holding. All of those are reasonable responses. None of them mean you should not have done the repair.

Repair Between Siblings

Sibling rupture is harder to repair, partly because the children are usually the same size emotionally, and partly because parents often try to make repair happen in the wrong moment.

The single most useful principle here is that the children cannot repair while either of them is still activated. The post-fight five minutes is not the repair window. The fight is just over. Bodies are still hot. Asking for an apology in this window almost always produces a half-hearted, resentful, performative apology that teaches the children that apologies are something you say to make adults stop nagging.

Wait. Let the bodies come down. Sometimes that takes ten minutes. Sometimes an hour. Sometimes a night's sleep. Then bring it up.

When you do bring it up, the parent is in the room as a structuring presence. Not as a judge. Not as a translator. As the adult who keeps the conversation safe.

A worked version, with two children, around eight and ten:

Parent: "I want both of you here for a minute. Earlier you had a really big fight in the kitchen. I am not going to make this a long thing, but I want each of you to tell the other one part. The first part is the part of what happened that you wish you had done differently. The second part, after both of you have done that, is one thing that you would like the other to do differently next time."

Older child: "I should not have called you stupid. I was angry but that was not okay."

Younger child: "I should not have hit you in the back. I was angry too."

Parent: "Okay. Now the second part. What is one thing you would like from the other next time?"

Older child: "Do not come in my room without asking."

Younger child: "Listen when I am talking, not just walk away."

Parent: "Both of those are reasonable. Anything else either of you wants to say?"

If the answer is no, the parent closes the moment with a brief connection move, often physical for younger children. "Okay. Thank you. I love you both."

What this conversation is doing is teaching repair as a skill. The children are learning that ruptures get followed by deliberate, structured repair, and that the repair includes both an acknowledgement of one's own part and a request for the other person's part. Over years, with practice, they begin to do this without the parent in the room.

PACE: A Lens for the Conversation

The clinical psychologist Daniel Hughes, working in attachment-focused family therapy, has spent decades developing a stance that he calls PACE.[2] It stands for Playfulness, Acceptance, Curiosity and Empathy, and it is one of the most useful single frames a parent can carry into a repair conversation.

Playfulness, in repair, does not mean making jokes about what happened. It means a tone of warmth, lightness where appropriate, that signals to the child that the relationship is not in danger. The repair conversation is not a tribunal. It is two people who love each other, sitting together to address something that went wrong.

Acceptance means meeting the child's experience without trying to argue them out of it. If they say the moment scared them, you do not say it was not that bad. If they say they felt unloved, you do not respond by reciting the evidence that you do love them. You accept what they tell you and let it land.

Curiosity means staying open about what was going on for them, rather than assuming you know. "Tell me what was happening for you when I came in." "What did you think when I raised my voice?" "What would have helped, in that moment, that I did not do?"

Empathy means putting yourself, briefly, in their experience and letting them know you have done so. "That must have felt awful." "I think it would have been confusing." "You must have felt like you could not do anything right."

PACE is not a script. It is a posture. The parent who has internalised it brings something different into a repair conversation than a parent who is approaching the conversation primarily as a problem to be wrapped up. The conversations land differently.

Common Mistakes in Repair

Several recurring mistakes are worth naming, because they take a repair that almost works and make it not work.

Repairing too quickly, while the child is still activated. The child is not yet able to receive the repair. The conversation produces resentment instead of resolution. Wait until the bodies have come down.

Repairing for yourself rather than for the child. The parent who comes in with their own guilt, in heavy emotional language, requesting comfort or forgiveness, has placed the burden of the repair back on the child. Repair is for the child. Your own guilt, real and reasonable as it is, belongs to your own self-work, not to the conversation with the child.

Wrapping the repair in justification. "I am sorry I yelled, but you really pushed me, and you know how I get when you do that." The justification cancels the apology. The child registers the second clause as the actual message and ignores the first. If you need to talk about what they did, do that as a separate conversation, not folded into the repair.

Demanding forgiveness. "Are we okay now?" "Do you forgive me?" The child, especially a younger child, will say yes because the parent is asking, regardless of how they actually feel. Repair is not a transaction. The forgiveness, if it comes, will arrive in its own time. Your job is to do the repair and trust the rest.

Over-explaining. A repair of two minutes does not need to become a thirty-minute conversation. The child is usually ready to be done well before the parent is. Watch for the moment they have heard what they needed to hear, and let the conversation close.

Making the same repair conversation about the same incident over and over again. Once the repair is done, it is done. Bringing it back up repeatedly turns it into a recurring source of anxiety for the child rather than a moment of healing.

Not repairing at all because you are not sure you got it perfectly right. Imperfect repair is enormously better than no repair. The standard is not flawless. The standard is that the child sees the parent come back.

When Repair Cannot Happen Yet

There are situations in which a clean repair is not immediately possible. They deserve naming honestly.

When you, the parent, are still too activated. If you cannot have the repair conversation without slipping back into defensiveness or another round of the original conflict, the repair is not ready to happen yet. Do your own regulation work first. Come back when you can hold yourself.

When the child is not ready. Some children, especially adolescents, will refuse the conversation when offered. Do not force it. Tell them, briefly, that you wanted to come back and acknowledge what happened, and that you are around when they are ready. Then leave it. Most children come back, in their own time, to receive the repair you offered.

When the rupture is not yet over. Some ruptures are still in progress. The behaviour is still happening. The household is still unsafe. Repair, in those situations, is premature. The first task is to address the underlying pattern. Repair becomes possible later.

When the rupture involves harm that is too large for a parent-led repair. Sustained pattern of contempt, physical harm, sexual harm, or behaviour that has produced clinical-level distress in the child. These situations need professional support, not a four-part conversation at the kitchen table. The clinician will help you figure out what an appropriate repair looks like and when it can happen.

Outside these situations, however, the bias should be toward repairing rather than not. Most parents err on the side of doing too little repair, not too much. If you find yourself wondering whether to repair a particular moment, the answer is almost always yes.

The Long View

There is a long-arc version of repair that is worth saying clearly, particularly for parents reading this book later in their parenting.

Repair is available across years, not just hours. A parent of an eighteen-year-old can repair a moment from when their child was eight, and the repair will land. A parent of a forty-year-old can repair a pattern from their child's adolescence, and the repair will land. The conversation is harder. The reception is sometimes longer in coming. But the move is the same one. Name what happened. Take responsibility. Validate the impact. Name what is different now.

Many adult children have spent decades waiting for their parents to do this work. Most parents who do it, even very late, find that it changes the relationship measurably. The adult child does not, in most cases, want a long apology. They want their parent to acknowledge, accurately, what they were inside as a child, and what the parent is now able to see that they could not see at the time.

If you are reading this chapter and recognising patterns in your own parenting, the same long-arc move is available to you. Repair is recoverable territory. There are very few situations in family life where repair, attempted in good faith, makes things worse than the silence it replaced.

What Helps

Lower the bar to entry. Repair does not require eloquence. Two minutes of plain language is enough. Most parents wait until they have a perfect script. Skip the script. Use ordinary words.

Repair the small things. Most repair work in a household is over small ruptures, not big ones. The sharp comment at breakfast. The dismissive reaction to a sibling. The phone you were on when the child wanted attention. These small repairs, done often, add up to a household that runs on repair as a default.

Practise on yourself. The parent who can name their own missteps, calmly, to themselves, has a much easier time naming them to a child. The internal practice supports the external one.

Co-repair where you are co-parenting. Where two adults are parenting together, repair is most effective when both are willing to do it. A child who watches one parent repair while the other holds the original line continues to receive a mixed message. Where you can, do the repair conversations together.

Notice the pattern of what you keep needing to repair. If you find yourself repairing the same kind of moment week after week, that is information. The pattern is the actual issue. Address it upstream. Sometimes that means more sleep, more support, less work, more help. Sometimes it means your own clinical work.

Do not measure repair by whether the child says you are forgiven. Measure it by whether the conversation happened. The forgiveness will come. The conversation is the move that matters.

Key Takeaways

Repair is the single most important practical move in this book. It allows every other piece of parenting work to be imperfect.

Tronick's research established that secure attachment is built less by parents who never get it wrong and more by parents who reliably return to connection after rupture. Repair is the actual mechanism.

A repair has four pieces: name what happened, take responsibility, validate the impact, name what you are doing about it. Most are short. Most can be done in two minutes.

After you have lost it with your child, repair is the move most parents avoid and most children most need. The voices that argue against it ("they seem fine now", "I do not want to make a thing of it") are the obstacles.

Sibling repair works best with the parent in the room as structuring presence rather than judge, and only after the bodies have come down.

Daniel Hughes's PACE stance (playfulness, acceptance, curiosity, empathy) is a useful posture for any repair conversation.

Common mistakes include repairing too early, repairing for yourself rather than the child, wrapping the repair in justification, demanding forgiveness, and not repairing at all because you are not sure you can do it perfectly.

Repair is available across years. Late repair, even with adult children, lands more reliably than parents expect.

The bar to entry is low. Two minutes, plain language, said often, will do enormous work over a childhood.

References

1. Tronick, E. (2007). The Neurobehavioral and Social-Emotional Development of Infants and Children. New York: W. W. Norton. (See also Chapter 10.)

2. Hughes, D. A. (2007). Attachment-Focused Family Therapy. New York: W. W. Norton.

3. Gottman, J. M., & Silver, N. (1999). The Seven Principles for Making Marriage Work. New York: Harmony / Crown Publishing.

CHAPTER 26
Accountability Without Shame

The Distinction That Changes Everything

There is a single distinction in this book that, once a parent has internalised it, changes how every difficult conversation with a child can go.

It is the distinction between guilt and shame.

On the surface, the words seem nearly interchangeable. We use them loosely in everyday speech. We say a child should feel guilty for what they have done. We say a parent feels ashamed of how they handled something. Most of us have never had the difference explained.

The difference, drawn from decades of empirical work, is one of the most clinically useful distinctions in modern psychology. Get it right and accountability becomes a tool for growth. Get it wrong and accountability becomes the very thing that hardens the behaviour you are trying to change.

This is the chapter where we take that distinction seriously and translate it into the parenting work.

Guilt and Shame Are Not the Same

The American psychologists June Tangney and Ronda Dearing have spent careers documenting what each of these emotions does inside a person, and how they differ. Their 2002 book Shame and Guilt remains the standard academic reference.[1] Brené

Brown's popular work, particularly Daring Greatly, has brought the distinction to a much wider audience.[2]

The distinction, in its simplest form, is this. Guilt focuses on the behaviour. Shame focuses on the self.

Guilt says, "I did something bad."

Shame says, "I am bad."

Those two sentences seem close. Inside the body, they are completely different states.

Guilt tends to motivate repair. The person feels uncomfortable about what they have done, wants to make it right, and has the cognitive bandwidth to think about how. They can apologise. They can take responsibility. They can talk about what happened. They are still themselves while they are doing it.

Shame tends to motivate concealment. The person feels that something is wrong with them at the level of their being. The discomfort is unbearable. The body's response is to hide, deny, defend, attack the person who triggered the shame, or shut down entirely. They cannot, in that state, sit with what they have done. They can only get away from it.

The implications for parenting are direct. A child who feels guilt about hitting their sister can usually engage with a conversation about what happened and how to repair it. A child who feels shame about hitting their sister cannot. They will deflect, deny, blame the sister, or collapse into the sense that they are a bad person who is beyond saving. Neither of those states is the place from which growth happens.

If you want a child to learn from a mistake, you need to keep them in the territory of guilt and out of the territory of shame.

What Shame Does to Accountability

Most parents who have struggled to get a child to take responsibility for something have, without realising it, been pushing the child further into shame, and then wondering why the child is not capable of the responsibility they are being asked to demonstrate.

The moves that produce shame are familiar.

Identity statements. "You are cruel." "You are a liar." "You are out of control." Each of these tells the child that the behaviour is who they are, not what they did.

Public correction. Being corrected in front of a sibling, a friend, a relative, a stranger. The shame is amplified by the audience.

Disgust on the parent's face. Children read facial expression accurately. A parent whose face says, in the moment of correction, that they find the child repulsive is delivering a shame message that the words may not have included.

Reaching for old failures. "This is just like what you did last month. You always do this." Generalising the current behaviour into a pattern of who they are.

Comparison with siblings or peers. "Why can your sister manage this and you cannot?" The implication is that something is wrong with this particular child.

Withdrawal of love. Going cold. Refusing eye contact. Sending the child to their room not for safety but for punishment. Telling the child, in tone if not in word, that they are not okay with you right now.

Each of these moves, on its own, is something most parents have done at some point. They become a problem when they are the default style of correction. A child raised in a household where correction routinely runs through these moves does not learn accountability. They learn to manage shame. The two are not the same skill.

What Shame-Free Accountability Looks Like

Accountability without shame has a specific architecture. The architecture is what allows a child to receive the correction, take the impact in, and do something useful with it.

It addresses the behaviour, not the identity. "That behaviour was unkind" lands very differently from "You are unkind." The first leaves the child intact while asking the behaviour to change. The second tells the child the behaviour is who they are.

It is delivered privately where possible. Correction in the absence of an audience is correction the child can metabolise. Correction in front of others becomes an event that is being witnessed, and shame piles on top of any genuine guilt that might have produced repair.

It comes from a parent who is regulated. The state of the parent matters more than the words. A regulated parent saying a hard thing lands as guidance. A dysregulated parent saying the same thing lands as attack.

It separates the behaviour from the relationship. The child needs to know, in the middle of the correction, that they are still loved. The relationship is not in question. The behaviour is the only thing on the table.

It invites repair rather than demanding it. "Let's work out how to make this right" is the invitation. "Apologise to your sister now" is a demand that almost always produces a hollow apology.

It ends. A correction that becomes a long lecture is a correction that has tipped into shame territory. The child stopped hearing it three sentences ago. Most useful corrections are short. Two minutes is plenty.

It is followed by repair where the parent has slipped. If, in the middle of the conversation, you crossed into shame territory, you say so. "I went too hard there. I should not have said it that way." The repair models the very behaviour you are trying to teach.

A Worked Conversation

The contrast between shame-based and shame-free correction is best seen in real time. Take the same incident and run it both ways.

The incident: a ten-year-old has, for the third time this fortnight, taken something from a younger sibling's room without asking. The younger sibling is in tears.

The shame version, ninety seconds:

Parent: "For God's sake. Why do you keep doing this? You know it is not okay. You always think the rules do not apply to you. Look at her. Look at what you have done. You are old enough to know better. I am sick of having this conversation. Go to your room. I do not even want to look at you right now."

What the child has heard: I am a bad child. I keep failing in the same way. My parent is exhausted by me. Looking at me is hard for them. There is something wrong with me. I should hide.

The shame-free version, ninety seconds:

Parent: "Mate. Come and sit with me for a second. I want to talk about what just happened. You went into your sister's room and took her thing without asking. This is the third time in two weeks. I need you to look at her face."

Child: "I just wanted it for a bit."

Parent: "I get that you wanted it. And taking it without asking is not okay, especially when she has asked you not to before. Look at how upset she is. That is what your action did. I am not telling you that you are a bad kid. I am telling you the behaviour has to change. What can you do right now to make this right?"

Child, after a pause: "Give it back. Say sorry."

Parent: "Yes. And what about the next time you want something of hers?"

Child: "Ask."

Parent: "That is what I need. Go and do that now. I love you. We will keep working on this."

Same incident. Same correction. Same accountability. The first version produces shame and a child who hides. The second version produces guilt, repair, and a child whose relationship with the parent is intact.

Notice what is the same in both. The behaviour is named. The behaviour is wrong. The behaviour has to change. Notice what is different. The first version attacks the child. The second version addresses the behaviour.

Restorative Practice in Family Form

The shame-free architecture is not a new invention. It overlaps significantly with what is known in schools and justice systems as restorative practice, a framework developed and elaborated through the International Institute for Restorative Practices and described in accessible form in Bob Costello, Joshua Wachtel and Ted Wachtel's Restorative Practices Handbook.[3]

Restorative practice rests on a simple shift. When something has gone wrong, the question is not, "Who is to blame and what should the punishment be?" The question is, "Who has been harmed, what do they need, and whose obligation is it to make it right?"

Translated into a family, the difference looks like this. A traditional correction asks, "Who started it? What rule was broken? What is the consequence?" A restorative correction asks, "Who has been hurt by what just happened? What do they need? What does the person responsible need to do to repair it? And what needs to change so this is less likely to happen again?"

The four restorative questions, written for parents, run something like this:

What happened?

What were you thinking and feeling at the time?

Who has been affected by what you did, and how?

What do you think you need to do to make it right?

Asked in a calm voice, with genuine curiosity, by a parent who is not interrogating but actually listening, these questions do enormous work. They move the child from defensiveness into reflection. They surface what was happening underneath the behaviour. They put the responsibility for repair, appropriately, in the child's hands. They keep the conversation focused on the people and the harm rather than on rules and punishments.

Some families find it useful to actually use these four questions, almost verbatim, as the structure of any conversation following an incident. Others adapt them. Either way, the underlying move is the same. Replace blame with repair, replace punishment with responsibility, and replace the shame-driven correction style with one that produces actual learning.

The Parent's Own Shame

There is a circular problem in this work that needs naming.

Most parents who recognise themselves in the shame-based correction style described above do not respond to that recognition by feeling guilty. They respond by feeling ashamed. They read the chapter, recognise the pattern, and immediately conclude that they are bad parents who have damaged their children.

If you have just had that reaction, please pause.

The very thing the chapter is asking you to give your child is the thing you have to give yourself. Shame about your own past parenting will not produce better parenting. It will produce a tired, defensive, self-attacking parent who is too busy feeling bad to actually change anything.

Guilt about specific moments you wish you had handled differently is useful. It motivates repair. It directs your attention to what you want to do differently next time. It does not require you to conclude anything about who you are as a person.

Shame about being a bad parent is useless. It produces nothing the children need.

The first repair, in many cases, is the one you do with yourself. "I have been doing some of this. I am going to do less of it. I am going to repair the moments I can repair, and I am going to keep going." That sentence, said honestly to yourself, is the start of the change.

If your own shame is too large to manage internally, that is also useful information. Many parents whose default correction style runs on shame learned that style from their own parents, who learned it from theirs. The pattern is intergenerational. Working with a clinician on the underlying material, in your own life, is one of the most useful pieces of family work you can do. It will be easier to give your child shame-free correction once you can give it to yourself.

When the Child Cannot Yet Hear It

Some children, in some moments, cannot receive any correction at all. The body is too activated. The shame is too close. The relationship is too strained.

Trying to deliver a beautifully crafted shame-free correction to a child in this state is a setup for failure. The conversation goes nowhere. The child shuts down or escalates. The parent gets frustrated and slips into the shame-based style they were trying to avoid.

When you are dealing with a child in this state, the move is not to push the conversation. It is to do the regulation work first.

Help them get their body down. A walk. A drink of water. A few minutes of being left alone. A small physical co-regulation gesture (a hand on the back, sitting near them without speaking). Whatever your child has historically responded to.

Wait. The conversation does not have to happen now. Most corrections work better when delayed by an hour, a day, sometimes a weekend. The cost of a brief delay is much smaller than the cost of trying to correct an unregulated child.

Repair the relationship before the correction. If you sense the child is convinced they are a bad person beyond saving, that is what needs addressing first, not the specific behaviour. "I want you to know I love you. We are going to talk about what happened, but I am not angry with you as a person. We will get through this." The correction comes after the relationship is steady enough to bear it.

Ask what they need. Sometimes children who cannot receive a correction can tell you what would make the correction land. "I want to talk about what happened earlier. What do you need from me first?" Some will say nothing. Some will say something useful. Either way, the asking has done some of the work.

What Helps

Notice your own correction style. Pay attention, over a week, to how you actually correct your children. Are you describing the behaviour or attacking the child? Are you private or public in your corrections? Is your face warm or hard while you are doing it? The honest answer is the data.

Substitute behaviour language for identity language. "You did X" rather than "You are X." This single shift, applied consistently, produces a different household within months.

Use the four restorative questions when something has gone wrong. They are short, transferable, and adaptable to almost any age and incident. They also model, every time you use them, the kind of reflection you want the child to internalise.

Do not punish the recognition of wrongdoing. A child who has come to you and admitted to something they did wrong has done one of the harder things a child can do. Reward the admission with a calm conversation, not a heavier consequence than they would have got if they had hidden it.

Repair the slips. When you have crossed into shame territory, name it and come back. The repair conversation from Chapter 25 applies here.

Be patient with the practice. A correction style takes time to change. The first few attempts at shame-free correction may feel awkward, performative, or unfamiliar. They land anyway. The habit becomes natural with practice.

Get help with your own pattern where it is needed. Some parents will not be able to deliver shame-free correction reliably while their own shame from their own childhood is unaddressed. Working on that material is part of the work.

Key Takeaways

Guilt and shame are different states. Guilt focuses on the behaviour and motivates repair. Shame focuses on the self and motivates concealment, denial or attack.

If you want a child to learn from a mistake, the work is to keep them in the territory of guilt and out of the territory of shame. Most parents, without realising, regularly do the opposite.

Common shame-producing moves include identity statements, public correction, disgust on the parent's face, generalising current behaviour into a fixed pattern, comparing with siblings, and withdrawing love.

Shame-free accountability addresses the behaviour rather than the identity, is delivered privately, comes from a regulated parent, separates the behaviour from the relationship, invites repair, ends, and is followed by parental repair where the parent has slipped.

Restorative practice, drawn from school and justice contexts, gives parents a useful four-question structure: what happened, what were you thinking and feeling, who has been affected and how, and what do you think you need to do to make it right.

The hardest version of this work is doing it on yourself first. Shame about your own parenting produces nothing the children need. Guilt about specific moments, by contrast, motivates change.

Some children, in some moments, cannot receive any correction. The move is to regulate first, repair the relationship before the correction, and let the conversation wait.

References

1. Tangney, J. P., & Dearing, R. L. (2002). Shame and Guilt. New York: Guilford Press. (See also Chapter 2.)
2. Brown, B. (2012). Daring Greatly: How the Courage to Be Vulnerable Transforms the Way We Live, Love, Parent, and Lead. New York: Gotham Books. (See also Chapter 2.)
3. Costello, B., Wachtel, J., & Wachtel, T. (2009). The Restorative Practices Handbook for Teachers, Disciplinarians and Administrators. Bethlehem, PA: International Institute for Restorative Practices.

CHAPTER 27

Decode First. Discipline Second. Repair Always.

The Three Moves

By this point in the book, the practical pieces are all on the table. Calm authority. Bigger, Stronger, Wiser, Kinder. The biological floor. Welcoming feelings while holding limits. Collaborative problem-solving. Engineering the peer environment. Holding the line with visiting adults. Repair after rupture. Accountability without shame.

What is missing is the synthesis. The single movement that draws all of those pieces into something a parent can carry into a hard moment.

The synthesis, in this book, is a three-move sequence:

Decode first. Discipline second. Repair always.

It is short enough to remember in the middle of a meltdown. It is deep enough that, once a parent has internalised it, almost any difficult parenting moment becomes navigable using its three pieces in order.

This is the chapter that walks through the three moves and runs them across four worked examples spanning toddlerhood through adolescence.

Decode First

The first move is to decode what you are looking at before responding to it.

Most parents, faced with a difficult behaviour, react to the surface. The hitting. The lying. The eye-roll. The slammed door. The behaviour gets named, the consequence gets delivered, the moment closes. The underlying signal, if there was one, never makes it into the conversation.

Decoding is the move that pauses the reaction long enough to ask what the behaviour is showing you. It draws on every chapter in the opening of this book. The wounds underneath (Chapter 6). The skill gaps Greene's CPS framework points to (Chapter 21). The biological floor (Chapter 16). The family system (Chapter 4). The peer environment (Chapter 11).

Practical decoding questions, useful in almost any situation:

- What is the child trying to get, avoid, communicate, or protect with this behaviour?
- What is the state of their nervous system right now?
- What might be lagging in their skill set that this behaviour is showing me?
- What is happening in the wider context (school, peers, household, sleep, food, screens) that might be feeding this?
- What old wound, if any, might this be sitting on top of?

Decoding does not require a perfect answer to all five questions. It requires the parent to slow down long enough to ask any of them. Even one accurate guess about what is going on changes the response that follows.

Crucially, decoding is not the same as excusing. The behaviour still has to be addressed. Decoding just makes sure that what gets addressed is the actual thing, not just the surface symptom.

Discipline Second

The second move is the response itself. The boundary, the correction, the consequence, the conversation, the limit. Whatever the situation requires.

What this book has been arguing throughout is that discipline, in the original sense of the word, is not punishment. It is teaching. The Latin root of discipline is the same as the root of disciple, meaning a learner. Discipline, properly done, is the process by which a child learns what is okay and what is not, what is theirs to repair when they have broken it, and what kind of human being they are growing into.

Discipline that runs on punishment, threat or shame produces compliance, sometimes, in the short term. It does not produce the deeper learning the word originally meant.

Discipline that runs on calm authority, clear limits, age-appropriate consequences, and shame-free correction produces the deeper learning. It is also less exhausting for everyone involved, because the household stops running on a constant stream of escalating consequences and starts running on standards that hold.

The discipline move is informed by the decode that came before it. A parent who has decoded that the child's hitting is sitting on top of unbearable shame about a failure at school will deliver a different limit (still firm, still clear) than a parent who has decoded the same hitting as a frustration-tolerance gap. Both responses include the boundary. Each is shaped by what is underneath.

The Australian parenting educator Maggie Dent, whose work on raising boys and on resilience is widely read across this country, makes a similar point in slightly different language.[1] [2] Effective discipline, she argues, is calm, consistent, connected, and pitched at the actual developmental capacity of the child. The phrase that captures it for many of her readers is parenting with both spine and heart. The spine without the heart produces harsh authoritarianism. The heart without the spine produces permissiveness. The combination produces something children can grow inside.

Repair Always

The third move runs through everything else.

Repair is not what you do when you have got it wrong. It is what you do every time the relationship has been temporarily strained by the work of decoding and disciplining. After a hard conversation, a held boundary, a meltdown, a consequence, a moment that has briefly disconnected the parent and the child, repair is the move that re-establishes the connection.

Repair, as Chapter 25 set out, has four pieces of its own. Name what happened. Take responsibility where there is responsibility to take. Validate the impact. Name what you are doing about it.

What makes repair always rather than repair sometimes is that the parent does not wait for a serious rupture to repair. They repair after small frictions. They repair after a sharp tone, a missed moment, a flicker of impatience. The household runs on a steady, almost invisible practice of small repairs. By the time anything large happens, the repair muscle is already strong.

Children raised in this practice grow into adolescents and then adults who repair too. They become capable of saying, in their own relationships, the words they watched their parent say. The intergenerational transmission of repair is one of the more powerful gifts a parent can give. It is also the gift most easily lost in households where ruptures are followed by silence.

The three moves run together. Decode. Discipline. Repair. The order matters. The first changes what the second looks like. The third makes both available the next time around.

Worked Example: A Three-Year-Old Who Has Hit Their Sister

The behaviour: a three-year-old has just hit their younger sister, who is now crying in the corner.

Decode. Three-year-olds are not strategic actors. The hitting is almost always a frustration-tolerance gap meeting an unmet need. Maybe she had a toy he wanted. Maybe he was tired. Maybe he is hungry. Maybe she did something that humiliated him in some small way only he registered. His nervous system is in fight mode. He has very little capacity, at this age, to translate frustration into words.

Discipline. The parent gets between the children. The harming child is moved away physically, gently. The harmed child is comforted first. "You are okay. Mum has got you." Then the harming child gets the response. The voice is calm. The face is neutral. "Hitting is not okay. Hitting hurts. We do not hit in this family." The child may be upset, may even be hitting at the air. The parent stays steady. "I can see you were really cross. It is still not okay to hit."

If the child cannot calm down, the parent stays with them. Not in punishment. In presence. "I am going to sit with you until your body comes down. Then we will go and check on your sister."

Repair. Once everyone is regulated, often within ten minutes at this age, the parent walks the child through the small reconciliation. "Let's go and see her. What can we say?" The child may be capable of a soft "sorry". They may not. They may need to give a hug instead. The parent makes the gesture happen, gently.

Then the parent's own repair, briefly. "You and I had a hard moment too. I love you. We are okay."

Notice what is not in this example. No long lecture. No shame. No drawn-out time-out alone. No identity statement ("you are aggressive"). The boundary was crystal clear. The child was held through it. The relationship is intact. He has had a small experience of the formula in action.

Worked Example: An Eight-Year-Old Who Has Lied

The behaviour: an eight-year-old has been caught in a lie about whether she finished her homework.

Decode. Lying at this age is almost always about the cost of telling the truth. The child has calculated, probably without realising she is calculating, that the consequence of admitting she did not finish is worse than the consequence of being caught lying. That calculation may be reasonable based on past experience. It may be exaggerated by a perfectionist temperament, or by a recent moment when telling the truth produced a sharp parental response. The decode question is not just why she lied. It is why the truth felt unsafe.

Discipline. Privately. Calmly. "I want to talk about the homework. You told me you had finished it. Your teacher emailed me to say you had not handed it in. I am not going to be cross with you for a moment. I want to understand. Why did the truth feel hard to tell?"

The child may stonewall. "I forgot." The parent stays curious. "That is possible. It is also possible something about telling me felt scary. If it was that, I would rather know."

Eventually, often after a long pause, the child says something more useful. "I knew you would be upset." "I did not want to do it." "I was tired." Whatever it is, the parent receives it without disputing. "Okay. That makes sense. The lying is still not okay. We need honesty in this family. We are going to work out together how to make telling the truth easier next time. And we are going to deal with the homework."

Then a short consequence proportionate to the actual issue. The homework gets done tonight, with the parent nearby. Screen time tomorrow is reduced because the time was spent on the homework that was supposed to have been finished. The child knows what the consequence is, and why.

Repair. "Thank you for telling me what was going on. I know that was not easy. I love you. We are going to keep working on the truth being safe to tell in this house."

Noticc thc work that just happened. The lie has been addressed. A consequence has been delivered. And the underlying issue, that the truth had become unsafe, has been named and put on the table for ongoing work. None of that is possible if the discipline move had come first, before the decode.

Worked Example: An Eleven-Year-Old Who Has Spoken With Contempt

The behaviour: an eleven-year-old has just rolled her eyes at her father's request and said, in a tone everyone in the room felt, "Whatever."

Decode. Eleven is the entry point to the years where peer culture begins to noticeably shift the child's vocabulary, tone, and posture. The contempt was almost certainly imported. From a particular friend group, an online creator she follows, a YouTube channel, a sibling, somewhere. The contempt is not, at this age, a settled feature of who she is. It is a borrowed style. She is trying it out.

What is also true is that contempt, even imported, has to land somewhere. If it lands without being addressed, the household is teaching her that the style is acceptable here. Over time, what was borrowed becomes hers.

Discipline. Not in front of an audience if there is one. Privately, calmly, soon after. "I want to talk about earlier. The way you said 'whatever' had a tone in it that I am not okay with. It was contemptuous. I would not say that to you. Your mother and I do not say it to each other. I do not want it in this house."

The child may push back. "Everyone says that." "It was a joke." "You are being too sensitive." The parent stays steady. "I hear you. It is still not how we speak in this family. I am not going to make a long thing of it. I am asking you to not use that tone with me again."

Notice the absence of escalation. The parent has not threatened a consequence. They have not said the child is rude or disrespectful as identity claims. They have named the behaviour, named the standard, and asked for it to stop. Most eleven-year-olds, at this point, will adjust. If the behaviour continues, the conversation deepens, and consequences may follow. Most of the time it does not need to.

Repair. Within the same conversation or shortly after. "That was a hard thing to bring up. I love you. I know you are growing into yourself. I want you to bring more of yourself, not less. The contempt is not the part I want more of."

What this conversation just modelled, alongside everything else, is how to address contempt with someone you love without using contempt yourself. That modelling is doing more work than the words.

Worked Example: A Fifteen-Year-Old Who Has Broken Curfew

The behaviour: a fifteen-year-old came home at one in the morning, two hours after the agreed curfew, after texting at midnight that he was on his way.

Decode. Adolescents push curfews. That is part of what the developmental period does. The question is not just whether he broke the rule. The question is what was happening for him that the rule did not survive. Was he with people he was finding it hard to leave? Was he scared something would happen if he left first? Was he safer staying than catching a late train alone? Was he testing whether the rule would be enforced? Was he trying to belong with a group whose currency includes lateness?

All of these are possible. The decode requires asking, not assuming.

Discipline. Not at one in the morning. The conversation at one in the morning is not productive for either of you. The curfew has been broken; the consequence is on the table. The conversation is for the next day, when both of you have slept.

The next morning, calmly, sitting at the kitchen table. "You came home two hours late last night. I want to hear what happened."

Adolescent: "I texted you."

Parent: "You did. You also did not actually come home for two hours. I want to understand what was going on."

Adolescent, after a pause: "I was with [friend] and her dad was supposed to drive me but he was having a fight with her mum and I did not want to ask in the middle of it. I waited."

Parent: "That makes sense. You could have called me. I would have come and got you."

Adolescent: "I did not want to make a thing of it."

Parent: "Got it. Here is the deal. I would rather have a phone call at midnight than a son who is two hours late and not communicating clearly. The rule is the rule. Curfew is the same. You are losing the next two weekends out, because the consequence has to mean something. After that, we are back to normal. And here is what I want you to take from this conversation. If something like that happens again, you call me. Even if you think it is going to make a thing. I would rather have the thing than have you stuck somewhere working it out alone."

Repair. "I love you. I am proud that you actually told me what happened. We will keep doing this."

Notice what just happened. The decode produced new information that the parent did not have. The discipline still landed. The consequence still stands. And the underlying lesson, that calling Mum or Dad in a difficult situation is the right move rather than the embarrassing move, got delivered explicitly.

This is the kind of conversation that, repeated over years, builds an adolescent who calls their parent when they are seventeen and stuck somewhere. The conversation that just punishes does not produce that adolescent.

When the Formula Does Not Land Cleanly

These four worked examples are clean. Real situations rarely are.

Sometimes the decode is wrong. You think the hitting was about frustration tolerance, and it turns out the child has been targeted at school all week and has been carrying the rage home. The discipline you delivered was technically correct but missed the actual issue. That is okay. You decode again, address the new information, and adjust.

Sometimes the discipline does not land. The child is too dysregulated, too angry, too humiliated, too tired. The conversation does not work. That is okay too. Step out. Let the bodies come down. Try again later. Not every moment is workable in real time.

Sometimes the repair is refused. Some children, especially adolescents, will not engage with a repair conversation when offered. Do not force it. Tell them you are around when they are ready, and leave it. Most come back in their own time.

Sometimes you, the parent, are the one who cannot run the formula in the moment. You are too tired. You are too activated. The day has been too long. That is okay. The decode and discipline do not have to be perfect every time. The formula is a guide, not a test. A messy attempt at the formula, repeated often, builds the household more than a perfect attempt would.

And sometimes, despite everything, the same problem keeps coming back. That is when the underlying pattern needs more than the formula can address. It needs the deeper work of the earlier chapters: looking at the family system, the wounds, the biological floor, the peer environment. It needs, often, professional help.

The Long Practice

Most parenting books offer techniques. The techniques work in the abstract. Real parenting happens at six in the evening, with everyone tired, the dinner half-cooked, and at least one child melting down about something inscrutable.

The formula in this chapter is not a technique. It is a stance the parent learns to carry into the actual evening. Decode first. Discipline second. Repair always. Spoken or unspoken, the three moves are running through the parent's head as the situation unfolds.

The practice gets easier. Parents who have been working on this for six months notice that the decode happens almost automatically. They are reading what is going on under the behaviour without having to consciously try. The discipline has become quieter, firmer, less escalating. The repair has become a regular practice rather than a special event.

Children growing up in this household notice the difference too. They begin to internalise the same three moves in their own dealings with siblings, friends, and eventually their own children.

The formula transmits across generations more reliably than almost any other parenting practice, because it is not a rule. It is a way of being with each other in the harder moments. That way of being is what the children take.

What Helps

Run the formula deliberately for a few weeks. Out loud, if it helps. "Let me decode this for a second. What is going on for him?" The deliberate practice makes the eventual reflexive use much faster.

Talk it through with your co-parent or a trusted friend. After a difficult moment, run through it. What did I decode? Was the discipline the right shape? Did I repair? The reflection compounds.

Notice when you skip a move. Most slips happen when one of the three moves gets dropped. Skipping the decode produces a discipline that misses the point. Skipping the discipline produces a permissive moment that lets the behaviour stand. Skipping the repair leaves the relationship subtly strained.

Use the formula on yourself. The same three moves work for the parent's own behaviour. Decode what was going on for you. Take the discipline (in the form of self-correction or a change you are going to make). Repair where you have crossed a line.

Be patient. The formula is not a switch. It is a practice that lands gradually. Six months in, it begins to feel native. Two years in, it is the way you parent.

Write the three lines on something you will see. Some parents put them on the fridge. Some on a phone wallpaper. Some on the inside of a kitchen cupboard. The repetition matters more than the location.

Key Takeaways

The synthesis of the practical work in this book runs as a three-move sequence: Decode first, Discipline second, Repair always.

Decoding is the move that pauses the reaction long enough to ask what the behaviour is showing. It draws on the wounds underneath, the skill gaps, the biological floor, the family system, and the peer environment.

Discipline, in the original sense of the word, is teaching, not punishment. Discipline informed by the decode is shaped to address the actual issue, not just the surface behaviour.

Repair runs through everything else. Small repairs, done often, build the household muscle long before any major rupture.

Worked examples across age stages (toddler, primary, tween, teen) show how the same three-move structure adapts to different developmental capacities while remaining the same underlying practice.

Real situations are messy. The formula tolerates imperfection, missed moments, mis-decoded situations and refused repairs. A messy attempt at the formula, repeated often, builds the household more than a perfect attempt would.

Where the same problem keeps recurring, the answer is rarely a better technique. It is the deeper work the rest of this book points toward, often supported by professional help.

The three moves transmit across generations. Children raised inside this practice tend to use it themselves with their own children. That is one of the more powerful gifts a parent can give.

References

1. Dent, M. (2017). Real Kids in an Unreal World: Building Resilience and Self-Esteem in Today's Children (2nd ed.). Murwillumbah, NSW: Pennington Publications.
2. Dent, M. (2018). Mothering Our Boys: A Guide for Mums of Sons. Murwillumbah, NSW: Pennington Publications.

CHAPTER 28
Belonging Without Self-Abandonment

The Question Underneath It All

If the rest of this book has been about how to keep harmful patterns out of a child's developing world, this chapter is about the deeper question that sits underneath all of it.

What kind of human being are you trying to raise?

Most parents, asked the question directly, can answer it. They want a child who is kind. Honest. Resilient. Confident. Capable of love. Capable of work. Capable of being themselves in the company of other people without dissolving into whoever those other people happen to be.

That last piece is the one this chapter is about. The capacity, in a child and then in an adult, to belong somewhere without losing themselves to it.

It is one of the harder developmental tasks a human being is asked to manage. It is also the task most directly threatened by everything this book has been describing. The bad apple effect runs through children whose internal anchor has not yet been built. They reach the room, find that the room has its own currency, and adapt to the currency at the cost of the self that arrived. The work of the parent is not to keep them out of the room. The world has too many rooms. The work is to give the child enough internal anchor that they can enter any of those rooms, recognise the currency, and decide whether and how much of themselves to spend on it.

why children, and adolescents in particular, are so willing to abandon parts of themselves to belong.

Belonging is not optional for a developing human. It is one of the deepest needs the species has. Children are wired, from infancy, to seek and maintain attachment to the people around them. The drive to belong is older than language, older than thought, older than reason. It runs underneath all of those.

When the choice is presented to a child between belonging on terms that cost them part of themselves, and not belonging at all, most of them will pay the cost. Their nervous system will pay it almost without consulting them. The cost may be paid in voice, in confidence, in interests, in friendships, in opinions, in the body's relationship with food, in the willingness to take up space.

This is not a moral failure on the child's part. It is a survival decision the body has made before the mind has had a chance to weigh in.

The work of parenting is not to override this drive. It cannot be overridden. The work is to provide a parallel, more reliable belonging from earlier in the child's life. A child who arrives at adolescence already belonging somewhere (to their family, to a sense of who they are, to a few rooms whose currency they recognise as good) has options when a new room arrives. They can choose. They can decide whether the cost is one they want to pay. They can leave a room without losing the entire experience of belonging.

A child who arrives at adolescence belonging nowhere reliably has none of those options. The first room that offers belonging at almost any cost will get the cost.

What Self-Abandonment Looks Like

Self-abandonment is the word for what happens when a child, to keep their belonging in a particular room, leaves part of themselves outside it.

It looks different at different ages.

In a five-year-old, self-abandonment may look like the child becoming whoever the louder child in the playgroup is that week. They drop a previous interest, take up the louder child's interest, copy their phrases, abandon a friendship to be in the new one. Most of this is normal developmental flexibility. It crosses into self-abandonment when the child loses access to their own preferences in the process and begins to assume that they have to be whoever the room is asking them to be.

In a nine-year-old, it may look like the child who has stopped putting their hand up at school because no one else does. The child who has put away the book they were excited about because someone else mocked it. The child whose laugh, around their friends, is no longer their laugh. The child who has begun to dress, talk, eat or move differently because the version of themselves they used to be is no longer landing.

In a twelve-year-old, it may look like the child who has gone quiet at the family dinner because their friend group has decided that family dinners are embarrassing. The child who has stopped showing you the things they make. The child who is, suddenly, mortified by you in public.

In a fifteen-year-old, it may look like the adolescent who is performing a personality at school that does not match the personality at home. The adolescent who has begun to drink, vape, scroll, opine or post in ways that match the group rather than the person. The adolescent who has, in some real sense, become unrecognisable to themselves.

Some of this is normal developmental shedding. Adolescents are supposed to try on identities. The shedding becomes self-abandonment when the underlying child is no longer accessible, even to themselves. They have not just tried on a new self. They have lost contact with the old one.

The job of the parent is to keep a thread to the original child available, even while the child experiments with the new versions, so that the child can come back to themselves when they are ready.

Identity as Anchor

The American developmental psychologist Erik Erikson, in his 1968 book Identity: Youth and Crisis, named identity formation as one of the central developmental tasks of adolescence.[1] His framework, with refinements added by James Marcia and others over the following decades, has organised most of what the field has thought about identity since.

What Erikson named, in clinical detail, was that identity is not just a feature a young person has or does not have. It is a process. The young person is not given an identity by their family, their culture or their peers. They build one over years, through trying things on, taking things off, returning to things, integrating contradictions, and slowly arriving at a working sense of who they are and what they want.

The healthier the process is, in Erikson's model, the more securely the young person ends up rooted in something. They can describe what they value. They can describe what they want. They can describe what they will not do. They have, in the body and in the mind, an anchor.

The less healthy versions of the process produce a young person who has either foreclosed (taken on an identity given to them by the family or peer group without testing it) or remained diffuse (unable to commit to anything because they have not yet found their own ground).

Both unhealthy patterns produce a young person who is more vulnerable to the bad apple effect. The foreclosed identity collapses the moment a louder room offers a different identity. The diffuse identity will adopt almost any room's currency in the absence of an internal one.

The parental work, then, is to support the building of the anchor. Not by handing the child a finished identity. By giving them the conditions in which they can build their own.

Building Internal Belonging Inside the Family

The first place a child learns whether they are someone, in their own right, is the family.

Internal belonging at home is different from being loved at home, and a household can give one without giving the other. A child can be deeply loved by their parents and still grow up without a clear sense of who they are inside their own household. The love alone does not build the anchor. The anchor is built by the family's daily practice of recognising and naming the actual child.

small and accumulative.

The parent who notices the things the child is interested in and treats those interests as worth taking seriously. The mother who learns the names of the dinosaurs because her son is in his dinosaur period. The father who watches the matches his daughter cares about because she cares about them. The parent who knows which book the child is currently reading, which song they are currently into, which show they are currently following.

The parent who asks for the child's opinion and treats the answer as data rather than as something cute. "What do you think we should do about this?" is a powerful sentence said to a six-year-old. It is even more powerful said to a sixteen-year-old.

The parent who can describe their child accurately. Not in glowing terms. Not in deficit terms. In specific, observed, individual terms. "You are someone who is patient with smaller children but loses patience with adults who are not following the conversation. You are funny in a dry way. You take longer to make decisions than your sister does, and you make better decisions when you take that time. You are not actually shy. You are private." A child who has been seen this accurately, repeatedly, knows themselves better than a child who has been generally praised.

The parent who lets the child be different from the parent. The hardest version of this is for parents whose own self-image is bound up in their child's likeness to them. The child who is quieter than the parent expected. The child who is louder. The child whose interests, sexuality, politics or temperament does not match the parent's. The capacity to receive a child accurately, including the parts that surprise you, is part of how the child learns that they are someone. If the parent can only meet the version of the child that confirms the parent's expectations, the child will, often quietly, begin to perform that version and put the rest somewhere else.

Named Values

One specific practice, drawn from family-systems work and from values-driven parenting traditions, is worth recommending here. It is the practice of naming, explicitly, what the family stands for.

Most families have implicit values. Honesty. Kindness. Hard work. Looking after each other. Standing up for people who cannot stand up for themselves. Treating animals well. Trying things even when they are hard. Telling the truth even when it costs.

The values are real. They are present in how the household runs. They are usually not, however, named.

Children raised inside an unnamed value system absorb most of it through observation. That is enormous, and it is not nothing. But children raised inside a named value system can do something more. They can carry the names with them into rooms where the parents are not present. They can use the names as a point of reference when they are deciding what to do. They can recognise, when a peer group's currency contradicts a family value, that there is a contradiction.

Naming the values is not a sermon. It is woven into ordinary moments. "In our family, we tell the truth even when it is hard." "In our family, we do not speak about other people behind their backs." "In our family, we look out for the kid no one else is looking out for." Said quietly, repeatedly, over years, these sentences become part of the child's internal furniture. They become things the child can later use to anchor themselves in the rooms the parent does not get to attend.

It is also worth being honest with yourself about which values are really yours, rather than which ones you think you are supposed to claim. The values that hold up in your family are the ones the parents live. A value spoken about and not lived produces a cynical child. A value lived, named, and occasionally articulated produces a child with a working compass.

Family Rituals

Underneath the named values, there is something even more foundational. The actual rhythms of the family week.

Most of the deepest belonging children carry into adulthood is built by repetition rather than by major events. The Friday night dinner that always happens. The Sunday walk. The birthday tradition that has been the same every year since they can remember. The way the house smells in the morning. The mug their parent always uses. The phrase one parent always says before bed. The annual trip somewhere familiar. The song the family always sings on a particular drive.

These rituals are usually unremarkable to the parents living through them. They are also some of the most powerful identity-building work the family is doing.

What rituals do, in the developing child's nervous system, is install a sense of continuity and recognisability that becomes part of the self. The child who has these rituals knows what their life is. They can describe it. They can return to it. They can tell people about it. The rituals become an internal home.

The child without rituals does not have this resource. Their week is a sequence of unrelated events. Their life, when they try to describe it, is harder to describe. Their sense of self has fewer hooks to hang on.

If your family has rituals already, protect them. They are doing more work than they look like they are doing. If your family does not have many, you can build some. They do not need to be elaborate. The most powerful family rituals are usually the most ordinary. Pancakes on Saturday morning. The same restaurant for birthdays. A specific walk after dinner on Sunday. The deliberate boring repetition is the point.

Helping Children Notice When They Are Self-Abandoning

All of the work above is upstream. By adolescence, you can also do something more direct. You can teach the child to notice, in themselves, when they are self-abandoning, and to give the noticing a name.

This is harder than it sounds, because most adolescents will not respond to a direct lecture about self-abandonment. The work is gentler.

When you notice your child has come back from a particular peer environment seeming smaller, quieter or less themselves, you can name what you have noticed. "I noticed you were a bit different at dinner. Like you were not quite there. I am wondering if something happened with [friend]." Not as accusation. As observation.

When your child describes a moment in which they did something that seems unlike them, you can ask, gently, what was happening for them. "What were you noticing in your body when [the thing] happened? Did it feel like you, or did it feel like you were performing something?"

When they have done something they regret, a few hours later, you can name the pattern without weight. "It is hard to be the only one who does not laugh at the joke when everyone else is laughing. I have been there. I do not always get it right either."

Over time, with enough conversations of this kind, the adolescent develops their own internal language for the experience. They start to be able to say, even to themselves, "That was not me. I was performing." Once they have that language, they have a tool the bad apple effect cannot easily get past.

What you are giving them is not a rule. You are giving them a self-noticing capacity that they can apply in any room they find themselves in for the rest of their life.

The Long Arc

the work in this chapter is the work of years, not weeks. A child does not arrive at a stable internal anchor by sixteen because their parents read this chapter when they were eight. The anchor builds slowly. The named values land repeatedly over years before they become internal furniture. The rituals are doing their work in the background even when the family is not noticing.

By young adulthood, in a household where this work has been happening, the difference shows. The young adult can describe themselves accurately. They have things they care about that are theirs. They can be in a room without disappearing into it. They can have a difficult friend without becoming the friend. They can take a stand without becoming preachy. They can love their family while disagreeing with them.

These young adults also tend to have something else. A capacity to recognise and seek out other people who have done similar work. They are drawn to friends and partners who are themselves. The currency they look for, in the rooms they enter as adults, is the currency they grew up inside.

That last point is the most powerful argument for the work this chapter is asking. The child you raise in this practice does not just become a more intact young person. They become an adult who chooses, in turn, partners and friendships and work environments where the same intactness is possible. The bad apple effect they were vulnerable to as a child has been replaced, in adulthood, by a relatively reliable taste for environments where they do not have to abandon themselves to belong.

That is, in some ways, the deepest gift this book is asking parents to try to give.

What Helps

See your child accurately. Not as you wish they were. Not as you fear they are. Specifically, in their actual particularity, including the parts that surprise you.

Take their interests seriously. Even the ones you find boring. Especially the ones you find boring. The taking-seriously is what tells the child their interests are real, and that they are someone whose interests are worth having.

Name the family's values. Quietly, repeatedly, in ordinary moments. The naming becomes internal furniture.

Protect the rituals. Build new ones if you do not have many. Boring repetition is the point.

Notice when your child has come home smaller than they left. Name it without weight. The noticing teaches them to notice for themselves.

Let them be different from you. The version of your child that surprises you is the most important version to be able to receive.

Stay in the long view. The work compounds. A six-year-old's anchor is barely visible. A sixteen-year-old's, in the same household, will be obvious.

Key Takeaways

Self-abandonment is what happens when a child, to keep belonging in a particular room, leaves part of themselves outside it. It is not a moral failure; it is a survival decision the body makes before the mind weighs in.

The job of the parent is not to override the drive to belong (which cannot be overridden) but to provide an earlier, more reliable belonging through the family, so the child has options when later rooms arrive.

Identity, in Erikson's framework, is built rather than given. The healthier the process, the more securely the young person ends up rooted. Foreclosed and diffuse identities, by contrast, are particularly vulnerable to harmful peer influence.

Internal belonging at home is different from being loved at home. It is built through the family's daily practice of recognising and naming the actual child.

Naming the family's values explicitly, in ordinary moments, gives the child portable furniture they can carry into rooms where the parents are not present.

Family rituals (Friday dinner, Sunday walk, the same birthday tradition) do enormous identity-building work. The boring repetition is the point.

Adolescents can be helped to notice when they are self-abandoning, gently, through observation and ordinary conversation rather than through lecture.

The work of this chapter is the work of years, not weeks. The compounding shows up by young adulthood as a young person who can be in a room without disappearing into it.

References

1. Erikson, E. H. (1968). Identity: Youth and Crisis. New York: W. W. Norton.

2. Marcia, J. E. (1980). Identity in adolescence. In J. Adelson (Ed.), Handbook of Adolescent Psychology (pp. 159–187). New York: Wiley.

3. Bowlby, J. (1969). Attachment and Loss, Vol. 1: Attachment. New York: Basic Books. (See also Chapter 6.)

CHAPTER 29

Becoming the Good Influence in the Room

The Reverse Contagion

Almost every chapter of this book has been about how harmful things spread through a system. Behaviour. Mood. Contempt. Vigilance. Shame. Dysregulation. The bad apple effect, in its worst forms, is the story of those things travelling efficiently through families, peer groups, classrooms and online environments, and shaping the children inside them.

What is also true, and what this final chapter is built around, is that the same mechanism runs in the other direction.

The biology that allows hostility to spread also allows kindness to spread. The contagion that carries contempt also carries warmth. The peer pressure that produces conformity to harm can produce conformity to integrity, when that is the currency of the room. The system that learned to organise around dysregulation can, with effort and time, learn to organise around regulation.

This is the reverse contagion. It is real. It is measurable. It is doing the bulk of the work this book has been describing in the protective direction.

And the parent who has done the work of the previous chapters is, whether or not they realise it, the engine of that work. The regulated parent regulates the household. The repaired family changes a sibling subsystem. The child who has been raised inside both becomes, in time, the regulated presence in their own peer group, in their own classroom, in their own workplace, in their own family. The contagion moves outward.

This is the chapter that brings the whole book home to that idea.

What a Regulated Child Does to a Room

Most parents do not get to see the effect their child has on the rooms the parent does not enter.

The teacher sees it, sometimes. The other parents on the side of the football field notice it. The grandparent who watches the cousins together on a holiday sees it. The first university tutor catches a glimpse. The friend's mother who is hosting a sleepover knows. But the parent themselves, on the whole, does not.

When a child who has been raised in something close to the practice this book describes walks into a room of their peers, several quiet things happen. Their nervous system, on the regulated end of the spectrum, sends a low-volume signal of safety to the other children present. Their face is slightly more relaxed. Their voice is slightly more even. Their willingness to listen is visible. Their lack of urgent need to perform is visible. The room, registering this, calibrates around it.

The child does not have to be the leader, the popular one, the loudest, or the most charismatic. They have to be regulated. The room calibrates around regulation more reliably than it calibrates around almost any other quality.

your child, when they walk into the next year of their life, is doing some of the same work you have been doing in your own household, in the wider world. They may not know they are doing it. The other children in the room may not know it is happening. The effect is, however, real.

Across years, this child becomes the kind of presence other children gravitate toward. The friend whose home other children's parents trust. The classmate who somehow takes the heat out of the bullying without making a scene. The teammate who is steady when the team is losing. The young adult whose presence in a difficult conversation makes the conversation more honest.

These children do not arrive in the world already shaped this way. They are made. The parents made them.

What a Repaired Family Does Across Generations

There is a longer arc than the room and the year and the friendship.

A child who has watched their parents repair, week after week, year after year, internalises repair as something families do. They use it with their siblings. They use it later with their own partners. They use it, eventually, with their own children. The practice has been transmitted.

The same is true, in the opposite direction. A child who watched their parents never repair has internalised something else: that ruptures are followed by silence and avoidance. They take that pattern into their own adult relationships. Their own children, in turn, will inherit the same default unless one of those generations interrupts it.

Most parents who pick up a book like this one are doing exactly that interrupting. They were raised in a household that ran on patterns they do not want to pass on. They are trying to give their children something they did not get. The work is sometimes lonely, often slow, occasionally invisible to everyone including the parent doing it.

The compounding, though, is real. The household that runs slightly more on regulation, repair and shame-free correction in this generation produces children who run slightly more of the same in the next, and significantly more of the same in the one after that. By three generations on, the pattern that the original parent worked so hard to interrupt is barely recognisable.

Most parents do not get to see the third generation. The third generation, however, is the one whose lives the work was for.

Three Degrees of Influence

There is a useful piece of empirical work that puts a number on this.

The American physician and social scientist Nicholas Christakis and the political scientist James Fowler, in their 2009 book Connected, summarised more than a decade of work on how behaviours, moods and patterns spread through human social networks.[1] Drawing primarily on data from the long-running Framingham Heart Study, they were able to track how a person's emotional state, health behaviour, and social patterns rippled outward through the people they were connected to.

Their central finding was what they called the Three Degrees of Influence Rule. Your behaviour, your mood, your health practices and your relational patterns measurably affect not only the people you are directly connected to (one degree) but also their friends (two degrees) and their friends' friends (three degrees). Beyond three degrees, the effect tends to fade. Within three degrees, the influence is real and measurable.

What this means, in plain English, is that the way you parent your child does not stop at your child. It reaches your child's friends. It reaches their friends' families. It reaches the rooms those families touch. The reach is not infinite, and it is not noisy. It is, however, present, and it is statistically detectable.

Your work is, in this sense, much larger than your own household. You will not see most of it. The children who pass through your home as your child's friends will be slightly affected by what they encountered there. The parents of those children will be slightly affected by what their children bring home. The teachers who have your child in class will register, even subconsciously, what kind of student your child is. The wider community is, at the level of three degrees, registering your work.

It is one of the more quietly hopeful findings in modern social science.

The Quiet Influence Children Become

Most parents, asked what they want for their child, will say something like, "I want them to be happy."

It is a worthy goal, and it is also a slightly limited one. Happiness is a state. It comes and goes with circumstances. A child raised exclusively for happiness can end up unprepared for the parts of life that are simply not happy.

A larger and more useful goal, and the one most of this book has been quietly pointing toward, is to raise a child who becomes a quiet good influence in the rooms they move through.

What does that look like in adult form?

It looks like the colleague who, when a meeting has begun to slide toward contempt, makes a small steady comment that pulls it back. It looks like the friend who can sit with someone in a hard moment without performing distress or rushing to fix. It looks like the partner who can be disagreed with without becoming defensive. It looks like the parent of a child themselves, decades from now, who can hold both halves of the line your child once heard you hold. It looks like the citizen who notices, in the wider room of their community or country, when the temperature is sliding, and who finds small ways to push it back without grandstanding.

These adults are not the loudest people in any room they are in. They are also, almost always, doing more work than the loudest people are doing.

Your child has the chance to become one of these people. Your work is part of how that chance becomes a likelihood.

The Parent's Long Reach

clearly, before this book closes, what the parent's work in the household actually amounts to.

You are not just managing a child. You are not just managing a series of behaviours. You are not just running a household.

You are, in real terms, shaping what kind of human being takes your work into the next half of the twenty-first century. You are shaping what kind of partner this person will be to someone you have not yet met. You are shaping what kind of grandparent they will become. You are shaping the household, two generations from now, that is not yet a household.

That sentence is not meant to add pressure. It is meant to honestly name the scale of what is happening on the days when the work feels small. The dinner you held together on a wet

Tuesday is doing more than you can see. The repair you did after losing your temper is doing more than you can see. The boring family ritual you kept up even though you were tired is doing more than you can see. The conversation you had with the difficult relative that you had been avoiding for years is doing more than you can see.

Most of the work of parenting is invisible to the parent doing it. That does not make it less real. It makes it more remarkable. You are doing something for people who do not yet exist, and you will not get to receive their thanks for it, and you are doing it anyway.

That is what parenting is. That is what it has always been. The book has tried to give you some tools. The using of them is yours.

The Frame Returns

The book opened with a line by Maya Angelou. "Do the best you can until you know better. Then when you know better, do better."

Almost every chapter has been an answer to that line. It has tried to give you the next piece of knowing better, alongside permission to have not known it before.

Several chapters in, we picked up a line from John Steinbeck. "And now that you don't have to be perfect, you can be good." That line, from Lee in East of Eden, has been the quiet companion to Angelou's. The Angelou line is the call. The Steinbeck line is the permission underneath it.

What the two lines together say, by the time you arrive at the end of this book, is something like:

You did not need to know all of this earlier. You did not need to be the parent you are now becoming, all the way back. The work begins where you are. The standard is not perfection. The standard is the willingness to keep doing better as you learn, and the willingness to be good rather than perfect.

On those terms, you are doing exactly what you are supposed to be doing. The fact that you read this book is, by itself, evidence of the willingness. The work has already begun.

A Note for the Reader Who Got Here Tired

If you have read this book straight through, or in fits and starts over weeks, or while a child was crying in another room, and you have arrived at this final chapter, you are tired.

Some of what you have read will have been useful. Some will not have landed. Some will have made you uncomfortable in ways that are still settling. Some may have produced, by now, a small but real shift in how you respond to the next difficult moment with your child. Most of it will, in the way of these things, take time.

Please do not use this book as one more thing to feel inadequate about. The point of it has not been to give you a longer list of ways you are failing. The point has been to give you a frame that makes the work doable, repairable, and survivable.

If you take only a few things into the rest of your parenting, take these:

Children are not bad apples. The pattern is the problem.

All feelings are welcome; not all behaviours are.

The child is often the signal, not the source.

Repair, not perfection, is the actual mechanism.

Decode first. Discipline second. Repair always.

The aim is not just to protect your child from harmful influence. The aim is to raise a child who can, in time, become a good one in the rooms they enter.

Most days, you will get some of this right and some of it wrong. The wrong parts are recoverable. The right parts compound. That is most of what you need to know.

Your child is luckier than they realise to have a parent who got to the end of a book like this. They will, mostly, never thank you for it. The work is not for the thanks. The work is for them.

Go gently.

What Helps

Re-read the chapters that landed hardest. The first reading is rarely the one that does the work. The second is.

Pick one practice. Do not try to change everything. The most reliable household change comes from picking one of the practices in this book and committing to it for three months. Then the next.

Find one other parent. Doing this work alongside another parent (a partner, a friend, a parent in your child's class) compounds the effect. You catch each other's slips. You notice each other's progress. You feel less alone.

Get help when you need it. The chapter on the parent who becomes the bad apple, and the chapter on protective supervision, both pointed at the same truth: some patterns are bigger than self-management can address. The right professional, in the right relationship, can make the work much faster and gentler than alone.

Be patient. The compounding takes years. You are unlikely to see the full effect until your child is well into adulthood. Trust that the work is doing its work even when you cannot see it.

Forgive yourself the days when you do not do any of this well. Those days are also part of the work. The repair is the next move.

Key Takeaways

The same mechanisms that allow harmful behaviour to spread also allow prosocial behaviour to spread. Regulated parents shape regulated children, who shape the rooms they walk into.

Christakis and Fowler's Three Degrees of Influence Rule documents that your behaviour and patterns measurably affect people up to three degrees of social separation away. Your work in your own household reaches further than you can see.

A child raised in something close to the practice this book describes does not become the loudest person in their future rooms. They become the quietly steady presence other people calibrate around.

The compounding of regulation, repair and shame-free correction across generations is one of the more powerful long-term gifts a parent can give. Most of it is invisible at the time.

The frame from Angelou and Steinbeck holds: do the best you can until you know better, then when you know better, do better. And when you do not have to be perfect, you can be good.

If you read only this list, take these: children are not bad apples; all feelings are welcome and not all behaviours are; the child is often the signal not the source; repair not perfection is the actual mechanism; decode first, discipline second, repair always; the aim is to raise a child who can become a good influence in the rooms they enter.

Your child is unlikely to thank you for this work. The work is not for the thanks. The work is for them.

References

1. Christakis, N. A., & Fowler, J. H. (2009). Connected: The Surprising Power of Our Social Networks and How They Shape Our Lives. New York: Little, Brown and Company.

2. Steinbeck, J. (1952). East of Eden. New York: Viking Press. (See also Chapter 10.)

Conclusion

There is no clean way to end a book like this, because the work it has tried to describe does not have a finish line. Children grow. Households change. The patterns shift. The chapters of this book that mattered most to you the first time you read them may not be the chapters that matter most when your child is fifteen, or twenty-five, or grown and raising children of their own.

What I would like to leave you with, on the way out the door, is a small handful of things.

Children are not bad apples. They never were. The metaphor of this book has always been about the pattern, the influence, or the culture, never about a person.

The bad apple effect is real. It runs through families, peer groups, classrooms and online communities. So does its opposite. The same biology that lets harm spread lets care spread.

You cannot remove every harmful influence from your child's life. The world will keep arriving with its own bad apples. What you can do is build the conditions in which your child develops enough internal anchor to recognise harmful patterns and choose differently. That work is mostly invisible. It is also mostly what works.

Repair is the engine. Almost every other piece of parenting is recoverable through repair. Almost no other piece of parenting is recoverable without it.

Decode first. Discipline second. Repair always.

All feelings are welcome; not all behaviours are.

The aim is not just to protect your child from the bad apple effect. The aim is to raise the good apple. The child who knows who they are. The child who can belong without abandoning themselves. The child who can recognise harmful patterns and choose another way. The child who, in time, becomes a steady, kind and courageous presence in the rooms they enter.

And if you got to the end of this book and feel nothing changed for you, that is also okay. Some books work on us in delayed ways. Some pages will return to you in moments months from now, when you need them, in ways you do not expect. The reading was not wasted.

Maya Angelou's line is the one I have come back to most often while writing this. "Do the best you can until you know better. Then when you know better, do better."

You are doing better. The fact that you are here is the evidence.

Go gently with your children. Go gently with yourself.

And when you get tired, remember the sentence Steinbeck gave us through Lee.

"And now that you don't have to be perfect,
you can be good."

Greg Doney

2026

Appendix A — The Four-Part Repair Script

This appendix collects the repair script from Chapter 25 in a single page, in case you want to keep it somewhere easy to find. Most parents who have used this regularly tell me they have it on the inside of a kitchen cupboard, on a phone wallpaper, or simply in their head, ready when needed.

A repair has four parts. They do not always have to happen in this order, but all four usually need to be present.

1. Name what happened.

Concretely, accurately, without minimising or generalising.

"I yelled at you when you came in from school today."

"I was sharp with you in the kitchen."

"I said something unkind about your friend, and you heard it."

"I was on my phone the whole time you were trying to tell me about your day."

2. Take responsibility.

Without the word "but". Without explanations that work as excuses. A short context line is allowed.

"That was on me. I was already stressed before that conversation, and I took it out on you. It was not okay."

"I got it wrong. The way I responded was not how I want to respond to you."

"I was tired and that is not a good reason to speak to you that way."

3. Validate the impact.

What it landed like for the child. The part most parents skip.

"I can see that hurt you."

"I think it scared you."

"I think it made you feel like I was angry with you as a person, which is not true."

"I can see you went really quiet for the rest of the afternoon."

4. Name what you are doing about it.

What is different next time. The part that turns the repair from an event into a practice.

"I am working on this. When I notice myself getting like that, I am going to step out before I say anything."

"I am going to keep working on it. I will get it wrong again, and when I do I will come back like this."

"I am sorry. I love you. We are okay."

A few notes on using it

The whole conversation, in most cases, is two minutes or less. Long repairs become uncomfortable for everyone and rarely add much.

Do not require the child to forgive you or comfort you. The repair is for them.

Wrap nothing in justification. "I am sorry I yelled, but you really pushed me" cancels the apology. The child only hears the second half.

Repair small things, not just big ones. Most repair work in a household is over small frictions, and those small repairs build the muscle.

If you have not repaired in a long time, the first repair conversation may feel awkward for both of you. That is normal. Keep going.

Repair is available across years. A late repair, even years after the rupture, lands more reliably than parents expect.

Appendix B — A Parent's Self-Audit

This appendix is a private tool, not a test. There are no scores. The questions are drawn from across the book, brought together so you can do an honest stocktake of where your household sits at this moment in time.

Most parents find it useful to do this audit twice a year. Some do it at the beginning and end of school holidays. Some do it at the start of each new school year. Some do it whenever they sense a drift.

Sit somewhere quiet for fifteen minutes. Read each section. Note down, in your own words, what you notice. The point is not to grade yourself. The point is to see clearly.

The Biological Floor (Chapter 16)

Are the children getting enough sleep, most nights, on most weeks?

Is their eating reasonably steady, with enough protein and not too much added sugar?

Are they moving every day, ideally outdoors, ideally in daylight?

Are screens contained, or have they crept back into bedrooms, mealtimes and the first thirty minutes of the day?

Are there enough unhurried moments of connection between the children and the adults?

Which of these is most clearly broken right now? That is usually where to start.

The Family System (Chapters 4 and 9)

How is the parental subsystem (whatever shape it takes) functioning right now? Cohesive, strained, drifting?

Are conflicts between the adults being resolved, or are they accumulating?

Are the children being pulled into adult tensions in ways that do not belong to them?

Has any one child become the household's identified problem?

Has any one child become the easy one whose needs are quietly going unmet?

Your Own State (Chapters 10, 17 and 25)

How regulated have you been, on average, in the last month?

What has triggered you most often, and where might that trigger have a longer history than the moment it appears in?

Are there particular times of day, or particular interactions, where you most reliably lose it?

Are you carrying any of the patterns from Chapter 10 (chronic anxiety, criticism, withdrawal, unpredictability, contempt, explosiveness) more than you would like?

When you have got it wrong with the children, have you been repairing?

Are you giving yourself the same shame-free accountability you are trying to give the children?

Drift and Neutralisation (Chapters 14 and 15)

What behaviour, in any member of your household, has become acceptable to you that would not have been acceptable a year ago?

What are you using one of the five neutralisations on? Denial of responsibility, denial of injury, denial of the victim, condemnation of the condemners, appeal to higher loyalties?

If a friend you trusted spent a week in your house, would they raise anything that you have not been raising with yourself?

The Wider Environment (Chapters 11, 12, 13 and 23)

What kinds of peer groups, classrooms or online environments are your children currently spending the most time in? What is the currency of belonging in each?

What kinds of adults are routinely in your home or your children's lives? Are any of them currently part of the harmful pattern rather than the protective one?

Are there environments your children would benefit from being in more (sport, music, scouts, surf life saving, service) that have slipped off the schedule?

Is there a conversation with a relative or visiting adult that you have been avoiding?

Repair and Connection (Chapters 18, 19, 24 and 26)

When was the last time you did a deliberate repair conversation with each of your children?

When was the last time you sat with one of your children, undistracted, for more than ten minutes?

Is there a relationship in your family that has cooled and that you have been telling yourself will warm up on its own?

Of the three moves in Chapter 27 (Decode first, Discipline second, Repair always), which is the one you are doing least?

What Comes Next

After running through these questions, pick at most two things to focus on for the next three months. More than two is a setup for failure. Two is workable.

Write the two things down. Tell your partner, or a friend, or a clinician, or simply yourself in a journal.

Come back to this audit in three months. See what has shifted. Pick the next two.

The parents who do this consistently, twice a year, find that the household has measurably changed within eighteen months. The work compounds. You do not need to do it all at once.

Appendix C — When to Seek Help

This book has tried, throughout, to be honest about its limits. There are situations in which the work it describes is not enough on its own, and trying to manage them inside the household is the wrong move. Bringing in clinical or specialist support is not a failure of parenting. It is part of what good parenting looks like.

This appendix collects the red flags scattered through the book and the Australian first-line resources for seeking help. If you are reading from outside Australia, the equivalents in your country apply.

Red Flags That Warrant Outside Help

Self-harm in any form, or talk of self-harm, in a child or adolescent.

Suicidal ideation, regardless of how passing or how dismissed by the child themselves.

Disordered eating: restrictive eating, binge eating, purging, or extreme preoccupation with food, body, or weight.

Substance use that has moved beyond experimentation into pattern.

Violence inside the home, between siblings or between adults and children.

Sexualised behaviour between siblings, especially with a developmental gap or any element of coercion or secrecy.

A child who has gone significantly quieter, more withdrawn, more anxious or more depressed in a way that is not lifting after a few weeks.

A teenager whose behaviour has changed sharply in a way that is not consistent with normal adolescent shifts.

Any disclosure by a child of harm caused to them by an adult, inside or outside the family.

Domestic or family violence, coercive control, or abuse of any kind in the household.

A parental crisis (mental health, addiction, untreated trauma, postnatal illness) that is interfering with your capacity to parent.

A pattern between a child and a particular adult that is making your gut tighten, even when you cannot fully explain why. Trust that signal.

Australian First-Line Resources

If you, your child, or another person in your household is in immediate danger, call 000.

Lifeline Australia: 13 11 14. 24-hour crisis support and suicide prevention.

Kids Helpline: 1800 55 1800. Free, confidential phone and online counselling for young people aged 5 to 25.

1800RESPECT: 1800 737 732. National sexual assault, domestic and family violence counselling service.

Beyond Blue: 1300 22 4636. Information, advice and counselling for anxiety, depression and suicide.

PANDA (Perinatal Anxiety and Depression Australia): 1300 726 306. Support for new and expecting parents.

13YARN: 13 92 76. Crisis support line for Aboriginal and Torres Strait Islander people.

QLife: 1800 184 527. Anonymous, free LGBTI peer support and referral.

headspace: www.headspace.org.au. National youth mental health service for ages 12 to 25, with centres around Australia and online support.

MensLine Australia: 1300 78 99 78. Telephone and online counselling service for men.

Getting Started With a Clinician

For most families, the first step is your GP. A General Practitioner can prepare a Mental Health Treatment Plan under Medicare's Better Access initiative, which provides rebates for sessions with a registered psychologist, social worker, or occupational therapist.

For children and adolescents, paediatric and child mental-health services include private psychologists, headspace centres, paediatricians, and state-funded Child and Adolescent Mental Health Services (CAMHS).

For families dealing with the harder situations covered in this book (sustained sibling harm, sexualised behaviour, sustained mental-health crisis), specialist services are appropriate. Your GP can refer or you can contact a state-based child and family mental health service directly. Brave Hearts (1800 272 831) and Bravehearts (1800 272 831) provide specialist support for families dealing with sexual harm involving children.

For couples and family-relationship work, Family Relationship Centres around Australia provide free or low-cost mediation, counselling and parenting support. Relationships Australia (1300 364 277) offers similar services in every state and territory.

For online safety concerns, the eSafety Commissioner (www.esafety.gov.au) is the federal regulator and provides free resources for parents.

If You Cannot Afford Private Care

Most of the services above are free or significantly subsidised. The Better Access initiative provides Medicare rebates for psychological care. Headspace is free. Relationships Australia and Family Relationship Centres are sliding-scale or free. Beyond Blue, Lifeline, Kids Helpline, 13YARN, MensLine, QLife, PANDA and 1800RESPECT are all free, confidential, and 24-hour or near-24-hour.

Public mental-health services in your state or territory are free, although waitlists may be long.

Most major employers offer an Employee Assistance Programme (EAP), which typically provides several free, confidential counselling sessions for employees and their immediate family members. Ask your workplace.

The cost of getting help should not be the thing that stops you. Australia has, despite its imperfections, one of the more accessible public mental-health systems in the world. Use it.

A Final Word

If you are reading this appendix because something in the book has surfaced for you, please do not put the book down without doing one thing.

Pick up the phone. Make the GP appointment. Call the helpline. Send the email.

The conversation you are about to put off is the conversation that, in three weeks, you will be glad you had today.

Made in United States
Troutdale, OR
11/03/2026

56844636R00225